LANDMARK VISITORS

Sri Lanka

Christopher Turner

Published by
Landmark Publishing Ltd
Waterloo House, 12 Compton, Ashbourne,
Derbyshire DE6 1DA England

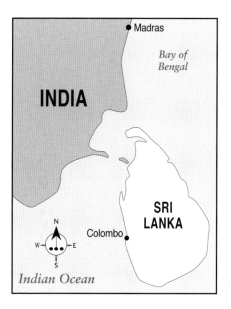

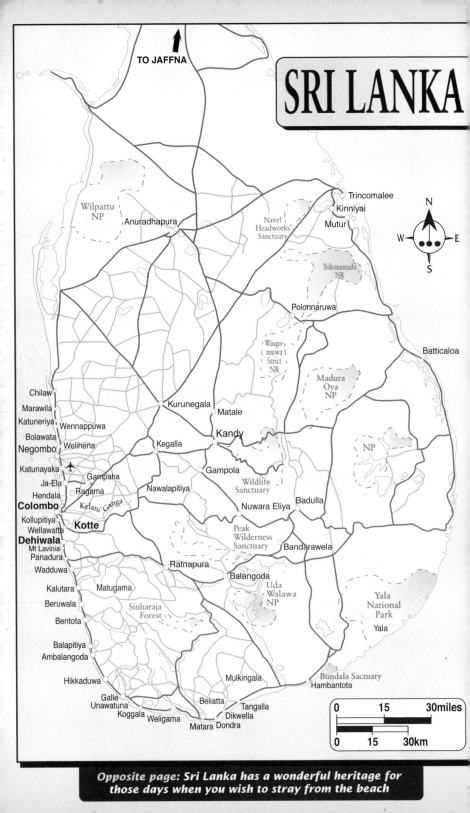

TO JAFFNA

SRI LANKA

N
W · · · · E
S

Trincomalee
Kinniyai
Mutur
Navel Headworks Sanctuary

Wilpattu NP

Anuradhapura

Trikonamadu NR

Polonnaruwa

Wasgomuwa Strict NR

Batticaloa

Madura Oya NP

Chilaw
Marawila
Katuneriya
Bolawata
Negombo
Katunayaka
Ja-Ela
Hendala
Colombo
Kollupitiya
Wellawatta
Dehiwala
Mt Lavinia
Panadura
Wadduwa
Kalutara
Beruwala
Bentota
Balapitiya
Ambalangoda
Hikkaduwa
Galle
Unawatuna
Koggala

Wennappuwa

Welihena

Gampaha
Ragama
Kelani Ganga
Kotte

Matugama

Sinharaja Forest

Kurunegala
Matale
Kandy
Kegalla
Gampola
Nawalapitiya
Wildlife Sanctuary
Nuwara Eliya
Peak Wilderness Sanctuary

NP

Badulla
Bandarawela

Ratnapura
Balangoda

Uda Walawa NP

Yala National Park

Yala

Mulkirigala
Hambantota
Bundala Sactuary

Beliatta
Tangalla
Dikwella
Matara Dondra
Weligama

0   15   30miles

0   15   30km

Opposite page: **Sri Lanka** has a wonderful heritage for those days when you wish to stray from the beach

LANDMARK VISITORS GUIDE

Sri Lanka

Christopher Turner

• CONTENTS •

Introduction   **6**

Location   8
Geology   8
Brief history   9
Internal unrest   11
Plants and crops   12
Animals and birdlife   13
Sri Lanka's people   14
Climate   15
Food and drink   17

1 Negombo   **26**

Trips to Colombo   27
Map: Negombo to Colombo   27
Negombo as a main
   beach resort   29
History   29
Map: Negombo   31
Negombo Beach   32
Negombo Town   33
Resorts north of Negombo   36

2 Colombo   **38**

Map: Colombo Town   39
History   40
Fort   41
The Pettah   45
Galle Face Green   48
Galle Road   49
Bambalapitiya   51

3 Mount Lavinia   **54**

Mount Lavinia Hotel   54
*Map: Colombo
   to Mount Lavinia*   55

**4 Wadduwa &
   Kalutara**   **59**

Panadura   60
Wadduwa   60
Kalutara   61
Ratnapura   61
Map: Wadduwa & Kalutara   62
Sinharaja Forest Reserve   65

**5 Beruwala
   & Bentota**   **66**

Beruwala   67
Map: Beruwala   67
Kaluwamodara   69
Alutgama   69
Map: Bentota   71
Bentota   72
Induruwa   74

**6 Kosgoda
   & Hikkaduwa**   **75**

Turtle hatchery   76
Ahungalla   77
Balapitiya   77
Ambalangoda   77
Map: Kosgoda & Hikkaduwa   78
Hikkaduwa   79

**7 Galle to
   Dondra Head**   **82**

Galle   82
Map: Galle & the South Coast   83
Map: Galle   86
Ramparts Walk   88
Unawatuna   91
Koggala   92
Koggala to Weligama   93
Matara   94
The southern coast   95
Dondra Head   96

**8 The South-East
   Coast & Yala
   National Park**   **98**

Tangalla   98
Map: Hambantota to Yala   99
Hambantota   100
Tissamaharama   101
Ruhunu (Yala) National Park   102

9 The Hill Country & Nuwara Eliya 103

Kataragama 104
The Hill Country 105
Map: The Hill Country 106
Horton Plains 107
Nuwara Eliya 109
Northward to Kandy 117

10 Kandy 118

Map: Kandy & Around 119
Map: Kandy 119
Kandy's concentrated attractions 120
History 120
Map: The former Royal Palace area 122
Temple of the Tooth 124
Kandy Lake 129
Walk to Arthur's Seat and viewpoint 131
West of Kandy 132
Hotels around Kandy 136

11 The Ancient Cities 139

Matale 140
Dambulla 141
Map: The Ancient Cities & Trincomalee 142
Sigiriya 144
Habarana 148
Polonnaruwa 149
Map: Polonnaruwa 150
Ancient City Tour 151
Mihintale 159
Anuradhapura 161
Map: Anuradhapura 163
Exploring Anuradhapura 164

12 Trincomalee 171

History 172
What to see in Trincomalee 172

FEATURE BOXES

Touts and Hustlers 16
Sri Lankan Dishes 19
Architecture 21
Buddhism in Sri Lanka 22-24
Sculpture 25
Cinnamon – spice worth more than gold 28
Day Excursions from Negombo 37
Colombo's National Museum 51
Who was Lavinia? 56
Adam's Peak (Sri Pada) 63/64
Historic Mansion Museum 88
Esala Perahera 121
The Sacred Tooth – An Itinerant Relic 126
Nathuma – traditional Kandy dance 134
Pinawala Elephant Orphanage 137
Sacred Bo-Tree (Sri Maha Bodhi) 166

FactFile 179

Accommodation 179
Currency Regulations 182
Electricity 182
Health 183
Holidays and Festivals 183
Money 185
Packing 185
Passports 186
Tourist Information 186
Travel 187

Index 188

Introduction

S ri Lanka, although primarily regarded as a winter sun resort, has so much more to offer than tropical beaches, splendid though they are. A great deal of the island's charm derives from its Buddhist and Hindu religions, with their joint heritage of temples, monasteries, rock carvings and, above all, enormous bell-shaped *dagobas*, some of which are almost 1,000 years old and rival the Egyptian pyramids in height.

Safaris to the island's twelve wild-life reserves provide opportunities to see elephants, buffaloes, crocodiles and, with luck, sloth bears and leopards, in their natural habitat.

Easily reached from the beach resorts, Sri Lanka's cool Hill Country reaches a height of just over 7600 ft (2,500 m). In the middle lies Nuwara Eliya, a 'time warp' colonial town surrounded by emerald-green tea plantations.

Colombo, the administrative capital, holds little of great interest for tourists, but the white city of Kandy, with its delightful lake and famous Temple of the Tooth, is a must for all first-time visitors. Further north, the ancient, now ruined, cities of Sigiriya, Polonnaruwa and Anuradhapura, hidden by jungle for centuries, are Sri Lanka's cultural highlight; many of their historic buildings are being restored by UNESCO.

It is natural that many expect Sri Lanka to resemble India, but in reality, in spite of their close proximity and the common ancestry of their people, the two countries differ widely. Both, of course, are classed as Third World, but in Sri Lanka

Forbidden areas

The number of tourists visiting Sri Lanka has now reached the pre-civil war level of the late 1970s, partly due to the Tamil Tigers' continued policy of not harming foreign visitors. At the time of writing, Trincomalee was the only east coast resort that could be reached, and the great plain that stretches northward from Anuradhapura to Jaffna, the Tamil Tigers' stronghold, could not be entered. In effect, this reduces 'tourist' Sri Lanka to roughly two-thirds of the country's total area but, apart from Wilpattu National Park, and Arugam Bay, this section fortunately contains all Sri Lanka's locations of greatest tourist appeal.

signs of poverty are far less conspicuous, corruption in general does not appear to be as prevalent, and standards of rubbish clearance are incomparably higher. In addition, the tourist beaches are cleaner and, primarily due to the protection of coral reefs, sea bathing is a more tranquil experience. Europeans, in particular, are delighted to discover that even in the 'dry' season the grass remains green.

Most visitors divide their time between a coastal resort and an escorted coach tour of the island's interior. Due primarily to cost advantages the majority of visitors to Sri Lanka opt for a package tour, and they can be certain of high quality accommodation and air-conditioned transport. Most tour operators offer either Negombo, Mount Lavinia, Beruwala or Bentota as their coastal base. Independent visitors will find a selection of recommended hotels and guest houses listed at the end of each chapter.

Few places in the world can offer so much diversity in such a small area as Sri Lanka, and there is a temptation to try to see too much, which can involve early morning departures and many hours travelling. The full descriptions of the locations in this book, all of which have been visited by the author, will prove invaluable in forming a Sri Lanka itinerary and, hopefully, provide an instructive and entertaining read on the beach – or during a long journey.

LOCATION

Sri Lanka, formerly Ceylon, is a tear-shaped island lying off the south-east coast of India. At its longest, the country stretches 270 miles (435 km) from north to south and at its widest 140 miles (225 km) east to west. Its area of 25,300 sqare miles (66,610 sq km) is similar to that of Ireland.

Lying between Mannar Island in the north-west of Sri Lanka and the Indian island of Ramaswaram, a distance of only 25 miles (40 km) are a string of islets and sand banks known as **Adam's Bridge**. The evidence of flora and fauna suggests that the two countries were linked at this point around 25,000 years ago, when they jointly formed part of the enormous land mass now referred to by geologists as Gondwanaland. In 1999, it was decided to blast a shipping lane through Adam's Bridge, which is currently navigable only by small craft, necessitating inconvenient and costly detours.

Island of many names

From ancient times, the island had been known as 'Lanka' to the Sinhalese, and 'Ilankai' to the Tamils. Roman merchants called it 'Taprobane', and Arab traders dubbed it 'Serendib' (the source of the English word 'serendipity' which means 'the faculty of making happy and unexpected discoveries by accident'). 'Ceilao' was a Portuguese corruption of Sinhala, which the Dutch spelt Ceylan and the British Ceylon. The prefix Sri added to Lanka is a term of deep respect.

GEOLOGY

Like south India, the island is made up mainly of Precambrian, crystalline rock. Most of it is low-lying, particularly in the north and east, and the only hills of importance rise abruptly from the middle of the southern half of the country, covering an area of around 39 sq miles (100 sq km). Although several peaks exceed 6000 ft (2000 m) in height, this is no arid wilderness: the tea grown at such high altitudes is greatly prized for its quality. As may be expected, many of Sri Lanka's important rivers have their source in the highlands, including the long-est, the Mahaweli, which flows northward for around 155 miles (250 km) before entering the Bay of Bengal at Trincomalee.

From the air, the country appears to be studded with lakes; almost all of these, however, are man-made reservoirs, or tanks, some of them thousands of years old, their prime function is to irrigate the rice paddies.

BRIEF HISTORY

ARRIVALS FROM INDIA

The earliest known inhabitants of Sri Lanka, the Veddah, were immigrant aborigines, probably related to the first occupants of south India. Some survive and live tribally, a few in Colombo and on the east coast; a tourist's best chance of seeing them will be in the vicinity of Anuradhapura. By tradition, Indo-European Aryans under the leadership of Prince Vijaya emigrated to the island from north India in the 5th century BC. The reason for this mass exodus is unknown, nor is it clear if they travelled overland or by sea, but eventually the Sinhalese immigrants took over from the Veddah. It is the north Indian Sanskrit base of their language that provides the only undisputed corroboration of the Sinhalese people's origins.

Invaders from Tamil south India probably began to settle in the north of Sri Lanka during the 1st century AD, although it has been suggested that some of them may actually have preceded the Sinhalese. The Tamil people and their language are Dravidian, as opposed to the Aryan Sinhalese.

Early settlements

The first great settlement in Sri Lanka was at **Anuradhapura**, which served as the capital from 437BC to 781AD; during the 3rd century BC its king was converted to Buddhism. Spasmodic attacks from south India, some of which led to lengthy periods of rule by Tamils, led to a transfer of power to Polonnaruwa, which served as the capital for 500 years. After it in turn had been abandoned, a succession of Sinhalese capitals followed, the most important of which was Kotte in the south-west; a separate Tamil kingdom, Eelam, was set up in the north in the 14th century.

COLONIAL RULE

In 1505, the Portuguese began their conquest of the island, and within a hundred years controlled most of it. The exception was the Kingdom of Kandy, which, in 1592, became the last Sinhalese bastion. In 1658, the Portuguese were ousted by the Dutch East India Company, which in turn was supplanted by the British East India Company in 1796. The country was made a Crown Colony in 1802, but Kandy continued to repel British attacks until 1815, when it was ceded to them by rebel chieftains. Following the expansion of its port, Colombo was soon made the capital of the whole island.

Above: The head of the Buddha towers over the houses as the Wewurukannala Vihara is approached

Right: Hand-made lace is produced on the Galle Road

Below: Elephants can be approached closely in the Elephant Orphanage at Pinnawala

The British introduced coffee in the 1830s but, although profitable at first, it was wiped out by disease within fifty years and replaced by tea, which proved to be a greater and longer lasting success. Sinhalese refused to toil on the tea plantations and so the British brought poor, mainly low-caste people, Tamils from south India, to do the work. Known as the 'Hill' Tamils, they still provide virtually all the labour force, primarily female.

INDEPENDENCE

In 1919, Sinhalese and Tamils combined to form the Ceylon National Congress, which proved to be the stimulant for the island's movement for independence. This was gained in 1948, a year later than India's, but not until 1972 was a republic proclaimed.

INTERNAL UNREST

Solomon Bandaranaike became Prime Minister in 1956, and by making Sinhala the official language in place of English he is seen by many to have ignited the fuse that led to years of civil unrest. Bandaranaike was assassinated in 1959, and his widow, Sirimavo, who became the world's first female Prime Minister, continued her husband's misconceived nationalisation policy: the economy degenerated alarmingly and foreign investors withdrew their money. Mrs Bandaranaike reduced the number of places allocated to Tamils in the universities and proclaimed Buddhism to be the state's foremost religion, thereby alienating the Tamils further.

CIVIL WAR

In 1976, the Tamil United Liberation Front was founded, its prime aim being the formation of an independent Tamil state, which would bear the historic name of Eelam. Some Tamils had already turned to the use of force to press their claim, and in 1983 Tamil Tiger guerrillas massacred an army unit outside Jaffna. Sinhalese retribution was terrible, up to 2,000 Tamils being mindlessly slaughtered throughout the country, with little intervention by the police or army on their behalf. From this point onwards the conflict escalated, innocent people lost their lives, and mass evacuations by Tamils from Sinhalese areas and Sinhalese from Tamil areas took place. Many Tamils emigrated to

Sri Lanka's famous stilt fishermen can be seen only between Ahangama and Weligama

India, but the Hill Tamils took no part in the conflict. At one point, the government seemed about to concede a Tamil state, but not only did the LTTE (Liberation Tigers of Tamil Eelam, generally known as the 'Tamil Tigers') insist on ruling the north of the island from their historic Jaffna base, but also a strip along the east coast, which was occupied almost equally by Tamil, Sinhalese and Muslim people. This, no national government could accept.

Indian intervention

In 1987, Prime Minister Jaya-wardene negotiated a deal with India, whereby an Indian peace-keeping force patrolled the Tamil areas in place of the Sri Lankan army. Within three years the Tamil Tigers had been practically eliminated but, in 1990, President Pramadasa, in order to please Sin-halese nationalists, ordered the Indians to withdraw.

Continued strife

Although the Tigers had promised a ceasefire in return for Indian withdrawal, hostilities immediately resumed, and President Pramadasa was assassinated, probably by the LTTE, in 1993. In 1989 and 1990 a revolt against the government by Sinhalese Marxists resulted in a wave of terror in the south of the country, particularly Colombo, which was only ended by ruthless measures. An estimated 17,000 lost their lives in this separate dispute.

The People's Alliance, led by President Kumaratunga, the daughter of the former Prime Minister Sirimavo Bandaranaike, pledged to end the violence, but talks broke down in 1995, and the bombing in Colombo of the Central Bank, in which 80 were killed and 100 injured, occurred a year later; primarily as a gesture, a bomb was detonated by the Tigers outside Kandy's Temple of the Tooth in 1998, with little loss of life or damage to the shrine.

PEACE MOVES

In 1999, both sides claimed to be seeking a political settlement, and hopes have once more been raised that this will be achieved. Well over 50,000 have been killed in the conflict, and the cost to the country, both in maintaining the army and in lost foreign investment, has been enormous.

And yet, tourists will not observe an obviously poverty-stricken nation; services are reasonably efficient – although some are not as efficient as before nationalisation – and road surfaces are much better than in most third world countries. Even so, an end to the strife should release so much money into the economy that in a relatively short time Sri Lanka would be barely recognisable as the country it is today.

PLANTS AND CROPS

Apart from the plants introduced by the British, such as tea and rubber, the coconut and, of course, rice, are the most important of Sri Lanka's crops, followed by a wide range of tropical fruits. Environmental measures have greatly restricted the activities of the logging industry, and teak, ebony and the rare satinwood, albeit in restricted numbers, still grow in the northern 'dry' zone. In the tropical forest of the south-west 'wet' zone almost 200 species of orchid grow amongst the trees.

Flowering trees are at their best in Sri Lanka between March and May.

The **Hill Country** is now dominated by tea plantations and market gardens, where the lower temperatures mean fruits, vegetables and flowers familiar to north Europeans are grown in abundance.

It has been estimated that during the 20th century the forested area of Sri Lanka fell by two-thirds; the main causes being the timber industry, land cultivation and irrigation schemes. Nature reserves, which now cover 10 per cent of the country, and environmental policies should help to preserve most of what is left, but the former appearance of the country can never be regained.

From their coastal resorts, most tourists will be able to visit a lagoon, where the dominant plant will almost certainly be the mangrove, its long roots visible above water level.

The cinnamon tree can still be seen growing on the south-west coast, but its crop, once more valuable than gold, is now of marginal importance, and plantations no longer exist. Pepper and other tropical spices such as cardamom are all harvested in sufficient quantity to export, but amounts of coffee and cashew nuts meet little more than local requirements.

ANIMALS & BIRDLIFE

MAMMALS

The majority of Sri Lanka's elephants still live wild in herds mostly within the country's twelve wildlife sanctuaries. Most working elephants seen by tourists are assigned to temples for ceremonial duties. By 1900, the 'sporting' activities of British big game hunters had reduced Sri Lanka's once enormous elephant population to 12,000, a figure that had dwindled to just 3,000 a century later.

The only evidence of the Asian lion being in Sri Lanka, a fossil, dates from the Pleistocene era. More recent inhabitants, tigers, were hunted to extinction in Sri Lanka long ago, and leopards are now the country's only surviving big cats; Yala National Park currently affords the best chance of seeing them. Of the remaining 84 species of mammal, the sloth bear, porcupine and sambar deer are of exceptional interest.

Monkeys are numerous, and can always be seen amongst the ruins of the ancient cities, where they cadge titbits from tourists; most common are the long-tailed langur and the toque macaque. Colonies of large bats, known as 'flying foxes', will be seen suspended upside down from the trees in the Botanic Gardens at Peradeniya near Kandy.

REPTILES & FISH

Crocodiles are still found in certain rivers, particularly those flowing through wildlife sanctuaries; only rarely are attacks on people reported. More dangerous are the venomous snakes: cobra, krait (Indian and Sri Lankan) and viper (Russell's and Saw Scaled), but they are frightened of man and do all they can to avoid contact.

Snorkellers, in particular, will be able to admire the vivid hues of the myriad tropical fish that inhabit the island's coral reefs.

A succession of rock-strewn bays between Dikwella & Tangalla provide some of the island's most attractive coastal scenery

BIRDLIFE

More than 400 species of bird can be seen in Sri Lanka, 21 of them indigenous. The country's location, at the southern extremity of south Asia, makes it a popular stopping off point for migrants. Outstanding amongst them are the Ceylon Blue Magpie, common in the Hill Country forests, the Kashmir Red-Breasted Fly Catcher, eye-catching Bee Eaters, the long-tailed Ceylon Paradise Flycatcher, the Red Faced Malkoha, the Brown-Capped Babbler, the Indian Golden Oriole, and the red-breasted Malabar Trogon.

Waterfowl and waders, such as Painted Storks, Egrets, Spoonbills, Cormorants, Plovers and Kites are commonly seen on Sri Lanka's tanks and lagoons. The Bundala Reserve is renowned for Pelican and great flocks of Flamingos.

At some time, most visitors are likely to see the Ceylon Junglefowl, Sri Lanka's national bird, which differs little from its Indian relative. Both have close similarities with the domestic chicken, which is descended from them. All birds are at their most active and visible at dawn, and bird watchers must be prepared to rise early.

SRI LANKA'S PEOPLE

The inhabitants of most tropical islands are laid-back, friendly and generally wreathed in smiles: Sri Lankans are no exception. Nearly all have Indian forebears and there has been a great deal of intermarriage between Sinhalese and Tamils – in spite of what might appear from the present ethnic confrontations.

Pure Sinhalese, with their northern, Aryan ancestry, are often paler in complexion than the Tamils, who came from India's deep south, and often have slightly flared nostrils, typical of Dravidian people. However, physical characteristics are not a reliable guide to identification.

POPULATION

In the last fifty years, Sri Lanka's population has risen from 7 to 18 million, resulting in a density of 270 per sq km, one of the highest in Asia. Almost 90 per cent speak, as a first language, either Sinhala (colloquial Sinhalese) or Tamil. Around 60 per cent of Sri Lankans are also reasonably proficient in Eng-lish, particularly those who live in Colombo and the tourist beach areas.

Sinhalese

Almost 74 per cent of the popula-tion are Sinhalese, the vast majority of whom follow Buddhism, but a few, particularly on the south-west coast, are Christian converts. They were spread throughout most of the country, although in recent years few have chosen to remain in the Tamil-dominated north of the island.

Tamils

The Tamil population makes up around 19 per cent of the country's total. Most live in the north or along the east coast and are Hindus. The 'Hill Country' Tamils are also mostly Hindu, but some are Christian or Muslim converts. The total Tamil population has fallen in the past few years due to emigration to India.

Minorities

Sri Lankan Muslims are descended from Arab traders and mostly still live on the coast. Malay fishermen are concentrated around Hamban-tota and are also Muslim; they speak Sinhalese or Tamil. Burghers are descended from the earliest European settlers, particularly the Portuguese; almost all are Christians and speak English. Before indepen-dence, the Burghers were fairly numerous, but so many have emi-grated in recent years that now they make up just 2 per cent of the population. Most live either in Colombo or Batticaloa on the east coast.

Fashion

An interesting fashion difference between Sri Lankan and Indian men is that while the latter almost without exception grow mous-taches as soon as they are able, the majority of Sri Lankans do not.

Male dress is less exotic than in much of India, and a turban is rarely seen; many men, however, instead of trousers wear the Indian dhoti – a single piece of cloth tucked in tightly at the waist that can be flapped to create a cooling draught. Buddhist monks, all of whom are shaven-headed, wear a toga-style robe that is either saffron or russet in appearance.

Sri Lankan women may wear European clothing or Indian saris, but the Sinhalese, particularly on occasions of importance, also wear the Kandy-style three piece *sujeewa*, which they regard as 'national' dress.

CLIMATE

THE MONSOONS

Low-lying areas of Sri Lanka differ little in temperature through-out the year, averaging around 27^0C (over 80^0F), i.e. hot. Rainfall, however, is a different matter. The south-west monsoon brings rain to the south-west coast and the Hill Country from May to Au-gust, and the north-east monsoon

• TOUTS AND HUSTLERS •

Everywhere in the world where tourists visit in large numbers, touts and hustlers will appear. In general, the poorer the country and the greater its unemployment the more numerous they will be. In addition, if, as in Sri Lanka, the state discriminates against tourists by charging them high prices to enter National Parks and monuments whereas Sri Lankans pay virtually nothing, touts will find little immoral in their own activities. In consequence, tourist areas in Sri Lanka are unduly plagued by these rogues.

They usually speak excellent English and claim to have a close friend or relative who owns a rental car, a souvenir shop or a hotel, all of which give extraordinarily good value for money. They should be completely ignored. Areas where they proliferate are outside the more expensive hotels, central Colombo, central Kandy and, of course, the beaches. A high proportion of drivers of taxis and three-wheelers become touts immediately they are rented by an innocent tourist. In Sri Lanka they are aided by the refusal of the authorities to insist on metering, and it is essential to find out in advance what the approximate fare should be.

Most tourists at some time will be confronted by a friendly gentleman bearing a large book in which are written the names of subscribers to a blind children's school. Do not donate: all are bogus collectors however 'authentic' their credentials may seem.

Single male tourists in certain beach resorts such as Negombo, Mount Lavinia and Hikkaduwa may well be approached by a particularly offensive type of tout offering sex with children. This has become quite an industry in Sri Lanka, and in consequence, many pederasts are attracted to the country. Poor fishermen seem to be the greatest offenders, many of them closely related to the child in question. It is best to decline as politely as possible rather than risk aggression.

affects the whole country, but particularly the north and east, from October to January. However, on occasions, either monsoon can arrive late. Between them there should be dry periods but, unlike India, these cannot be guaranteed.

A CLIMATE CHANGE?

It appears that Sri Lanka's climate has become increasingly unpredictable during the last 10 years. For example, those who spent a holiday on the popular south-west coast of the island during the second half of January 1998 had day after day of unbroken sunshine, whilst during the same period in 1999 there were ten continuous days of leaden skies and heavy downpours, with hardly a glimpse of the sun. Even the so-called 'dry' Zone, which includes the Ancient Cities and Trincomalee, received heavy rainfall in 1999 for much of February and March.

Writer Sir Arthur C Clarke, who knows a lot about these things and has lived in Colombo for many years, says that he doesn't know what is happening and doubts if anyone else does. An obvious suspect is, of course, global warming, which may be exaggerating the movement of the Inter-Tropical Convergence Zone. This is a wide band of heavy cloud, which can spread up to 10 degrees north and 10 degrees south of the equator at any time. Virtually all of Sri Lanka, but only the most southerly tip of India can be affected by this.

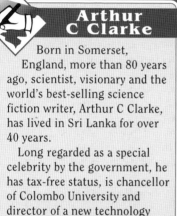

Arthur C Clarke

Born in Somerset, England, more than 80 years ago, scientist, visionary and the world's best-selling science fiction writer, Arthur C Clarke, has lived in Sri Lanka for over 40 years.

Long regarded as a special celebrity by the government, he has tax-free status, is chancellor of Colombo University and director of a new technology park. For many years he had the island's only satellite dish; and his walled compound in Colombo is linked by the most sophisticated technology to global communications networks.

FOOD AND DRINK

Food lovers, particularly those who are familiar with Indian cuisine, will be disappointed to discover that Sri Lanka has one of the most limited national cuisines in the world. Hotel buffets almost exclusively comprise 'Continental' (i.e. European) dishes. On rare occasions, Sri Lankan curry and rice or devilled meat may be included among the main courses, and curd (yoghurt)

with honey or *wattalapam* with the desserts. For breakfast, the better hotels sometimes offer hoppers or, more frequently, string hoppers. And that is it!

CURRY AND RICE

A genuine Sri Lankan meat or fish curry is prepared with so many chillies that few foreigners, including Indians, find it palatable. In consequence, tourist hotels always prepare a milder version unless requested otherwise. The curry is not only accompanied by rice but also a selection of blandly prepared vegetables, fruits and condiments served in separate bowls, which may include: shredded cabbage with dried fish, dhal (without chillies), pumpkin, potato, aubergine, ladies fingers, banana flower, ground coconut, pineapple and mango. Condiments such as *sambol* (ground coconut with small fish), and *ambul thiyal* (marinated tuna), together with Indian-style pickles and *ambarella* (similar to lime chutney) often accompanying the meal.

Very little variation to this dish apart from quality can be expected. If possible, select chicken as the meat for a curry, as in Sri Lanka it is almost always free range and succulent. The New Oriental Hotel at Galle, on the south coast, serves the finest chicken curry in Sri Lanka.

EUROPEAN DISHES

The mainstay of the ubiquitous hotel buffet, Sri Lanka's 'Continental' dishes vary enormously in authenticity and quality. Unfortunately, in order not to offend the bland palates of north Europeans, particularly the Germans and Dutch, the food generally lacks flavour.

Buffet food must, of course, be kept warm in tureens, sometimes for many hours, and towards the end of the session much of it becomes stale and limp. Those who prefer to eat late may find it better to opt for à la carte meals whenever possible. Interestingly, a popular dish of the 1950s, Chicken Maryland, is a Sri Lankan revival.

Vegetables are usually restricted to carrots, onions, green beans and, surprisingly, leeks; they can be expected to be served undercooked, presumably to meet the current taste for 'crunchy' vegetables.

Seerfish, a splendid white fish, which inhabits the shores of Sri Lanka and south India, will frequently be served, but Sri Lankan chefs seldom remove the skin, which tastes rather 'fishy'. Be sure to do so. Lobster (crayfish) and Tiger prawns are expensive and tasteless, butterfly prawns will be much cheaper and more flavoursome.

CHINESE FOOD

When Sri Lankans eat out, they generally choose a Chinese restaurant, and many hotels – even some guest houses – provide a selection of Chinese dishes. Unfortunately, Chinese vegetables and many of their sauces (apart from soy) cannot be obtained, and noodles are usually soggy. Also lacking are Chinese dishes such as Peking Duck; pork, apart from in Christian areas such as Negombo, is rarely available.

ETHNIC FOOD

Some hotels hold special Indonesian, Japanese, Italian, etc. nights, and

Fishermen haul in the nets at Hambantota – many of them are of Malay origin

• SRI LANKAN DISHES •

Devilled meat
The meat should be marinated in a chilli sauce, but for tourists, who are not expected to like chillies, tomato ketchup is usually substituted – with detrimental results.

Curd with honey
This delicious form of rich, creamy yoghurt is made from buffalo milk; it is generally accompanied by 'honey', which is a sweet syrup with a caramelized flavour, that has been tapped from a type of palm tree. It appears to be identical to the *Miel de Palma* of the Canary Islands.

Wattalapam
This soft cake, with the texture of bread pudding, resembles the *bebinca* of Goa, made from layers of coconut-flavoured pancakes. It can be served as a dessert or ordered with afternoon tea.

Hoppers
Only served at breakfast, these pancakes are soft in the middle and crisp around the edges; they can be topped with a fried egg or curry (usually fish). As the mix for the hoppers has to ferment, orders must usually be given the night before.

String Hoppers
Also a breakfast dish, string hoppers resemble a bird's nest of vermicelli. As the mix is not fermented it is unnecessary to order in advance.

their chefs make a brave stab at preparing what are to them completely unknown dishes. Don't expect the real thing.

TROPICAL FRUIT

During the main tourist season, papaya, mango, pineapple and custard apple provide a not-to-be-missed treat, but the more exotic rambutan, jack fruit, mangosteen and durian only become available during the summer months.

BREAKFAST

Hotel breakfasts in Sri Lanka are so good that one recalls Gertrude Stein's recommendation to a friend on a first visit to England "Eat breakfast three times a day". Again, the buffet system is employed, but eggs, toast and sometimes bacon are generally cooked individually. Not only is a very full English breakfast provided but also, for European tastes, cakes, cold meats and cheese.

Strangely, although bacon always comes from the pig, sausages are normally of beef or chicken. Another idiosyncrasy is that some chefs prepare *pommes lyonnaise* (potatoes sautéed with onions) in the mistaken belief that this is a European breakfast dish.

Fruit juices in the more expensive hotels are rarely made from fresh fruit; the give-away is a chilled dispenser. Fresh orange juice will never be found, but fresh pineapple and papaya juices in jugs are often provided at the less expensive hotels. An honourable exception to the purveyors of manufactured 'juices' is the Aitken Spence group, whose hotels frequently offer unusual juices from native Sri Lankan fruits such as Belli and Sour Sap.

Brown's Beach Hotel at Negombo must be awarded the 'best breakfast in Sri Lanka' prize – they even make their sausages from pork.

BEVERAGES

Soft drinks

Unless a hotel provides purified water (some of the better hotels do), drink bottled mineral water rather than tap water, which may cause sickness. Ensure that the bottle cap is sealed.

Tea and coffee

Ceylon Tea is, of course, famous, but Sri Lankans, like Indians, prefer their tea mixed with water, milk and sugar and brought to the boil; this results in a bitter sweet-tasting brew, which few visitors enjoy. Always ask for black tea with cold milk and sugar separate. The cold milk will usually be powdered, as fresh milk is boiled for health reasons; neither does much for the taste of the otherwise delicious tea, which,

in consequence, is much better taken black and not too strong.

The good fresh coffee usually offered will be less affected by whatever form of milk is added. It will always be made from locally-grown beans.

Alcoholic drink

Alcoholic beverages are freely available and, in contrast with India, most European brands of spirits can be obtained. Due primarily to a 38 per cent import tax, prices are fairly high, but most tourists will have purchased the generous allowance of tax-free spirits at Colombo airport for their evening drinks on the hotel balcony.

Locally brewed lager-type beers are quite acceptable; brands include Lion, Three Coins, Golden Brew (the strongest). Carlsberg, Becks and Heineken are imported, and much more expensive. Some may be tempted to try the local firewater, *arrack*, made from distilling the coconut bud. The older the arrack, the smoother it will be, but little flavour ever seems to develop. Take care, a little too much can be lethal.

Schweppes tonic, imported from Singapore, is stocked by some hotels, but the local Club tonic is not a bad alternative; Elephant tonic, a tasteless fizz, should be avoided. Note that Sri Lankans refer to cool, never cold, drinks and may not understand when the latter is requested.

· Architecture ·

From the 2nd century BC buildings of Anuradhapura to the last major construction period at Polonnaruwa in the 13th century AD, Sri Lanka's religious buildings changed little in appearance. It is true that the introduction of mortar permitted higher structures of brick or stone, but there is no evidence that these ever exceeded three floors; anything above this had to be built of timber.

ARCHITECTURAL GLOSSARY

Dagobas

These hemispherical buildings, usually of solid brick and immense size, are Sri Lanka's most impressive architectural contribution. Dagobas can form part of any Buddhist religious foundation but must contain a relic of the Buddha; this is usually buried within the structure but can be erected on top of it.

Each dagoba is surmounted by a finial in the manner of the dome of a church or mosque. Originally, all were plastered and coated with a white lime wash, but most examples in the Ancient Cities have lost this, some even being covered by vegetation, which gives them the appearance of a natural hillock.

Vihara

The term technically refers to a Buddhist monastery, but is often used to denote an image house as opposed to a dagoba. Image houses generally incorporate a reclining figure of the Buddha, a seated Buddha, and scenes painted from the Buddha's life.

Vatadage

This is a circular relic house consisting of a small central dagoba surrounded by columns, which originally supported a wooden roof.

Devale

These temples are built in south Indian style, usually for Hindu worship.

Gedige

This is a Buddhist temple with walls that are so thick that a flight of steps can be incorporated into them. Roofs are decorated with corbel brackets.

- BUDDHISM IN SRI LANKA -

Not only is Buddhism by far the most widely followed religion in Sri Lanka, but the majority of Buddhists throughout the world regard the country as pre-eminent in matters regarding their faith. Only by staying within the confines of a large hotel at a major beach resort can tourists avoid contact with some aspects of the religion; most visitors, of course, travel widely in search of the country's outstanding examples of Buddhist architecture and sculpture.

LIFE OF THE BUDDHA
Birth and death

The Buddha (meaning enlightened one) was born Gautama, the son of Suddhodama, ruler of the Sakya warrior class. Another name, Siddhartha (he who has achieved his aim) was added later by his followers. There is much disagreement on the precise dates of the Buddha's birth and death: 624 to 544 BC and 560 to 480 BC both have their advocates, but neither may be correct.

However, few dispute that his place of birth was the Lumbini Gardens, now Rummindei, which lies just within Nepal. Here, Mongol features are predominant, which may be why the Buddha is generally depicted as oriental rather than Aryan. After a lifetime of missionary work, the Buddha returned to the district of his birth, where he is said to have died and attained nirvana, aged 80, at Kusinagara; its ruins lie near the modern town of Kasia.

From prince to mendicant

Gautama, who had lived a very sheltered life, became greatly disturbed on first coming into contact with poverty, disease, old age and death. At the age of 29 he is said to have secretly renounced his life of luxury, cropping his hair, donning a simple robe, and abandoning his wife and child to seek religious understanding and a way of extinguishing human suffering.

The Prince became a disciple of two Hindu wise men and lived an ascetic life for six years, undergoing penances that weakened him almost to the point of death. He then abandoned current religious teachings, and meditated, eventually gaining enlightenment beneath a Bo-tree, at a town in north India now called Buddh Gaya. By his enlightenment, Gautama would henceforth be known as the Buddha and devote the rest of his life to teaching. Followers believe that the Buddha had three previous existences, and one is yet to come.

TEACHINGS OF THE BUDDHA

It is not possible in this book to deal more than superficially with Buddhist beliefs, which are highly complex and, at least some of them, controversial. One must bear in mind that although the Buddha lived in the 5th or 6th century BC, his teachings (*dharma*) were not written down until the 1st century BC; before this, they had been handed down orally.

The Buddha taught that all life, from birth to death, involves suffering. Selfish desires for objects that are expected to relieve this suffering only increase it, and the pleasure that they appear to give is an illusion. Only by mastering one's own mind so that selfish desires are banished completely can suffering be extinguished and true happiness gained.

The Buddha did not advocate extreme self-denial, but a path between it and worldly life, which is known as the 'Middle Way'. All must strive to develop the 'noble eightfold path' of right views, right thoughts, right speech, right action, right aspiration, right effort, right awareness and right composure. Reincarnation occurs until the 'noble path' of increasing goodness has been completed and supreme enlightenment attained. The reward is salvation, the cycle of rebirth ends, and nirvana – a state of oneness with all – is reached.

No soul, no god

It is not easy for Westerners to comprehend the Buddhist view of reincarnation, primarily because no unvarying 'soul' is involved but a consciousness that some have likened to Sigmund Freud's 'id'. As the Buddha did not believe in the existence of a supreme being or god, it can be argued that Buddhism should be defined as a philosophy and moral code rather than a religion.

DEVELOPMENT AND RECORDING

The Buddha's teachings, which only existed in oral form as the Three Pitakas, were first recorded in Sri Lanka on talipot palm leaves, around 80 BC, translated into Pali, the canonical script, early in the 5th century AD and added to the existing commentaries on them.

Buddhist events in the country are referred to chiefly in the *Maharamsa*, (Genealogy of the Great Dynasty) which was written by monks in the 5th century and covers the period from the arrival of Prince Vijaya in the 5th century BC until the end of the Anuradhapura period. The *Cularamsa* (Genealogy of the Lesser Dynasty) continues the history up to 1758.

In the *Maharamsa* it is stated that the Buddha made three visits to Sri Lanka, but there is no corroboration of this. Mahendra, son of the Indian Buddhist emperor Ashok, undoubtedly did visit the country as a missionary in the 3rd century BC and converted the Anuradhapura king at Mihintale. Within a very short time, Buddhism had replaced Hinduism as the national religion, and temples and monasteries were built; almost all this early work has been lost due to Hindu invaders from south India who demolished Anuradhapura's religious buildings and expelled the monks.

Chief periods of stability and Buddhist supremacy occurred during the reigns of Dutugemunu (2nd century BC), Mahasena (3rd century) and, at Polonnaruwa, Kings Parakrama and Nissanka Malla (both 12th century). Most of Sri Lanka's ancient Buddhist structures of importance to have survived were built in the reigns of these four kings.

Continued on page 24...

- BUDDHISM IN SRI LANKA -

SCHOOLS OF THOUGHT

The *Theravada* school of Buddhism is followed in Sri Lanka, where it developed shortly after the people had been converted from Hinduism. Also known as the 'doctrine of the elders', or the 'small vehicle' school, it is in many ways the most austere and demanding form of the religion.

Followers are held individually responsible for achieving enlightenment, and Buddhist ritual together with all forms of image worship are condemned. However, Buddhism is nothing if not tolerant, and figures of Hindu gods can often be seen in Sri Lankan Buddhist temples, Vishnu, Siva and Kataragama (or Skanda) being the most popular. There appears to be no doctrinal reason for their appearance, rather the reverse, but many Sri Lankans seem reluctant to give up gods completely, just in case, and regard the Hindu deities as 'Buddhist gods'. All most puzzling and incomprehensible to the visitor. Theravada Buddhism is also followed in Tibet, Thailand, Burma, Vietnam, Laos and Cambodia.

The second most important school, known as the *Mahayana*, or the 'large vehicle' school, has few adherents in Sri Lanka, even though it developed on the island in the 2nd century BC when, it is claimed, new religious texts in Sanskrit were discovered. Basically, it is far less rigorous, as the individual is given reduced responsibility, faith being regarded as sufficient to ensure eventual salvation. Theravada Buddhists regard this as heresy. Followers of Mahayana predominate in Tibet, Japan, Vietnam, China and Korea.

DECLINE AND REVIVAL

Although today Buddhism appears to have an unassailable position in Sri Lanka, during the colonial period of the Portuguese and Dutch it declined to such a degree that when the British arrived in the 1790s the religion appeared to be a spent force.

Revival began as recently as 1875, when Buddhism began to be associated with Sinhalese independence, and threats to its continued existence from other religions were feared. For reasons of national pride, the theory was promoted that Sri Lanka had been chosen by the Buddha during the last of his three visits, to preserve and promote the purest form of Buddhism.

Inevitably, the religious leaders became somewhat less tolerant and began to involve themselves in secular matters. Since independence, many Sinhalese politicians have had to take note of their demands: failure to do so being almost certain to invite canonical disapproval and consequent lack of support from the Sinhalese electorate. On occasion the activities of some monks during the recent Sinhalese/Tamil disputes can hardly be said to have followed Buddhist teaching.

· S c u l p t u r e ·

As may be expected, Sri Lanka's most highly regarded sculptures represent the Buddha, many of the most important being carved from natural rock face.

SCULPTURAL FEATURES

Buddha figures

The earliest existing figures were carved from limestone, a material that weathers badly, and have lost their original crispness. The Buddha can be depicted either seated with crossed legs, reclining (a representation of his achieving nirvana) or standing.

Hands cupped on the lap indicate meditation, a raised hand depicts protection, hands touching against the chest represent teaching and a hand pointing downwards indicates that the Buddha is watching (the witness attitude).

Moonstones

With just one exception discovered so far, moonstones (not to be confused with the semi-precious gemstone) are semi-circular in shape. They stand at the entrance to a building or at the foot of the stairs leading up to it and have been defined as a stone doormat. The design content is invariable, with bands of creatures, each symbolising the Buddhist view of life.

Stylised flames enclose the bands, which proceed from the elephant (birth) to the horse (old age), lion (illness), bull (death), serpent (lust) and goose (purity). The central lotus flower is a reference to the search for enlightenment.

Guardstones

These stone panels flank the entrance to a building and depict a mythical *Naga* (cobra) king who holds an object with auspicious attributes and is accompanied by dwarfs. Some of Sri Lanka's finest examples of carving can be seen on guardstones at Anuradhapura.

Balustrades

Several examples of balustrades decorated with dwarfs and the mythical beast, the *makara*, can be seen at Anuradhapura.

Mandapaya

A temple forecourt decorated with columns.

Buddhist Arts

As Theravada Buddhists do not approve of art for art's sake, architecture and carving rather than painting and music provide the prime examples of Sri Lankan religious art.

Negombo

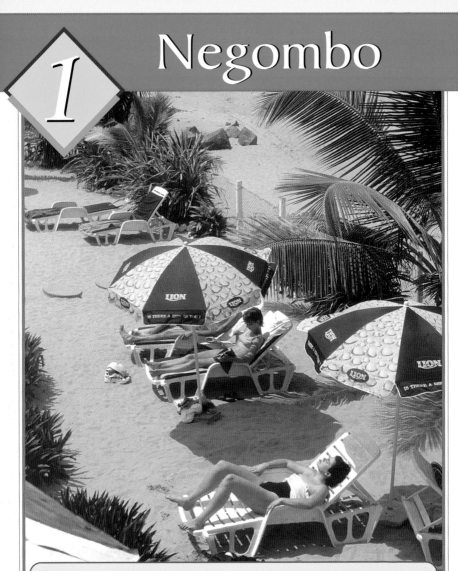

Negombo is partly a beach resort and partly a large fishing town refreshingly detached from tourism. The resort area, a 2 mile (3 km) long stretch of hotels, is separated from the town by half a mile (1 km) of not very enticing beach. As might be expected, the further from the town, the cleaner the sand becomes, and for this reason almost all the better hotels are located at the extreme north end.

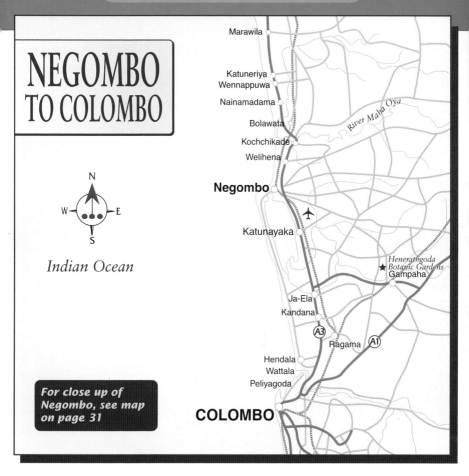

NEGOMBO TO COLOMBO

N
W — E
S

Indian Ocean

Marawila

Katuneriya
Wennappuwa

Nainamadama

Bolawata

Kochchikade

Welihena

Negombo

Katunayaka

River Maha Oya

*Henerathgoda
Botanic Gardens*
★ Gampaha

Ja-Ela
Kandana

Ⓐ3

Ragama Ⓐ1

Hendala
Wattala
Peliyagoda

COLOMBO

For close up of Negombo, see map on page 31

TRIPS TO COLOMBO

As it lies just 23 miles (37 km) north of Colombo and there are direct road and rail connections with the city, Negombo would appear to be ideal for those wishing to pop into the metropolis from time to time: for a top class dinner in a five-star hotel, for example. However, journeys take much longer than would be expected. By car, 50 minutes to the city should be allowed, even at quiet times, but the fare will be around 1500 rupees return. Express, air-conditioned buses take around an hour following the same route, but unfortunately the vehicles are small, and queues to board them will be lengthy in the rush hour. You may have to strap-hang, and queuing can take as long as the journey. Local buses are uncomfortable and

CINNAMON – SPICE WORTH MORE THAN GOLD

Apart from the south-west coast of Sri Lanka, the cinnamon tree is only indigenous to India's Malabar coast and the west coast of Burma. This rarity, combined with the great popularity of cinnamon from ancient times until the early 19th century led, at one period, to its price exceeding that of gold.

The spice played an important part in the Egyptian mummification process, and in medieval Europe Christians employed cinnamon as a fragrance during Mass. Internationally, cinnamon was most frequently used as a flavouring for food and wine and as a component of medicines. It was by far the most profitable spice traded by the Dutch East India Company.

In North America and the United Kingdom cinnamon is now used primarily to flavour cakes, apple pies and biscuits, and, combined with brown sugar, as a tasty coating for boiled ham. Elsewhere, it is still included in some curry dishes. A small amount of oil is contained in cinnamon, which can be distilled from trimmings and incorporated in drugs, liqueurs, perfumes and foods.

Extracting the spice

The evergreen cinnamon tree, a bushy relative of the laurel, can attain a circumference of 3 ft (1 m) and a height of 30 ft (9 m). To obtain the spice it is necessary to remove the outer bark from the shoots, which are cut into rods 42 inches (107 cm) long, and dried for up to five days. Further drying and bleaching takes place before the process is completed and the fragrant sticks are ready for transportation.

In Sri Lanka, cinnamon is harvested during the period of the south-west monsoon, June to August, and few tourists, therefore, are able to observe the process. Nearly all Sri Lanka's remaining cinnamon trees grow in private gardens; commercial plantations, as introduced by the Dutch, are no longer financially viable.

stop everywhere, and infrequent trains all take at least 90 minutes to Fort Station. For these reasons, most tourists make fewer journeys to Colombo than they might otherwise have planned.

ACCESS TO
THE AIRPORT

It is in its proximity to Bandaranaike International Airport that Negombo gains over all the other beach resorts in Sri Lanka. Tourist coaches or taxis cover the 4.5 mile (7 km) journey in less than 20 minutes. Compare this to more than 3 hours for the 60 mile (90 km) crawl southwards along the Galle Road to Sri Lanka's most popular resort complex at Beruwala/Bentota – quite a journey to endure after a long intercontinental flight. Because of its ease of access, many opt either to begin or end their Sri Lankan holiday at Negombo.

NEGOMBO
AS A MAIN
BEACH RESORT

It must be said that from the visitor's viewpoint no beaches north of Colombo, including Negombo's, match those of the popular resorts to the south. They are less clean, less picturesquely 'tropical' and mainly the preserve of fishermen, with all the paraphernalia – much of it odiferous – that their activities involve. In spite of this, Negombo has now regained its popularity, which had diminished somewhat as other coastal resorts were developed and their accommodation upgraded.

Apart from having a convenient location, much of the resort's success lies in the great value offered by its hotels, even though only one, the **Royal Oceanic** has an official rating as high as four stars, and none provides satellite television in the bedrooms. It takes just under an hour to walk along the sands from the main hotels to the town, 2.5 miles (4 km) distant, but as the beach is dead straight and some-what featureless it is more usual to take a three-wheeler; this will follow Porutota Road to Lewis Place and Sea Street, a route that runs parallel with the beach, ending at the Fish Market.

Negombo is currently regarded as the gay capital of Sri Lanka and, presumably in consequence, the number of reported cases of Aids is relatively high.

HISTORY

The importance of cinnamon throughout the 17th century was pivotal to the growth of Negombo, formerly a small fishing community. From the town, cinnamon trees grew in profusion along the southwest coast, and Negombo's natural waterfront became extremely important to its exportation.

The Portuguese arrived at Negombo in 1640, soon building a fort and setting about the conversion to Catholicism of the local Karava people, who it is believed migrated to Negombo from north India around 1000AD. Little force was needed due to the Portuguese policy of rewarding converts with many benefits. Most Karavas have remained Christian, as evidenced by the wealth of impressive churches in the town, which has earned it the

Continued on page 32...

NEGOMBO

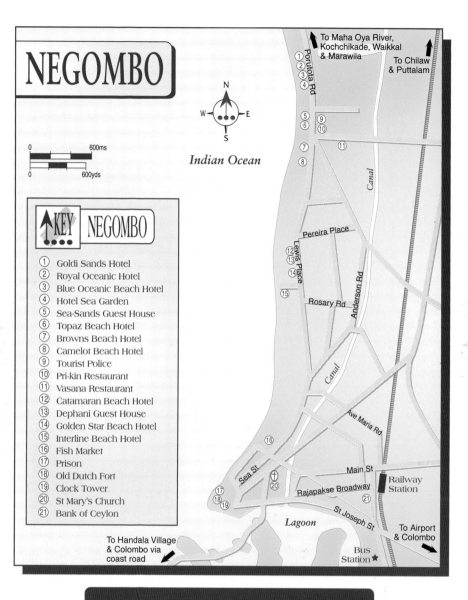

Indian Ocean

0 — 600ms
0 — 600yds

KEY NEGOMBO

1. Goldi Sands Hotel
2. Royal Oceanic Hotel
3. Blue Oceanic Beach Hotel
4. Hotel Sea Garden
5. Sea-Sands Guest House
6. Topaz Beach Hotel
7. Browns Beach Hotel
8. Camelot Beach Hotel
9. Tourist Police
10. Pri-kin Restaurant
11. Vasana Restaurant
12. Catamaran Beach Hotel
13. Dephani Guest House
14. Golden Star Beach Hotel
15. Interline Beach Hotel
16. Fish Market
17. Prison
18. Old Dutch Fort
19. Clock Tower
20. St Mary's Church
21. Bank of Ceylon

To Maha Oya River, Kochchikade, Waikkal & Marawila

To Chilaw & Puttalam

Poruota Rd

Canal

Pereira Place

Lewis Place

Anderson Rd

Rosary Rd

Canal

Ave Maria Rd

Sea St

Main St

Rajapakse Broadway

St Joseph St

Railway Station

To Airport & Colombo

Lagoon

To Handala Village & Colombo via coast road

Bus Station

Opposite; Top: Sri Lanka's ladies wear either the sari, left or, more formally, the 'national', Kandy-style sujeewa

Middle: Negombo's Canal, excavated by the Dutch settlers to transport cinnamon

Bottom: Brown's Beach Hotel, Negombo, looks directly over the beach

nickname 'Little Rome'. Portuguese and English names are particularly common amongst the Karavas, practically always indicating that he or she is a Christian.

When the Dutch East India Company ousted the Portuguese in 1658, they built their own churches, for Protestant rather than Catholic worship, strengthened the fort and built a canal to facilitate the transportation of cinnamon along the coast. This also helped the settlers transport Ceylon gemstones, which were another major export, particularly to India.

By 1796, when the Dutch handed over Negombo to the British, the demand for cinnamon had fallen considerably, and attempts were made by the new settlers to compensate by growing sugar cane; however, the conditions proved unsuitable. Fortunately, the new settlers were soon to introduce another crop to Ceylon that would prove somewhat more successful: tea!

When trunk roads and the railway between Colombo and Negombo had been laid out by the British, the Dutch-built canal lost its relevance to the export trade. Of prime importance to the region, of course, was the construction of Sri Lanka's international airport at Katunayaka, just 6 miles (10 km) south-east of Negombo. Plans for further expansion of the airport bode well for local employment. Nevertheless, apart from fishing, tourism is Negombo's main industry, even though, like Sri Lanka's other coastal resorts with the exception of Mount Lavinia, its development is comparatively recent.

NEGOMBO BEACH

Past the short jetty at the northern end of the hotel zone, fishermen operate their single-sail boats, known as *oruvas*, which resemble Arab dhows and feluccas. Early Arab traders may in fact have inspired the design of the oruva, a vessel that Sri Lankan fishermen are said to have used on the south-west coast for at least 2,000 years. Most oruvas are small, but they can attain a length of 33 feet (10 m) and accommodate a crew of eight. If its hull is made of jack wood (from the jack fruit tree) and regularly waterproofed with shark or coconut oil, it is possible to operate an oruva for up to 20 years.

The **Goldi Sands Hotel** marks the northern extremity of the beach front hotels. Immediately behind them runs Porutota Road, in the district of Ethukala, and a few somewhat cheaper hotels and guest houses have been built on the opposite side; from these, of course, the road must be crossed to get to the beach. Just south of Goldi Sands are two sister hotels operated by the Jetwing Group – the **Royal Oceanic Beach** and the **Blue Oceanic Hotel**. All rooms in both hotels are air-conditioned and, a rarity in Negombo, fitted with mini-bars. The Royal Oceanic Beach incorporates an Ayurvedic Health Centre, and is the only four-star rated hotel in Negombo. Yet a third Jetwing hotel follows, **Sea Garden Hotel,** much smaller and aimed at the budget tourist; however, its guests may use the facilities of the adjacent Blue Oceanic.

Facing Negombo's best stretch of sand, **Brown's Beach Hotel,** a member of the Aitken Spence travel group, has 140 air-conditioned rooms (4 of them suites) but, due to its popularity, rarely has vacancies in the high season. This predominantly low-rise hotel, the largest in the area, stretches a lengthy distance along the beach, fronted by bars and restaurants, which is why it never appears to be crowded, in spite of the many guests accommodated. Diners may choose from an à la carte menu (excellent smoked chicken) or a buffet.

The extraordinary breakfasts would be hard to beat anywhere. Apart from Sri Lankan curries, 'English' breakfasts always include: freshly-grilled bacon, sausages, kidneys, tomatoes, fried potatoes, and, of course, eggs cooked as required. As in other Aitken Spence hotels, guests are given the opportunity of tasting fresh juice from little-known local fruits such as the Belli and the Sour Sap: unappetising names but delicious flavours, which are never watered down.

Cocktail-lovers should make a point of visiting its beach bar, particularly when the sunset looks promising. Barmen shake the finest and cheapest margaritas, made with Mexican tequila and French cointreau, east of Acapulco.

South of Brown's Beach it should be noted that the former Golden Beach Hotel has changed its name to Camelot. The best of the remaining hotels are **Catamaran Beach Hotel** and the **Interline Beach Hotel** both of similar standard, with, between them, the higher-rated **Golden Star Beach Hotel**, fully air-conditioned and boasting a rooftop night-club. After passing the last group of guest houses on the periphery of Negombo town, the sand becomes decidedly grubby.

NEGOMBO TOWN

The town occupies a triangular promontory delineated by the Indian Ocean to the west and a lagoon to the south; it is bisected by the Dutch-built canal. Negombo's oldest sector lies between the sea and the canal, while the newest, which incorporates the railway and bus stations, is located east of the canal.

FISH MARKET

The market is held daily, except Sunday, in the open air, sea breezes fortunately dispersing much of the fishy smell, which some would otherwise find nauseating. Many visitors will already have seen a **tropical fish market**, but Negombo's is particularly special, due to the exotic specimens on display. Hues are brilliant, as if an exotic aquarium had been emptied; one wonders what the names of those yellow, blue, red and green fish might be and, even more important, how they taste. Presumably, locals with eclectic tastes enjoy them, but most are reputed to be somewhat boney; at any rate, their appearance on the menus of tourist hotels should not be expected.

Below the market, winding around the coast to the lagoon, fishermen and their families live in shacks, outside which they beach their oruvas. It is a very intimate area, and there is no path, but visitors are welcome to look around and take photographs without any hassle.

THE FORT SECTOR

From the Fish Market, follow Sea Street to its end: ask directions for the **prison**, not the fort, as the local people know nothing of the former fort – they will think you mean 'port'. The prison, with its formidable gates, was built by the British, and the building still serves its original purpose. Opposite the entrance is all that survives of the fort: a brick portal dated on both sides 1678 – therefore presumably built by the Dutch rather than the Portuguese – and beside this a stretch of wall on which stands a slender clock tower inscribed 'VR', indicating that it was erected by the British (who were keen on clock towers) in the reign of Queen Victoria. The fort commanded both the ocean and the lagoon.

A short distance to the east, overlooking the lagoon, visitors can usually be shown around the **Dutch Reformed Church** by a guardian.

NEGOMBO CENTRE

Follow St Joseph Street eastward from the north side of the lagoon's bridge. The first turning, left, follows the canal, which cuts through the middle of the town to Main Street, and continues to **Puttalam**, 60 miles (96 km) to the north; from the south end of the lagoon, the canal continues to Colombo, 22 miles (35 km) distant.

At Main Street, a right turn leads to Negombo's commercial area, with its banks and shops. Some may be tempted to buy brassware, which is the most important local craft.

The **railway and bus stations** face the east end of Broadway, which runs parallel with and to the south of Main Street. There is not a great deal of outstanding interest for tourists in this part of Negombo, and some will prefer to turn left from the canal at Main Street, crossing to the west side of the canal.

On the left rises **St Mary's Church**, the most impressive of the many Catholic churches in

Lagoon

Negombo's 7.5 mile (12 km) long lagoon, one of the most important in the south, is famous for its freshwater crustaceans. Much of its east bank is bounded by the airport, and in clear weather tourists will have a good view of the lagoon from their plane just before landing. A bridge from the town crosses the lagoon, via islands, to the narrow strip of land that cuts it off from the sea and runs half way to Colombo. This is a much more interesting route from Negombo to the city than the main road, and if a car is available every effort should be made to persuade the driver to follow it in one direction at least – he may charge a small premium for doing so.

The residents of **Duwa Island**, which is linked to Negombo by the lagoon's bridge, all take part in a passion play that is held each year – a sort of eastern Oberammergau. A get-away-from-it-all hotel is Blue Lagoon, located on the lagoon at **Talahena**, 5 miles (8 km) south of Negombo.

An additional advantage of taking the lagoon road is that it approaches Colombo via **Hendala**, a picturesque canal-side village.

Right: Brilliantly marked tropical fish are the attraction at Negombo's fish market

Below: Sorting out the fishing nets at Negombo

Negombo. Built in 1874, the pink-painted structure's west end is flanked by square twin towers, a popular architectural feature locally. Within, panels over the aisle's walls are decorated with scenes from the life of Christ; the barrel-vaulted roof is distinguished by three paintings of the Virgin, the work of a local artist. It is hard to believe that the altarpiece is not made of fondant icing sugar. Negombo's Fisher's Festival takes place in the monsoon month of July and, therefore, is witnessed by few tourists.

From the church, Sea Street is a short walk away.

RESORTS NORTH OF NEGOMBO

Between Negombo and Marawila, a distance of 12.5 miles (20 km), several beach front hotels have been built recently. They appeal primarily to tourists looking for a 'non-resort' holiday, with only marginal facilities outside their hotel – but plenty of fishermen to be seen hauling in the nets. As already mentioned, their beaches are not the island's most appealing.

Just 2.5 miles (4 km) from Negombo, at **Palangathurai**, a suburb of Kochchikade, both the **Oceanic Garden Hotel** and **Seashells Hotel** offer fully inclusive terms that are reminiscent of cruise liners as they include: breakfast, lunch, dinner buffets, afternoon tea, snacks, 'midnight' snacks, local spirits, soft drinks and mineral water!

Located 7.5 miles (12 km) from Negombo, the three-star **Club Hotel Dolphin**, in Waikkal Village, provides air-conditioned rooms in the main block or non air-conditioned cottages. It is popular with package tour operators and sports enthusiasts. Like the Seashells Hotel, inclusive terms are *very* inclusive. Nearby, **Ranweli Holiday Village** is a chalet development that also specialises in sporting activities.

Marawila, located 12.5 miles (20 km) north of Negombo, is perhaps too out of the way for most first time visitors to Sri Lanka, but value for money at the hotels is exceptional and there are signs that it will eventually develop into a popular resort. **Mario Beach Hotel** and **Sanmali Beach Hotel** have recently been joined by the **Aquarius Beach Hotel**.

ADDITIONAL INFORMATION

Restaurants

Most visitors adopting Negombo as their main beach resort will have taken inclusive terms that include a buffet dinner. In spite of this, many people like to eat out from time to time. The succulence of Negombo shellfish, renowned throughout Sri Lanka, can be appreciated more cheaply away from the top hotels.

Just behind Browns Beach Hotel is the highly recommended Vasana Restaurant for reliable steaks and tasty crab. On the opposite side of the road, Pri-Kin serves Chinese food in larger than usual portions: the fish, prawns and soups are highly recommended. As might be expected, restaurants along Negombo Beach change regularly, and local advice plus observation will undoubtedly result in the discovery of additional first rate eateries.

• DAY EXCURSIONS FROM NEGOMBO •

Most visitors using Negombo as their beach resort base take coach excursions around the island lasting several days, which they have booked before leaving home. However, day excursions of interest can easily be made by those who prefer to limit their touring. Exceptionally popular are the Elephant Orphanage at Pinawala, the Botanic Gardens close to Negombo at Henerathgoda, and boat trips up the Maha Oya to the north. Most hotels can arrange these excursions, but in any case obtain their advice on price and duration.

Henerathgoda Botanic Gardens

The gardens lie near **Gampaha**, off the A3 Colombo-Kandy road; from Henerathgoda station it is just 1 mile (1.6 km) to the entrance. Lovers of antique furniture will be interested to see hardwoods such as ebony and satinwood thriving. However, the rubber trees are more significant, as it was here, in 1876, that they were first grown successfully in Sri Lanka.

Plants reached Henerathgoda from Kew Gardens, where they had germinated from Brazilian seedlings smuggled to England via France by Sir Charles Wickham. Within twenty years, rubber had become a major crop in Sri Lanka, from where the first rubber tree plants were sent to Malaya, thus founding that country's vitally important rubber plantations.

Note that the Botanic Gardens of **Peradeniya** , near Kandy, are more spectacular if a decision has to be made to visit one or the other.

Maha Oya River

Boatmen will take tourists on river trips up the Maha Oya, which runs out to sea 3 miles (5 km) north of Negombo. The verdant scenery is attractive, but it is the bankside activities of the villagers that are of greatest interest, the highlight usually being the traditional manufacture of rope from coir (coconut husks). With luck, the tapping of coconut trees for toddy will also be seen.

2 Colombo

I n January 1996 the commercial heart of Colombo was devastated by a Tamil Tiger bomb. Young military personnel, bristling with guns, now bar pedestrians as well as vehicles from approaching the Harbour, and it is at their blockades that visitors are most forcibly reminded that a civil war is still in progress.

Only British tour operators are still unable to provide their clients with accommodation or excursions to Colombo due to recommendations by the United Kingdom Government. All other nationalities are free of such restrictions. However, there is nothing to stop British tourists visiting Colombo providing they make their own arrangements.

Even without such restrictions, however, it cannot be said that Colombo offers extensive tourist attractions, and few will wish to allocate more than two days of their vacation exploring it. Having said this, it would be a shame to leave Sri Lanka without seeing something of its administrative capital, particularly as, with the exception of Kandy, there will be no opportunity of exploring another metropolitan area of importance – there is none.

Another reason for visiting Colombo, particularly for independent visitors, is its convenience for

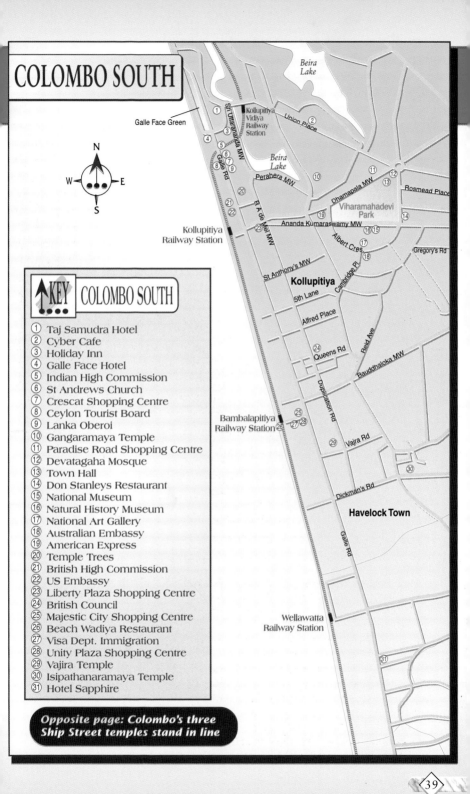

COLOMBO SOUTH

Beira Lake

Galle Face Green

N
W — E
S

Kollupitiya Vidiya Railway Station

Union Place

Sri Uttarananda MW

Galle Rd

Beira Lake

Perahera MW

Dhamapala MW

Rosmead Place

Viharamahadevi Park

R A de Mel MW

Ananda Kumaraswamy MW

Kollupitiya Railway Station

St Anthony's MW

Kollupitiya

Albert Cres.

Cambridge Pl.

Gregory's Rd

5th Lane

Alfred Place

Reid Ave

Queens Rd

Bauddhaloka MW

Duplication Rd

Bambalapitiya Railway Station

Vajira Rd

Dickman's Rd

Galle Rd

Havelock Town

Wellawatta Railway Station

KEY COLOMBO SOUTH

1. Taj Samudra Hotel
2. Cyber Cafe
3. Holiday Inn
4. Galle Face Hotel
5. Indian High Commission
6. St Andrews Church
7. Crescat Shopping Centre
8. Ceylon Tourist Board
9. Lanka Oberoi
10. Gangaramaya Temple
11. Paradise Road Shopping Centre
12. Devatagaha Mosque
13. Town Hall
14. Don Stanleys Restaurant
15. National Museum
16. Natural History Museum
17. National Art Gallery
18. Australian Embassy
19. American Express
20. Temple Trees
21. British High Commission
22. US Embassy
23. Liberty Plaza Shopping Centre
24. British Council
25. Majestic City Shopping Centre
26. Beach Wadiya Restaurant
27. Visa Dept. Immigration
28. Unity Plaza Shopping Centre
29. Vajira Temple
30. Isipathanaramaya Temple
31. Hotel Sapphire

Opposite page: Colombo's three Ship Street temples stand in line

booking and confirming flights, arranging itineraries, hiring a car, changing money at favourable rates, purchasing a Cultural Triangle ticket, and, above all, because it cannot be done elsewhere, obtaining a visa extension to the permitted 4 or 6 week stay in the country.

Five-star international hotels proliferate in Colombo (there are few elsewhere in Sri Lanka) and they are not excessively expensive; rates, in fact, significantly undercut those of similar establishments in nearby India. Bargaining, particularly at weekends, is worth trying in order to get a better deal.

Colombo is only 18 miles (30 km) from the international airport, and as there are direct buses to the middle of town, many independent visitors make immediately for the city. However, the attractions of a beach resort may prove irresistible, particularly after a long flight. Negombo, only 6 miles (10 km) from the airport, is preferred by some as their initial destination before facing the big city.

HISTORY

Before the usual progression of Portuguese, Dutch and British settlers of south Asia, Colombo was an insignificant port from where, since the 8th century, Arab visitors had shipped cinnamon stripped from the trees that grew wild in profusion nearby. Colombo had been incorporated in the Kotte Kingdom, the country's most important, when the Portuguese arrived in the 16th century. Initially, they merely displaced the Arab traders, but eventually the Portuguese became 'protectors' and virtual controllers of Kotte's rulers. In 1656 the Dutch

arrived and, together with the Kandyans, threw the Portuguese out of Colombo. Like their predecessors, the Dutch were primarily interested in Colombo's cinnamon trade, initiating the plantation system.

For the first time, a wall was built enclosing the area overlooking the waterfront, which is still known as **Fort**. The Dutch were also responsible for laying out the adjacent **Pettah** quarter of Colombo, primarily as a residential area for their merchants. However, it was the British, who arrived in 1798, who were chiefly responsible for Colombo reaching its pre-eminence, constructing throughout the 19th and the first half of the 20th centuries new roads, the railway, administration buildings and, above all, developing the quay and its international port.

In this period, Colombo became the capital of Ceylon, and it remained so following independence. However, in the 1980s, a purpose-built parliament house was constructed at **Kotte**, to the south-east, and this town has become once again the legislative capital of the country. Its official name is Sri Jayawardenepura Kotte.

Colombo, due to its pre-eminence, has suffered grievously throughout the troubled 1980s and 90s, several bomb outrages culminating in the January 1996 blast, in which 80 were killed and 100 injured. Perhaps the most destructive event, however, occurred at the beginning of the Sinhalese/Tamil strife when, in 1983, Sinhalese mobs in reprisal for a Tamil massacre of an army patrol, laid waste to much of the Tamil-occupied Pettah district.

FORT

Although only fragments of the defensive walls survive, the commercial heart of Colombo is still known as Fort; its streets, laid out in a grid pattern, will take little time to explore.

A WALK AROUND FORT

From the south, Fort is heralded by the **Ceylon Intercontinental Hotel,** a convenient starting point for an exploration of the middle of town, which will begin with the tall office blocks that sprawl on either side of Janadhipathi MW, formerly Queen Street.

Visitors approaching the city either by car or bus via the long **Galle Road,** which runs parallel with the coastline, will be dropped close to the hotel. Those arriving by train at Fort Station will generally prefer to take a rickshaw to the hotel, as the railway station, in spite of its name, is located in the Pettah. Alternatively, visitors journeying to Colombo by long distance buses will be deposited at termini sited on the eastern edge of the Pettah, and many, therefore, prefer to explore the Pettah first before proceeding westward to Fort.

The Ceylon Intercontinental Hotel is one of three luxury-class hotels that run in an almost straight line from west to east, the other two being the **Galadari,** now restored after suffering major damage from the Central Bank bomb blast of 1996, and the **Colombo Hilton,** the most luxurious (and the most expensive) of the city's hotels. All have excellent swimming pools, the Hilton's being dramatically overlooked by Colombo's gleaming new skyscrapers.

Checkpoint

Marine Drive, a surprisingly quiet thoroughfare, follows the sandy shore northward immediately behind the Intercontinental in the direction of the **Galle Buck Lighthouse.** However, the reason for its tranquillity becomes apparent well before the lighthouse: a military checkpoint blocks the road to unauthorized pedestrians and vehicles, and a return must be made to the Intercontinental. Visitors are thereby deprived of close proximity not only to the lighthouse, built around 1960, but also, behind it, the white **Buddha Jayanthi dagoba,** raised 65.5 ft (20 m) off the ground on stilts – an outstanding Colombo landmark.

The reason for the road block is not only to prevent terrorist attacks on the quay but also on the President's Residence from the rear. Much of Janadhipathi MW, from which the Intercontinental is entered, was demolished by the 1996 Central Bank bomb but, like a phoenix rising from the ashes, a cluster of slender tower blocks has been built recently around the thoroughfare to provide Colombo with the obligatory 'modern' skyline demanded by major Asian cities as evidence of their importance.

But the killing has not ended, and one prays that the confidence exhibited by the Sri Lankans in reconstructing the city's commercial area, at enormous expense, will not prove to be unwarranted. All three towers, semi-circular in plan and clad in rather fetching pale blue glass will, of course, accommodate offices.

Thankfully surviving the destruction in Janadhipathi MW, **Steuart**

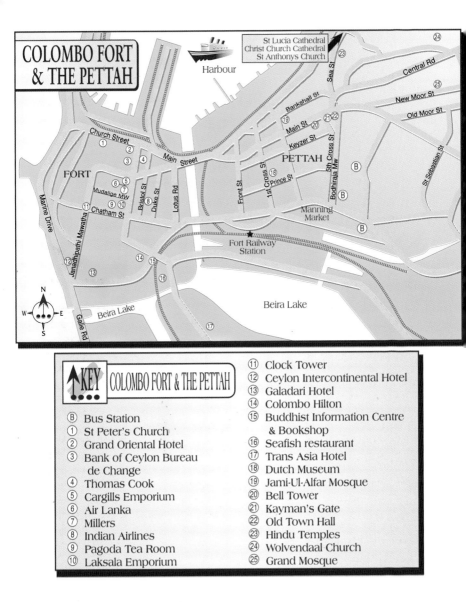

COLOMBO FORT & THE PETTAH

St Lucia Cathedral
Christ Church Cathedral
St Anthonys Church

Harbour

KEY COLOMBO FORT & THE PETTAH

Ⓑ Bus Station
① St Peter's Church
② Grand Oriental Hotel
③ Bank of Ceylon Bureau de Change
④ Thomas Cook
⑤ Cargills Emporium
⑥ Air Lanka
⑦ Millers
⑧ Indian Airlines
⑨ Pagoda Tea Room
⑩ Laksala Emporium
⑪ Clock Tower
⑫ Ceylon Intercontinental Hotel
⑬ Galadari Hotel
⑭ Colombo Hilton
⑮ Buddhist Information Centre & Bookshop
⑯ Seafish restaurant
⑰ Trans Asia Hotel
⑱ Dutch Museum
⑲ Jami-Ul-Alfar Mosque
⑳ Bell Tower
㉑ Kayman's Gate
㉒ Old Town Hall
㉓ Hindu Temples
㉔ Wolvendaal Church
㉕ Grand Mosque

House, founded in 1835 and now the headquarters of a travel company, retains much of its Regency style, the Classical Greek key frieze being a rare decorative feature in Sri Lanka.

Note that all westbound interconnections with the street are blocked, including the Chatham Street junction at the clock tower.

Clock Tower

The wife of Sir Henry Ward, Governor of Ceylon 1855-60, designed the **clock tower** ahead, which was erected in 1857 – as a lighthouse. It was always intended to incorporate a clock, but 50 years were to pass before funds became available for its installation.

Mariners were able to view the revolving light, originally a double oil lamp, up to 17 miles (27 km) away. However, by the mid-1950s, tall office blocks were obstructing the view, and the Galle Buck Lighthouse was erected on Marine Drive as a replacement.

Post Office

North of the clock tower, Janadhipathi MW is dominated on the right hand side by the enormous white **Post Office**, built in 1895 but looking at least half a century earlier. Its architect, H. F. Tomalin, employed Greek themes throughout, with Ionic pilasters to the ground floor, twin sets of Corinthian columns and pilasters to the first floor and Greek swags enlivening the attic. Within, the main hall is exceptional, once again Greek-inspired, and with a semi-circular wooden counter that is reminiscent of the old booking halls in railway stations.

President's Residence

No pedestrians or vehicles may pass the west side of the road opposite the Post Office as it fronts the heavily-guarded **President's Residence**. Built in the 18th century, the house became the British Governor's Residence, and was known either as King's or Queen's House depending on the gender of the reigning monarch. It is now the official residence of Sri Lanka's president. Even without the restrictions, due to the trees around it, only glimpses of the building are possible from the road.

A bronze monument to **Sir Edward Barnes**, a Battle of Waterloo hero and Governor of Ceylon 1824-31, stands at the north entrance.

From this statue, all distances between Colombo and elsewhere are measured.

North of the President's Residence, facing the Ministry of Foreign Affairs, **Gordon Gardens** was laid out as a public park in 1889 by Governor Arthur Gordon, to commemorate Queen Victoria's Silver Jubilee two years earlier. Unfortunately, the gardens now lie within the restricted zone.

Distinguished by its elephant head frieze, the **Standard Chartered Bank**, adjacent to the Post Office, opened in 1880, immediately prospering thanks to the success of Ceylon's tea and rubber planters, many of whom became extremely wealthy. Formerly, the site was occupied by a Portuguese monastic establishment. Most of the present building dates from 1930s remodelling.

The road now curves sharply eastward, changing its name to Sir Baron Jayatilaka MW. On the curve lies the white, colonial building that now accommodates the country's Ministry of Foreign Affairs – a most picturesque scene, but no photographs are permitted. Before parliament moved to Kotte, the Prime Minister's and Cabinet Offices were incorporated in the complex.

Many tourists may wish to take advantage of **Thomas Cook's** travel office on the north side of the street, or the **Air Lanka** office which faces it. In the latter, the young ladies behind the counters are deliciously attractive, which is just as well, due to the slow-moving queues for service which must usually be endured. Any queries regarding flights to India are more speedily dealt with at the **Indian Airlines** office (4 Bristol Street). Be sure to bring a passport, even for simple flight confirmations!

BAZAARS AND DEPARTMENT STORES

Neither Fort nor the Pettah are shopping meccas for tourists, as most outlets operate for the convenience of Sri Lankans. Those seeking European-style shopping areas will find them in Galle Road, to the south of the city.

Almost opposite Air Lanka, **Sathosa** is typical of the 'bazaar' type of store that can be found in most important towns. Within, an apparently illogical combination of goods is sold; although few will have great appeal to foreign visitors, cricket enthusiasts will find high quality cricket balls an easily transportable bargain in the sports section.

Cargill's, located on the south corner with York Street, is Sri Lanka's most famous department store, and now has branches throughout the country. It was founded here in 1844, originally accommodated in an ancient Dutch-built house; the store now occupies the entire block between York Street and Chatham Street.

In the late 19th century it became fashionable to paint the bricks of Colombo's buildings red, or in red-and-white candy stripes, and Cargill's retains the decoration from this period. An attractive feature of the store is its shady arcades, beneath which sundry traders ply their wares. Cargill's only section of interest to most tourists is its supermarket – a reliable and economical source of spices, pickles and cashew nuts – unsalted for cooking, salted for snacks. Note that all large bags must be left at the entrance, and that for goods other than food, *four* separate counters must be visited in order to complete a purchase. This is a good example of the south Asians' love of unnecessarily complicated systems, which their visitors find so incomprehensible – and often so infuriating.

Southward, on the Mudalige MW corner, **Millers** is another long-established department store, even more old-fashioned than Cargill's.

Laksala emporium

Noteworthy as the exception to the general rule, **Laksala**, near the York Street/Chatham Street intersection, does appeal directly to tourists. A government-run emporium on two floors devoted to Sri Lankan crafts, all the items are sold at prices that are fixed and fair. Just the place for tourists determined to return home with carved wooden elephants, brass Buddhas, painted dance masks, batik materials – or simply a pack of Ceylon (as it is still called, rather than Sri Lanka) tea.

Further westward along Chatham Street, those in need of sustenance may like to visit the **Pagoda Tea Room** for an egg and bacon breakfast, a simple rice and curry lunch or mid-afternoon tea and cakes. Dinners, however, are not on offer, the establishment closing at 6pm (2.30pm on Saturdays). Self-service or waiter service is available and prices are very Sri Lankan, their contrast with those demanded for similar dishes in the international tourist hotels explaining how locals can dine out on Sri Lanka's abysmally low wages.

ST PETER'S CHURCH

On leaving the hotel and turning left into Church Street, one is confronted by a military barrier. Fortunately, on this occasion, pedestrians are allowed to pass for a short distance in order to visit **St Peter's Church.**

With its colonnaded facade, the exterior of the building has no obviously ecclesiastical features; this is because no significant alterations were made to it in 1804, when what had been the dining-hall of the Dutch governor's 18th century residence was adopted by the British garrison as its church. Not until 1812 was St Peter's dedicated.

Within, immediately right of the entrance, a monument commemorates William Tolfray (1778-1817), who had served as an officer under Arthur Wellesley, the future Duke of Wellington. He later translated part of the Bible into the local Pali and Sinhalese languages.

Adjoining the church is the **Missions to Seamen** building; its bar is open to all mariners. No further progress is permitted along Church Street.

Many will find this a convenient point at which to bargain ferociously with a three-wheeler driver for a tour of the Pettah district – an hour should be sufficient. Alternatively, some may prefer to return to the Ceylon Intercontinental Hotel and continue southward to explore the Galle Road area of Colombo.

THE PETTAH

Pettah, a corruption of *pita* (Sinhala) and *pettai* (Tamil), both meaning outside, i.e. outside the fort, refers to Colombo's extensive area of bazaars, by far the largest in Sri Lanka. It was created in the 16th century, when the Portuguese, and later the Dutch, started building their residences to the east of the fort's confining walls; merchants and Arab traders soon added warehouses.

Colombo's 'hidden' Harbour

On no account to be missed is the stunning, **panoramic view of Colombo Harbour** from the fourth floor Harbour Room/Harbour Bar of the **Grand Oriental Hotel**, 2 York Street, Colombo 1, ☎ 320391, Fax 447640, where a great value lunchtime buffet is available. To reach the hotel, return northward along York Street, continuing to its end, a five minute walk.

Neither particularly grand in style nor oriental in decor, the hotel, formerly known as the Taprobane (the Roman name for Sri Lanka) is by far the oldest in central Colombo, having been founded in 1837. Walls of the more extensive building constructed in the late 19th century featured red and white candy stripes, but remodelling in 1991 removed all trace of this. In 1890, the Russian playwright Anton Chekhov stayed at the hotel during his 6-day tour of Ceylon.

This is the only point in Colombo from which visitors may view the Harbour, but what a view! The hotel directly overlooks its central jetty, providing a symmetrical vista that is quite breathtaking. In spite of the hotel's bulk it has only 32 rooms, but all are air-conditioned and moderately priced.

The Prince of Wales, later Edward VII, laid the foundation stone of Colombo Harbour, which was begun by the British in 1875. Approximately 3,000 vessels a year use the facilities of its six terminals; however, air travel has greatly reduced the importance of passenger arrivals and departures.

As within Fort, a grid pattern of streets evolved, the widest being Main Street, which is traversed, from west to east, by First, Second, Third, Fourth and Fifth Cross Streets, in the manner of New York. Each street was allocated a specific trade, following the tradition of medieval European cities.

A WALK AROUND THE PETTAH

Most visitors will find the general hustle and bustle of the Pettah's narrow thoroughfares, with their constant traffic jams, more memorable than any of its individual buildings.

Main Street begins at the junction with York Street, facing the Grand Oriental Hotel, soon crossing the short canal that links the quay with **Beira Lake**, before branching right at the Khan Clock Tower. First Cross Street, right, leads to Prince Street, left, where, at No. 95, the central city's only **museum** of much interest is found.

Dutch Period Museum

The colonnaded building that houses this museum was constructed as Colombo's town hall in 1796, the last year of Dutch rule. Since then, chameleon-like, it has served as: private residence, orphanage, hospital, police station and post office. In 1977, aided by Dutch finance, restoration and conversion of the building began to provide the present museum, which opened in 1982.

Artefacts from the Dutch period, 1685-1796, are exhibited. Above the door, inscribed in Latin, is text from Psalm 127: "Unless the Lord builds a house the work of labourers is in vain." The usual discriminatory entrance charge for foreigners is imposed.

Jami-Ul-Alfar Mosque

Second Cross Street returns northward, and continues past the Main Street junction to this enormous **mosque** on the righthand side, which dominates the quarter. Constructed in 1908, the building is a good example of Colombo's

The Jami-Ul-Alfar Mosque, Colombo

red-and-white candy stripe exteriors.

Kayman's Gate

Return to Main Street where, towards its east end on the south side stands a tiny Portuguese belfry, all that survives of **Kayman's Gate**, which was originally located further south, overlooking Beira Lake. The lake, now reduced in size, was once infested with crocodiles – to which the Portuguese allegedly threw their prisoners for speedy, untraceable disposal! The Dutch transferred the belfry to its present position in the 18th century: the name 'Kayman' is Dutch for crocodile.

Old Town Hall

A few steps further east is the **Old Town Hall**, which was built by the British in the 19th century, and converted to house a museum of Colombo ephemera in 1984. Of greatest interest to most will be the examples of early public transport displayed at the rear of the building.

Sea Street Temples

Sea Street, which leads northward, has been at the heart of Colombo's gem trade for more than 100 years, but owes its tourist interest to the three Hindu temples (*kovils*) which, unusually, are located close to each other in a straight line on the west side of the street. Visitors are welcome to enter the temples, all of which date from the 19th century.

The first, which faces Andival Street, is dedicated to **Ganesh** the elephant-headed god, whilst the next two, the **Old and New Kathiresan**, both pay tribute to the war god Skanda. Restored in 1999, the entrance to the New Kathiresan is a splendid example of filigree wood carving – it is usually open for puja around 12.30am, when the other two are closed.

Wolvendaal Church

The most appealing ecclesiastical building in Colombo is the Dutch **Wolvendaal Church**, erected in 1749, as inscribed on the exterior. Although externally there is little of interest, the interior has been perfectly preserved.

Vel Festival

In late July or early August, to coincide with the Buddhist Esala Perahera at Kandy, the Hindu Vel festival takes place in Colombo, its highlight being a procession led by Skanda's gilded chariot from the Kathiresan temples to other temples dedicated to the same god at Bambalapitiya, a southern suburb of Colombo.

The church, which lies a short distance to the east of the Sea Street temples, is entered from its east end – an attendant is usually on duty to open up after 9.30am. Original wood furnishings and fittings include a gallery and a typical Dutch pulpit, complete with sounding board. At the west end, plain stone floor slabs give way to reused 18th century tombstones, many of them finely carved.

Roman Catholic Churches

Located north of the Wolvendaal Church are the Roman Catholic churches of **St Anthony's**, close to the quay, and the domed **St Lucia Cathedral**, begun in 1872 but not completed until 1906; its nave alone can accommodate a congregation of 6,000. However, non-Catholics with limited time available may well opt to give both a miss as they are not of compelling interest.

To the south, on the edge of the Pettah, lie the **BM and CTB bus stations** and the **Fort Railway Station**, built in 1867; all three can be approached from Wolvendaal Church via the Grand Mosque.

Those who have opted to explore Pettah before Fort may now continue westward to the Ceylon Intercontinental Hotel, from where the walking tour of Fort as already described can begin. The hotel is also a good starting point for a three-wheeler tour of the Galle Road area south of Colombo.

Just before crossing an arm of Beira Lake, the classical brown stone bulk of the **Secretariat** is seen to the left. It was built by the British in the 19th century to house parliament, which sat here until the transfer to Kotte. Outside the Secretariat stand three bronze figures of statesmen connected with Ceylon's struggle for independence: prominent is that of the country's first Prime Minister, Dudley Senanayake.

GALLE FACE GREEN

Stretching ahead for 1 mile (1.6 km), this narrow rectangle of open land, bordered by the Indian Ocean, is a popular recreation area for Colombo's citizens. It was laid out in 1859 by Governor Sir Henry Ward for ladies and children of Colombo, as commemorated by a stone in the middle of the green. Now,

more energetic pursuits, primarily cricket, football and kite flying are enjoyed by Colombo youths.

Many visit the green on Sunday afternoons, when they are fed by street vendors and entertained by snake charmers. Mass, held on Galle Face Green by the Pope in January 1995, was attended by several thousand Roman Catholics. All these activities took their toll of the 'green', which became almost bereft of grass until, in January 1999, the long-promised returfing began at the south end. However, it would appear that some restrictions will have to be made if the new grass is to flourish permanently.

A further cluster of luxury hotels begins towards the south end of Galle Face Green.

Taj Samudra Hotel

The **Taj Samudra** looks across the green towards the Indian Ocean; on this side its balconied rooms benefit from wonderful sunsets. Extensive grounds and a large pool are a feature of this hotel, which offers the Taj Group's usual five-star luxury.

Even if not staying at the hotel, visitors who mistakenly believe that Indian specialities will be available throughout Sri Lanka should be sure to visit the hotel's Navratna restaurant – it will be their only chance to enjoy top quality food in an Indian restaurant on the island. Excellent Mogul buffets are also, however, a feature of the nearby Holiday Inn, and Indian specialities are available at the Mount Lavinia Hotel.

Galle Face Hotel

This large hotel, which opened at the south end of the green in 1864, maintains a colonial charm in its extensive public areas. The south wing has been closed for many years, awaiting finance for complete remodelling, and only 77 rooms (22 of them suites) are available; for this reason, it is extremely difficult to obtain accommodation here in the season.

Gracious, colonnaded terraces and a sea-water swimming pool facing the ocean are the hotel's highlights. Some of the suites are huge – try at least to see the Commonwealth Suite – but run-of-the-mill rooms are somewhat disappointing, which accounts for the hotel's relatively lowly three-star rating in spite of its apparent magnificence. Visitors to the hotel's bar will be able to appreciate the old-world atmosphere best in the early evening, when sea breezes frequently waft across the central lawn.

Two large plaques in the foyer list, respectively, the names of famous visitors and major events in the world's history that have occurred since the hotel opened. British tourists will be interested to note the inclusion, on the first plaque, of theatrical giants Laurence Olivier, Vivien Leigh, Trevor Howard and Noel Coward, whilst Americans will observe that Gregory Peck, John D. Rockefeller and Cole Porter have stayed at the hotel.

GALLE ROAD

Galle Road, the A2 trunk route, sweeps past the east flank of the hotel, linking Colombo not only with Galle, but also with every beach resort in the south. Accompanying Galle Road, hugging the coast as far as **Matara** where it terminates, the railway line provides an alternative method of transport which some visitors prefer.

Several tall shopping areas have been constructed along Galle Road, but only the most recent are entirely western in concept; early examples tend to comprise large numbers of small units, inhibiting the display and range of goods on offer. Galle Road is built up almost along its entire length, giving the impression that Colombo's suburbs are never-ending. The majority of tourists who travel by road from the airport directly to their chosen beach resort, and must of necessity use Galle Road, will find the journey somewhat tedious.

In spite of recent road widening, progress from Monday to Saturday afternoon is generally slow, and every attempt should be made to avoid Colombo's 'rush' hours – when vehicles hardly move at all, let alone rush. It is partly for these reasons that international tour operators seldom base their clients further south than Bentota.

A short distance from the Galle Face Hotel, on the same side of Galle Road, long queues denote the **Indian High Commission**; the queues are for visas to enter India. Unfortunately, visitors who decide they might like to pop over to India during their holiday – there is a short and economically-priced flight to Trivandrum – must think again. Such a simple measure is quite beyond the scope of India's infamous red tape. An Indian visa applied for by a foreigner in Sri Lanka can take around three months to process: somewhat too late for most holidaymakers, and those intending to visit India must therefore obtain a visa before leaving home.

St Andrew's Church

Built of stone in 1842 as the **Scots Kirk**, battlements reinforce the building's highland castle appearance. This was the first Presbyterian church to be built in Colombo.

The tall **Lanka Oberoi**, next to the church, is one of Colombo's largest and most luxurious hotels. Unusually, 212 of its 416 rooms are singles, indicating the Oberoi's popularity with businessmen. Designed around a central atrium, in the modern fashion, the hotel has a direct link with the **Crescat Shopping Centre**.

Crescat, opened in 1999, is the Sri Lankan shopping area that most closely resembles western examples. Units are larger and goods, particularly clothing, appear to be aimed at overseas visitors. The basement is worth visiting at lunchtime, where a 'village' of small restaurants offers a variety of dishes quickly and cheaply.

Ceylon Tourist Board

Almost directly opposite Crescat are the offices of the **Ceylon Tourist Board**, where a wide selection of posters and brochures may be purchased. However, if possible, it is better to obtain the brochures from Ceylon Tourist Board offices outside Sri Lanka, where they are free of charge. Visitors cannot expect much assistance here, and in 1999, frustrated Sri Lankan hoteliers mounted a campaign to privatise the marketing of the country's tourism, and the situation, hopefully, will improve. Some much needed personnel changes have already been made.

Further south, on the same side of the road, the **British High Commission** provides assistance to UK

The museum opened in 1877, and its gleaming white building, designed by James Smither, remains one of Colombo's most impressive colonial structures.
All aspects of Sri Lankan craftsmanship are covered within the museum.

In the grounds, facing the entrance, a bronze figure of Sir William Gregory commemorates the British governor responsible for the creation of the museum.

Within the foyer, facing the entrance, the seated **Toluvila Buddha** is regarded by many as the finest statue discovered at the ancient capital of Anuradhapura, where Sri Lankan art attained its zenith. The Buddha's ethereal expression of repose is deeply satisfying – not only to Buddhists.

In the corner left of the entrance, the standing figure of Buddha in wood dates from the much later Kandy period.

Brass figures and carvings in ivory, horn and tortoiseshell from the 17th to 19th century Kandy period occupy Gallery 6. The appearance of the Hindu swastika emblem will be noted on some Buddhist artefacts.

In Gallery 7, a Kandy manuscript box decorated with arabesques

visitors in difficulties or seeking to do business in Sri Lanka.

Prime Minister's Residence

Immediately opposite, **Temple Trees** is the official residence of the Prime Minister. Little can be seen through the screen of exotic frangipani trees, and neither pedestrians nor motor-

evokes English Jacobean work. Collections of ancient coins and chinaware (from China) are followed by a horrendous selection of gifts presented to Prime Minister Mrs Bandaranaike by visiting heads of state; they include a silver space shuttle (USA), a wooden kangaroo (Australia) and a model cannon (USSR); Britain's silver rose bowl is probably the least offensive. Most specimens resemble prizes awarded for rifle shooting in a rundown fairground.

The next room, Gallery 8, half-panelled in wood, displays important items relating to the Kandy monarchy. Contemporary portraits of the monstrous Vikrama Raja Sinha, the last king of Kandy, and his Queen flank the 17th century royal throne, crown, footstool and ceremonial swords, all of which are protected by glass. After the British had defeated the Kandy Kingdom in 1815, these symbols of monarchy were removed to Windsor Castle, where they remained until George V returned them to the country in 1934.

Sanni ceremonial masks decorate the stairway to the upper floor. Each of the eighteen separate designs depicts a specific malady, presumably the reason for their sinister appearance.

The first of the upper floor's galleries features an outstanding collection of Sri Lankan musical instruments. Masks and costumes used in **Kolam dancing** are displayed in the larger room: reminiscent of the satire of Gilbert and Sullivan, self-important politicians, police officials and military leaders are among those derided in the performances.

Puppets of the world are an important feature of the **children's section** of the museum in the adjacent room. Suspended from the ceiling is the skeleton of an enormous Blue Whale (earmarked for eventual removal to the Natural History Museum when a sufficiently lofty area becomes available).

An extensive collection of bronzes, both Buddhist and Hindu, and gold ornaments are shown in the rooms that follow.

Swastika

The swastika is an ancient symbol, associated for Hindus with good fortune. It is also important for Buddhists and Jains. When the top bar faces right, the swastika indicates the day, when it faces left, the night. Only rarely will the swastika be seen facing left.

---

ists may proceed along the east side of Galle Road at this point.

Continue southward to the first turning left, at the end of which **Liberty Plaza** is a large but rather old-fashioned shopping development. It faces the long R.A. de Mel MW where, at No. 39, Levis sell their jeans at prices that are much lower than in the West.

BAMBALAPITIYA

Roughly 2 miles (3 km) south of Liberty Plaza, Galle Road passes through the suburb of **Bambalapitiya**, which can be reached easily by bus or train; it is one stop from **Kollupitiya station**.

Galle Road is linked to **Bambalapitiya Station** by the short Station

Road, the entrance to which is flanked by two of Colombo's major shopping malls: **Unity Plaza** and **Majestic City**. The latter is probably the best one-stop mall in Colombo for purchasing clothes, as Leather Collection, Odel, Benetton and Cotton Collection have branches here. The basement restaurants are highly recommended for a reasonably priced lunch.

On the south side of the road is the Visa Department of **Sri Lanka's Immigration Office**, the only venue in Sri Lanka where visas may be obtained to extend a stay.

At the end of Station Road cross the railway line ahead to Colombo's best-known fish restaurant, **Beach Wadiya**, which overlooks the beach towards the sea. Reservations are recommended at weekends.

Two other shops in Bambalapitiya which may be of interest are: **Barefoot** (handicrafts of quality), 704 Galle Road, just north of Majestic City, and **Toys For U** (beautifully made toys, many of wood) 385 Duplication Road.

Duplication Road runs to the east of and parallel with Galle Road; from its south end, in Havelock Town, Dickman's Road branches eastward to Isipathana MW, where the **Isipathanaramay Buddhist Temple** is renowned for its frescoes.

From Liberty Plaza, a fifteen-minute walk or a three-wheeler will take visitors eastward along Ananda Kumaraswamy MW to Albert Crescent and Sri Lanka's most important museum.

Approached by a path from the National Museum is the **National Museum of Natural History**, which lies behind it. Unless interested in somewhat dusty stuffed animals, few will wish to spend valuable vacation time in this unremarkable museum. It faces **Viharamahadevi Park**, Colombo's most popular park, and is adjacent to the National Art Gallery, but for incomprehensible reasons the gateway providing access to both is kept locked, and visitors wishing to reach them must return to Albert Crescent, turn right, and right again to Ananda Kumaraswamy MW.

National Art Gallery

Located in a low, cream-painted building, works of art exhibited, both permanent and temporary, are indeed 'national', with the emphasis on portraits. Do not expect to find internationally regarded masters represented.

Cross the road to the park.

Viharamahadevi Park

Laid out by the British in the 19th century as Victoria Park, this attractive green oasis was renamed in 1951 to honour the mother of Dutugemunu, who liberated Anuradhapura from the south Indians in the 2nd century BC. The exotic trees flower profusely in the spring, when, unfortunately, most tourists have departed.

Working elephants are frequently bathed and scrubbed by their owners in the pool located in the south-west corner of the park, particularly on Sunday afternoons. Large, but very nervous monitor lizards, known locally as *talagoyas*, inhabit the park and can often be seen lurking beneath shrubs at the north end, near the gold Buddha seated on a plinth. As may be expected, the park caters for children; there is a small funfair and a zoo in the middle, and a mini-train runs around the perimeter.

Overlooking the park to the right, the domed **Town Hall** is a splendid example of British neo-classicism of the 1920s. It was built in 1927, as proclaimed on the facade in Roman numerals, and re-placed the function of the old town hall in the Pettah. Due to its civic importance, the building is kept in gleaming white condition.

Paradise Road

Facing the Town Hall, at 213 Dharmapala MW is the strangely-named Paradise Road, possibly **Colombo's most appealing store** in which to browse. Occupying a Victorian period house, antiques, embroidery and ceramics are in-cluded amongst the wide range of locally-made goods displayed. On the second floor, an excellent cafe serves soft drinks – even fresh fruit juice – and snacks daily until 6pm.

The **Devatagaha Mosque** stands behind the Town Hall, but a more interesting religious building (at least to non-Muslims) is a short three-wheeler ride away to the west where, just off the south end of Sir James Pieris MW stands **Colombo's most appealing temple**.

Gangaramaya Temple

As Colombo is a relatively modern city there are no ancient temples to be found there. This **Buddhist temple** comprises the usual vihara and dagoba, together with a museum and two courtyards. The main court-yard is packed with religious stat-ues, whilst the second is frequently occupied by the temple's elephants, which can usually be seen munch-ing branches of palm trees.

Brightly painted frescoes in the vihara depict scenes from the Buddha's life, and there is an enormous reclining Buddha. For some visitors this will be the first Buddhist temple seen in Sri Lanka; it is very typical, as most tend to be virtually identical in form and content, apart from the ancient ex-amples within the cultural triangle.

ADDITIONAL INFORMATION

Not a great deal of further interest lies in the area around Colombo, however, some may wish to visit the important school of Buddhist teaching at **Kelaniya**, 4.5 miles (7 km) north-east of the city. It is easily reached by bus 226, which begins its journey in front of the police station.

Raja Maha Vihara Temple, Kelaniya

By tradition, the Buddha preached here during his first visit to Sri Lanka 2,000 years ago, and this is commemorated in Kelaniya each January by the *Duruthu Perahera* procession which begins at the temple.

The dagoba is one of Sri Lanka's rare hollow examples. Originally, it is believed to have accommodated a throne from which the Buddha had preached. Set with precious stones, this was lost many years ago, probably following a south Indian invasion. The damaged dagoba was rebuilt in the 13th century but destroyed 300 years later by the iconoclastic Portuguese. Nineteenth century restoration may have incor-porated fragments of the original structure, but this is not certain. The vihara houses a greatly venerated reclining Buddha; frescoes depict scenes from his life, together with important events in Sri Lanka's Buddhist history.

Mount Lavinia

Mount Lavinia, formerly a fishing village known as Galkissa, is located 8 miles (13 km) south of Colombo centre – although few who approach it from Galle Road will comprehend the distinction. Indeed, the high tower blocks of the city can be seen clearly from the seashore, and behind the hotels there is undoubtedly a suburban feel. Nevertheless, Mount Lavinia is regarded as a beach resort in itself, and, occupying its promontory, the Mount Lavinia Hotel, from which the area gained its name, remains the most famous hotel in Sri Lanka.

MOUNT LAVINIA HOTEL

For most, the interest of Mount Lavinia begins and ends with this historic hotel, still redolent of colonial times in spite of recent additions and renovations. Although the huge complex now boasts 275 bedrooms, there is rarely a vacancy between December and March due to constant demand, particularly from British tourists to whom Mount Lavinia has become something of a legend. The legend is reinforced immediately on arrival, by doormen

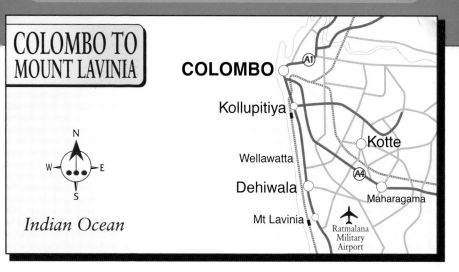

in pith helmets and gold braid uniforms as worn by the Governor's staff in 1823.

GOVERNOR'S BUNGALOW

Lieutenant-General Sir Thomas Maitland, the second British governor of Ceylon, was responsible for the first building on the site, a rustic, but well-appointed bungalow, completed in 1806, which he referred to as his 'place in the country', and named Mount Lavinia House; parts of this still survive as the core of the structure. 'Mount' was a reference to the bulging rock on which the bungalow was constructed but is no longer apparent due to subsequent construction work; in the 17th century the rock was referred to by Dutch mariners at sea as 'the pregnant wench'.

In 1824, the then governor, Sir Edward Barnes, extended Maitland's bungalow; what are now known as the Governor's Staircase and Governor's Wing survive from his work. Soon after Barnes had completed the extensions, demolition of the building was ordered by the government for some unknown reason. In the event, after falling into disrepair, it was sold and converted to the Grand Hotel, which opened in 1877. During the Second World War, the hotel served as a military hospital, and some scenes from this period were re-enacted in the building during the making of the film *Bridge Over The River Kwai*; although set in Burma, the film was made in Sri Lanka.

Governor's Wing

Furnished in colonial style, the exclusive Governor's Suite has been created on two levels of the Governor's Wing. However, many of the other rooms in this block may be considered rather spartan in view of the tariff demanded. In the spring of 1999 there were no signs of the lift in the Governor's Wing being renovated or replaced, although it had been out of action for some

A romantic tradition, for which there is some evidence, explains the British governor's puzzling choice of Lavinia for the name of his country house. Sir Thomas Maitland, a confirmed bachelor in his mid-forties, was a workaholic despot who treated his staff with an arrogant strictness that earned him the nickname 'King Tom'. Conversely, his sense of fair play endeared him to the under-privileged: during his governorship he introduced trial by jury, repealed discriminatory laws against Catholics and forbade the local insistence that some low caste women had to bare their breasts at all times.

Although Maitland worked hard he also played hard: the soirées held at his new house were renowned in Colombo for their opulence. In the nearby fishing village of Galkissa, a beautiful young girl named Lovina Aponsua was the star attraction of a dancing troupe run by her father; she was from mestizo (Portuguese/Ceylonese) stock, and as such regarded as low caste. It has been suggested that Maitland first saw Aponsua's dancers when they entertained at one of his soirées, and was immediately smitten by Lovina. In a short period rumours of a romantic liaison between the dancer and the crusty British governor became rife in the village.

Apart from local tradition passed on by word of mouth the only 'corroboration' of the affair is the certain existence of a tunnel from the wine cellar of Maitland's house to the village. Part of this was exposed and bisected when the railway cutting was excavated in the mid-19th century; the house end of the tunnel was bricked up as recently as 1957.

Lieutenant-General Sir Thomas Maitland, George III's Governor of Ceylon, was a Scottish nobleman, the second son of the Earl of Lauderdale, and it is hardly surprising, therefore, that no documentation of an amorous adventure with a half-caste girl, if one ever existed, has been discovered. Extreme secrecy would have been paramount: no meetings in public, not even a nod and certainly not a wink would have been possible – hence the reason for the tunnel.

It is said that Maitland built a small house for Lovina in Galkissa, and ordered a tunnel to be excavated from his wine cellar (not an unusual occurrence), ending at the top of the well in Lovina's garden. She would probably have been aided to and from the tunnel's entrance by her father who, it is said, approved of the relationship and no doubt would have been well rewarded for his connivance.

Having completed five years service in Ceylon, Maitland returned to England in 1811 before being appointed Governor of Malta two years later. He died in 1824, still unmarried. It is not known what happened to 'Lady Lovina', as the dancing girl seems to have been called locally: some say she died of a broken heart, or even that she committed suicide, however, there seem to have been no rumours of a love-child.

A single member of the Aponsua family survives but refuses to discuss the matter. If there is no truth in the story, the reason why Maitland named his house Lavinia (an anglicised version of Lovina) remains a mystery. Apparently no member of his family, nor any of his few female acquaintances bore that name. Undoubtedly, Puccini would have done wonders with a libretto based on the tale.

months, a quite unacceptable situation considering there are five levels involved. Check the current situation.

Bay Wing

Those who expect 21st century amenities should specify the Bay Wing, all its 100 rooms being air-conditioned and fitted with satellite television, a mini-bar and a canopied bed. Honeymooners find the romantic history of the hotel hard to resist, most of them are Sri Lankans, but each month on average eight couples from overseas spend at least part of their honeymoon here.

The hotel's rooftop swimming pool overlooking the sea, has recently been renewed and is now one of the finest in the country. From its terrace there is access to the 'private' beach. The 'public' beach, to the north, (both are really public) can only be approached from the hotel garden – an attendant will unlock the gate in response to loud shouts.

RESTAURANTS

Some of Sri Lanka's best food is served in the Mount Lavinia Hotel's wide range of restaurants. This is because close proximity to Colombo attracts many business clients, who demand higher standards than those provided by hotels catering mainly for foreign holidaymakers. The hotel has been fortunate in retaining as its executive chef since the late 1950s the legendary Publis; he is regarded as the master of Sri Lankan cuisine, and local dishes such as *ambul thiyal* (marinated tuna) and devilled prawns are prepared in the authentic manner – chilli content will be automatically reduced for foreigners.

There are three beach front restaurants within the complex. At **Seafood Cove** diners make their choice nightly from the 'Seafood Market'; beach barbecues here are a major attraction. As might be expected, the **Texan Grill** offers steaks (imported), whilst the **Bamboo Curtain** provides Chinese food both at lunchtime and in the evening.

The Clipper oriental restaurant offers Sri Lankan and Indian dishes, some of which also appear, combined with western dishes, on the menu of the hotel's all-purpose **Governor's Cafe**, a 24-hour coffee shop, in which the hotel's substantial buffet breakfasts and dinners are provided.

On occasions, 'theme' cuisines are served in the Governor's Cafe, although the **Regency Room** is preferable for these if possible. The Regency Room can accommodate 200 and is one of the hotel's three banquet and conference venues, the others being **La Fontaine** (160 capacity) and the galleried **Empire Room** (capacity 500) which is illuminated by an enormous chandelier. On Friday and Saturday nights **The Little Hut** night-club and disco, with top-class local bands and DJs, attracts the more affluent Colombo youngsters in addition to hotel guests.

LOCATION AND BEACHES

It will soon become apparent that trains run directly behind the hotel, but very little noise from them penetrates the building. The beach to the north, which stretches all the way to Colombo, presents clear views of the ancient trains, which here can be somewhat noisy. Unless staying at the Mount Lavinia Hotel, the beach can only be reached from the town, or vice-versa, by walking across the railway line – take good care if doing so. Few will find this part of the beach very appealing as it is backed by the shell of a multistorey hotel that was burnt out in the communist riots of the 1980s; now condemned, demolition is awaited. In front of it huddle a cluster of beach shacks offering food and drink, which has become a meeting place for gay locals and tourists (even though in Sri Lanka, as in most Third World countries, homosexuality remains illegal).

The 'private' beach on the south side of the hotel is manicured regularly by its staff, however, a great deal of flotsam is washed in, presumably from Colombo, and the sea here will have little appeal for fastidious bathers.

EXCURSIONS

The railway station is conveniently located behind the Mount Lavinia Hotel, and visitors will find that trains either to Colombo or the southerly beach resorts an economical and convenient way of making excursions. Establish departure and return times in advance from the station; avoid rush hours and Sundays if possible.

A great advantage of rail over road travel along this part of the southwest coast is that for much of the journey there are uninterrupted views of the beaches from the trains, whilst the Galle Road offers little more than brief glimpses between almost unbroken stretches of ribbon development.

Dehiwala Zoo

Dehiwala, a Colombo suburb, lies 1.5 miles (2 km) north of Mount Lavinia, from which its zoo is easily reached by three-wheeler. Those who have visited Asian zoos before will not expect to find acceptable accommodation for the big cats, and they will be right. Most will also fail to see the point of caging monkeys, which scamper freely a short distance inland. An elephant show at 5pm is really something out of a circus.

OTHER HOTELS AT MOUNT LAVINIA

In spite of the pre-eminence of the Mount Lavinia Hotel, there are, surprisingly, many other hotels and guest houses in the area, all however, are separated from the beach by the railway track. For those who would like to sample the luxuries of the Mount Lavinia Hotel but are unable to obtain a booking or prefer more economically-priced accommodation, it is possible, of course, to stay close by and make daily visits – anyone may use the restaurants and bars and, for a daily fee, the pool and beach facilities.

Additional Information

German Restaurant
De Saram Road, Mount Lavinia
☎ 01-716034

4 Wadduwa & Kalutara

Glorious golden sands are typical of the south-west coast

S oon after continuing southward from Mount Lavinia, the Galle Road passes Ratmalana Airport on the left. Until quite recently this served as Sri Lanka's domestic airport, from which there were flights to the remoter parts of the island. Now, however, it is the preserve of the military. Civilians may no longer fly anywhere within Sri Lanka.

The airport is located on the west side of **Bolgoda Lake**, an arm of which brushes Moratuwa en route to the sea. **Moratuwa** is famous for furniture manufacture, and many of its showrooms face Galle Road; ample supplies of superb, locally-grown hardwoods still appear to be available, styles are generally conservative.

PANADURA

After Moratuwa, a bridge crosses the wide Panadura River, at the end of which the town of **Panadura** nestles against its estuary. Whilst there is little of interest to see in the town, wildfowl enthusiasts will enjoy the lake nearby, and the road from Panadura to **Ratnapura 'gem city'** (see below) 70 miles (111 km) distant follows one of the most idyllic routes in Sri Lanka.

For all its present serenity, Panadura's history mirrors important events in the country, some of them violent. Early Arab traders sheltered from the monsoon in the estuary, those who decided to stay probably being the first to settle in the country. Tamils from South India invaded Panadura in the 12th century but were quickly repulsed. In the 17th century, Dutch invaders

en route to Colombo from Kalutara managed to cross the Panadura River, but waiting for them on the north bank was a Portuguese army: and half the Dutch force of 3,000 perished.

WADDUWA

This small town, located between Panadura and Kalutara, has two luxury hotels, which, together with its splendid, palm-fringed sands, qualify Wadduwa as a beach resort.

Unlike Mount Lavinia and to a certain degree Negombo, buildings do not intrude here, and the water is absolutely clean; Wadduwa is really where Sri Lanka's famous 'tropical' south-west coast beaches can be said to begin. However, the beach is dead straight and for this reason rather less picturesque than those further south.

The Blue Water, a member of the Jetwing Group, and one of Sri Lanka's few five-star beach hotels, is superbly appointed, as might be expected. **Villa Ocean View**, located in Molligodawatte, 2.5 miles (4 km) from Kalutara, offers a choice of three-star villas or four-star rooms in the new wing, and is much less expensive.

KALUTARA

Kalutara's beach accommodation spreads 12.5 miles (20 km) from the area known as Mahawaskaduwa, north of the town, to Katukurunda, but the majority of the better hotels are found in what is referred to as **Kalutara North**. Here, the beach at last becomes more picturesque and sea bathing is excellent. As may be expected, most amenities are provided by the hotels, where life revolves around the swimming pools. Top of the range are the **Royal Palms Hotel** and the brand new **Golden Sun Resort** both with air-conditioned rooms, which include satellite TV and a mini-bar. Their superb pools both incorporate jacuzzis.

The Kalu Ganga meets the sea at Kalutara, to which it has curved from its source on **Adam's Peak**. An islet bisects the estuary proving a useful staging point for the bridge that crosses both arms of the river. Visitors will notice the modern **Gangatilaka Vihara** at the end of the bridge, which marks the site of an ancient Buddhist temple. Although it takes the form of a dagoba, the white structure is hollow and encloses no relic. It may be entered – to reveal another 'dagoba' and paintings of the life of the Buddha. Buddhist motorists frequently halt to pray here for a safe journey, so expect company! Outside stands the usual Bo-Tree, at which pilgrims make offerings.

Kalutara is no longer the spice area it was in the 17th century, when cinnamon trees grew in profusion. Bamboo baskets and coir mats are now, apart from tourism, the chief industry. In summer, many people's popular tropical fruit, the purple mangosteen, is an important crop: for some reason Kalutara's mangosteens are particularly succulent, but sadly they ripen too late for most tourists to sample.

RATNAPURA

Established in the 13th century, **Ratnapura** (meaning 'gem city') is regarded by Buddhists as a holy site. It is most easily reached from Panadura, on the west coast, by following the A8 highway inland. This road eventually leads to **Haputale**, and provides one of the most attractive tourist routes to the hill country.

Soon after leaving Panadura the scenery takes on a pastoral nature, its attractive villages being dependent on agriculture for their existence; the contrast with the heavily built up Galle Road is highly pleasing. In the region are many rubber plantations, the latex from which is processed in local factories (75 per cent of Sri Lankan rubber is exported).

Sri Lanka's gems

Remember that diamonds, red rubies, deep blue sapphires, emeralds and topaz are not found in Sri Lanka. Most local stones tend to look rather pale and watery. They include sapphires, cat's eyes, alexandrite, aquamarines, zircons, moonstones, spinels and garnets.

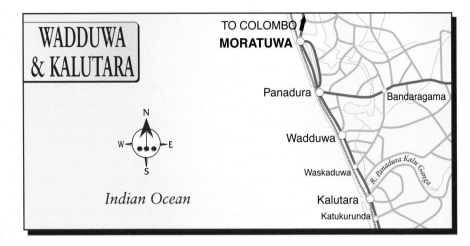

Small groups of men may be observed from time to time searching for gems in river beds and valleys that are lined with a specific seam of gravel in which they can be found.

GEM TRADERS AND MUSEUMS

Ratnapura itself offers little of tourist interest in spite of being the central trading point for Sri Lankan gemstones. Only professional dealers or experts are likely to find a bargain and, as can be imagined, the streets are filled with con-men looking for gullible tourists – beware! Only stones are sold in the town, never settings, and visitors wishing to buy them are advised to purchase only from government approved establishments, but preferably in Colombo, where they are likely to be cheaper.

Those with time available may wish to visit a gem museum whilst in Ratnapura; all offer free admission, however, some are little more than sales outlets for gems. Polishing can often be observed, but never cutting. The best, both located on the outskirts of town, are the **Gem Bureau Museum and Laboratory** at Getangama, and the **Gemmological Museum** at Batugedera, where the owner's exceptional collection of gemstones and interesting exhibits, including the model of a gem pit, are displayed.

Staying in Ratnapura

Accommodation in Ratnapura is surprisingly limited, but the two-star **Rathnaloka Tour Inn**, nearly 4 miles (6 km) outside the town at Kahangama, can be recommended. There are 52 air-conditioned rooms, de-luxe being worth the supplement as standard rooms are rather small. The swimming pool (closes at 6pm) is attractive, however, culinary delights should not be expected in the restaurant, where typical package tourist fare is offered. Excursions to the **Sinharaja Rain Forest** can be arranged at the hotel.

– ADAM'S PEAK (SRI PADA) –

Overlooking Ratnapura, to the north-east, is Sri Lanka's most
sacred mountain, Adam's Peak. Pilgrims climb to its summit
between December and April, when there is the best chance of fine
weather. During this period they are joined by tourists, who must be
physically fit and enthusiastic. Whilst it is possible to begin the
ascent from Ratnapura, an easier route, which takes 2 hours less,
begins at the village of Dalhousie, on the Badulla/Hatton/Nuwara
Eliya road, and most, therefore, will prefer to wait until they visit
the Hill Country before making this exhausting expedition.
However, views of the distinctive peak, shaped like the Matterhorn
(but without snow) are more impressive from just outside
Ratnapura, due to the lower level of the land on the west side; the
weather is generally clearer
in the morning.

*Adam's Peak, a pilgrimage site for the
four religions – but what a climb!*

Continued on page 64...

– ADAM'S PEAK (SRI PADA) –

Climbing the mountain

Adam's Peak is located in the 60,000 acre (24,000 hectare) **Peak Wilderness Sanctuary**. Surprisingly, entry is open to anyone at all times – even foreigners are not charged. Climbers from Ratnapura will pass through the Carney Estate, and should allow 6-7 hours to complete the 5 mile (8 km) ascent; this means beginning at around 11.30pm in order to reach the summit by dawn – the preferred arrival time. Warm clothing will be needed in the early hours.

Annual holidays and *Poya* (full moon) days should be avoided by tourists, as then they will be joined by up to 20,000 pilgrims and progress will be slow.

In March and April, enormous flocks of butterflies can be seen on the mountain, which have given it yet another name: *Samanale Kande* (Butterfly Mountain).

Climbers are lulled by the initially gentle approach, but the steepness soon increases until only a seemingly endless flight of steps is left to ascend. During the season, the routes are well illuminated at night, and refreshment stalls, most of which offers very strong, very sweet tea, are found at intervals.

Although, when clear, the views from Adam's Peak (the name selected by the British) are impressive throughout the day, it is at dawn and shortly afterwards that the effect is truly spellbinding. As the sun rises it casts an arrowhead shadow of the peak on the layer of mist below, which can reach almost as far west as Colombo. Dawn, like sunrise, is a swiftly passing event in the tropics, and once the shadow has reached its maximum extent it moves back on itself surprisingly quickly until completely disappearing.

On the summit stands a small Buddhist temple, and a postbox, just so that visitors can prove they have made it to the top. The original footprint, however, can no longer be seen, as it has been covered by an oversize copy in cement. Pilgrims who have come from Ratnapura are understandably proud of themselves for taking the longest and most arduous route up the mountain – some even appear to be totting up the celestial 'brownie points' they will be awarded for their religious zeal.

Sacred Peak

For over 1,000 years, pilgrims of various religions have climbed the 7,378 ft (2,249 m) high **Adam's Peak** to venerate the 'footprint' in the rock at the summit. To Buddhists, the **Sri Pada** (Sacred Footprint) was made by the Buddha when he visited Sri Lanka; to followers of Islam, the footprint is Adam's (Muslims believe that Adam and Eve were banished to Sri Lanka from the Garden of Eden); Hindus avow that the footprint belongs to Lord Siva; whilst Roman Catholics see a connection with the alleged visit of the apostle St Thomas – 'Doubting' Thomas – to south India. It seems probable that no other location in the world is regarded as sacred by the followers of so many important religions.

SINHARAJA FOREST RESERVE

This 13 mile (21 km) long reserve lies between Ratnapura and the south coast. Botanical enthusiasts are particularly attracted to Sinharaja as it is the only remaining lowland virgin rain forest in Sri Lanka. It has been estimated that more than 60 per cent of the trees in the reserve are native to the country, and many of its plants will rarely be found elsewhere. UNESCO declared the forest to be a World Heritage Site in 1989.

Around 50 small villages in the reserve are linked by roads and footpaths, but these intrude little on the virgin nature of the area. *Sinha Raja*, meaning 'Lion Prince', probably refers to royal ownership of the region, as the Asian lion has not existed on the island since the Pleistocene era.

Day trips to Sinharaja can be arranged from Ratnapura or some of the south coast resorts. A car with a knowledgeable guide/driver is the most rewarding way of exploring the rain forest. Yes, it rains heavily – seemingly at any time; mornings are likely to be drier as, of course, is the December-April 'dry' season.

Beruwala
& Bentota

Beruwala (sometimes spelt Beruwela) and its twin re
sort Bentota share a glorious 4.5 mile (7 km) coastline. The calm beaches, protected by reefs, are varied
and picturesque; it is little wonder, therefore, that
many tour operators book all their Sri Lanka clients
into Beruwala's and Bentota's comfortable hotels. The
authorities must be congratulated on rigorously limiting
the height of the buildings that line the beach, and hiding,
or at least screening them with palm trees.

Midway between Kalutara and
Beruwala, the Galle Road crosses
the railway for the first time, and
apart from a short stretch at
Bentota, it continues to hug the
coast as far as Galle. In consequence, motorists – or at least their
passengers – have fascinating

coastal views for most of this stretch.

Around a mile (2 km) before
Beruwala a mosque has been built
on a headland at **Kechchimale**.
Within, a shrine is said to contain
the body of a Muslim saint that
had been found on the beach
below in 1000 AD. By tradition, this

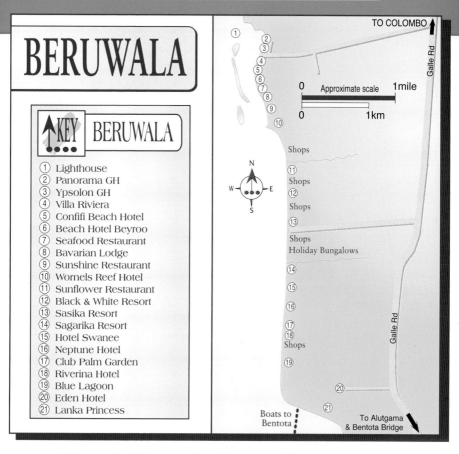

BERUWALA

KEY BERUWALA

1. Lighthouse
2. Panorama GH
3. Ypsolon GH
4. Villa Riviera
5. Confifi Beach Hotel
6. Beach Hotel Beyroo
7. Seafood Restaurant
8. Bavarian Lodge
9. Sunshine Restaurant
10. Wornels Reef Hotel
11. Sunflower Restaurant
12. Black & White Resort
13. Sasika Resort
14. Sagarika Resort
15. Hotel Swanee
16. Neptune Hotel
17. Club Palm Garden
18. Riverina Hotel
19. Blue Lagoon
20. Eden Hotel
21. Lanka Princess

TO COLOMBO
Galle Rd

Approximate scale
0   1 mile
0   1km

Shops
Shops
Shops
Shops
Shops
Holiday Bungalows
Shops
Galle Rd
Boats to Bentota
To Alutgama & Bentota Bridge

stone shrine was built by Sri Lanka's earliest recorded Muslim settlers, who landed in 1024.

BERUWALA

Approaching Beruwala the coastline, up to now dead straight, abruptly bulges 1 mile (2 km) seaward, while the main road continues ahead. For this reason, the northern sector of Beruwala's hotels are located some distance from the Galle Road and can only be reached from it by winding side streets.

Not only is Beruwala's beach protected by the headland, but semi-circular reefs of dead coral at the north and south ends create shallow pools, which are ideal for children and those who prefer to splash about in a warm sea without the excitement of suddenly being buffeted by waves. Islets out to sea, on one of which stands the lighthouse, and what appears to be a high island to the south but is actually a promontory, all contribute to the picturesque quality of the beach, which is one of Sri Lanka's most attractive. As it is just under 2 miles (3 km) long, the entire stretch can be explored easily in a morning.

Virtually all Beruwala's tourist accommodation is located on the beach, allocated to tour operators, and extremely popular with Germans. A visitor who has not pre-booked will have great difficulty in finding a room during the season. Guest house accommodation is extremely limited.

MORAGALLE

Almost all Beruwala's beach lies within its Moragalle suburb, the northern sector of which is primarily occupied by two and three-star hotels, the central sector, between two streams, by restaurants and shops, and the southern sector, before the Bentota River estuary is reached, by upper range hotels.

Although tourism, of course, is Beruwala's main industry, many locals can be seen intrepidly climbing 30 ft (9 m) high palm trees, to tap their sap (toddy). Some of this will be distilled to produce the fiery but somewhat tasteless *arrack*. Apparently, the rights to tap for toddy are handed down from father to son.

There are also an unusual number of jewellers' shops in the area, many of which are owned by descendants of the first Arab settlers. Prospective purchasers should take great care and haggle rigorously if a fair price is to be gained. Remember that in Sri Lanka 'Museum' and 'Factory' usually mean shop, whether the articles are jewels, batik, handicrafts, masks, shells, silk or lace.

BERUWALA BEACH, NORTH

Two guest houses, the **Panorama** and the **Ypsylon**, are followed by the Villa Riviera , a Jetwing hotel in the mid-price range with a large garden/swimming pool. Next comes the **Confifi Beach Hotel**, the highest-rated of the northern sector's hotels. For some reason, the sand at this point is rather coarse, but it becomes fine once more as the reef ends. Also with a pool, but much cheaper, is the long-established **Beach Hotel Bayroo**; all its 100 bedrooms are air-conditioned.

Two beach restaurants follow, with, between them, the Bavarian Lodge guest house which, as its name suggests, attracts a predominantly German clientele. If a Sri Lankan curry rather than 'Continental' food is required at any of Beruwala's restaurants, this can usually be arranged, but only by ordering in advance.

Wornel's Reef Hotel has two stars and falls into the economy range.

BERUWALA BEACH, MID-SECTION

After a stream has been crossed, sundry restaurants and shop developments take over until a holiday bungalow development appears just before the second of two streams. There is little direct access from the beach to the Galle Road, however, midway between the two streams a path runs inland beside the Sasika Restaurant; the half-hour walk to the main road is of little interest, but a three-wheeler can usually be found.

BERUWALA BEACH, SOUTH

The Sagarika, primarily a restaurant, lets out rooms, and the **Hotel Swanee**, that follows is also economical in spite of its swimming pool and two-star rating. Two much larger and grander hotels, Aitken Spence's Neptune and Confifi's **Club Palm Garden**, where terms are all inclusive, have more than 100 rooms, are three-star rated and offer all the expected facilities.

KALUWAMODARA

Another Confifi hotel, the luxury **Riverina**, marks the beginning of Beruwala's Kaluwamodara quarter. All 192 rooms are air-conditioned and fitted with TV and mini-bar as befits the hotel's four-star status. More shops are followed by the Blue Lagoon Restaurant/guest house and then the Confifi Group's **Eden Hotel**, Beruwala's only five-star establishment; the deluxe rooms have their own butler!

A short street links the hotel with Galle Road, which has swung seaward at this point. Ahead, boatmen wait along the shores of the **Bentota Ganga** estuary, which ends the beach. Most offer a ferry service across the short stretch of water to the narrow isthmus on which stand Bentota's hotels. Some, however, specialise in more ambitious river excursions.

ALUTGAMA

This market town, sometimes spelt Aluthgama, spreads for a mile along the north bank of the river's estuary, between Beruwala and Bentota. Alutgama is responsible for administering much of the isthmus on which Bentota's most northerly beach hotels stand and these, therefore, have an Alutgama rather than a Bentota address, which can be misleading.

Alutgama market is held near the bridge, which crosses the river to Bentota, and is particularly lively on Mondays. The Matugama Road leads inland towards Alutgama railway station, passing the cinemas and **Lalith's Bazaar**, a gems and handicrafts shop that is popular with tourists. If travelling by rail to and from Beruwala or Bentota, Alutgama is the station to make for, as faster trains, which usually ignore Beruwala and Bentota stations, all stop here. There are a few guest houses in Alutgama, but their distance from the beach limits their appeal to tourists.

Excursions up the Bentota Ganga

Hotels can arrange river trips of varying lengths, the most common being a 2-hour excursion to the mangrove swamps. Unfortunately, this usually includes a stop at **'Bentota Zoo'**, for refreshments and the opportunity to observe pitiful monkeys and peacocks locked in small cages. If this does not appeal, insist in advance that it is omitted from the schedule.

Further up the river, picnics can be arranged at **Galpota**, where the Buddhist temple was founded in the 12th century. More ambitious is a much longer cruise, at the end of which, with luck, crocodiles may be seen basking on the river banks. Passengers are assured that the sinister-looking reptiles never torpedo the boats. Look out for large monitor lizards which like to shelter in the trees from the sun, particularly after heavy rain.

Above: The Taj Exotica at Bentota is one of Sri Lanka's most luxurious resort hotels

Below: Boat trips along the coast are tourist attractions at Beruwala and Bentota

BENTOTA

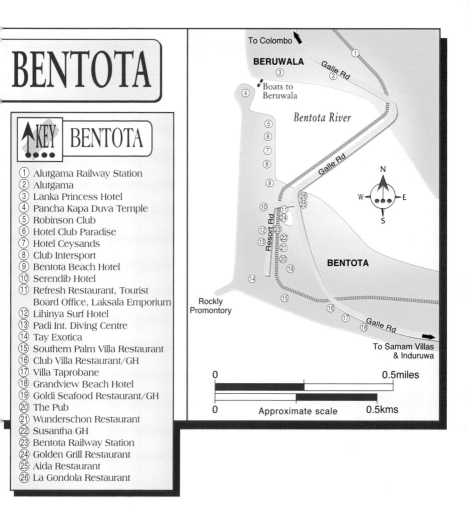

KEY BENTOTA

1. Alutgama Railway Station
2. Alutgama
3. Lanka Princess Hotel
4. Pancha Kapa Duva Temple
5. Robinson Club
6. Hotel Club Paradise
7. Hotel Ceysands
8. Club Intersport
9. Bentota Beach Hotel
10. Serendib Hotel
11. Refresh Restaurant, Tourist Board Office, Laksala Emporium
12. Lihinya Surf Hotel
13. Padi Int. Diving Centre
14. Tay Exotica
15. Southern Palm Villa Restaurant
16. Club Villa Restaurant/GH
17. Villa Taprobane
18. Grandview Beach Hotel
19. Goldi Seafood Restaurant/GH
20. The Pub
21. Wunderschon Restaurant
22. Susantha GH
23. Bentota Railway Station
24. Golden Grill Restaurant
25. Aida Restaurant
26. La Gondola Restaurant

The Brief

Midway between Beruwala and Bentota, the Alutgama/Matugama road leads inland. Reached after 7 miles (10 km) is The Brief, the former home of landscape painter **Bewis Bawa**. Bawa, an enthusiastic gardener, opened the grounds of The Brief to the public in 1970, and since his death in 1992 it has also been possible to explore the bungalow itself.

Within, all has been kept as it was at the artist's death. Work by the Australian painter Donald Friend, with whom Bawa was well acquainted, is displayed, adding a contemporary note.

BENTOTA

As far as tourism is concerned, Bentota is much more than just the sandy isthmus protruding from the south side of the estuary. Adjacent villages such as Rabolgoda, Pita-ramba and Aturuwella now promote themselves as being part of Bentota; even **Induruwa**, a resort in its own right, frequently attaches the name of Bentota to itself, although it is located 3 miles (5 km) away.

For practical purposes, however, Bentota is generally regarded as the area between the sea and the Galle Road that stretches southward from the Bentota Ganga estuary to the headland on which stands the Saman Villas hotel. A wide, unbroken, sandy beach, almost 2 miles (3 km) long, fringes the entire coastline.

BENTOTA GANGA RIVER ISTHMUS

Visitors approach Bentota from the north either by fishing boat from Beruwala, hotel ferry boat from Alutgama, or via the Galle Road, which crosses the long bridge over the Bentota Ganga, running parallel with the rail bridge. On the Bentota side, the Galle Road is joined, first right, by Resort Road, which passes the rear of some of the beach hotels and terminates at the Taj Exotica, central Bentota's only five-star hotel.

Taj Exotica

The Taj Exotica has the finest beach site in Bentota, arguably in all Sri Lanka. Built around a triangular rocky promontory, all its 161 rooms are air-conditioned and provided with satellite TV and a mini-bar. Each has a private balcony with stunning sea views – either to the north, or to the east, as the Exotica has been located precisely where the beach changes direction. The swimming pool is raised above the beach, and its terrace wall provided with furniture.

Although the hotel is popular with UK tour operators the majority of clients are usually German. Presumably for this reason, most food served, both in the restaurant and the coffee shop, is 'continental' and rather bland, which suits the German taste. The layout and ambience of the Taj Exotica are so outstandingly attractive that visitors to the coast, even if not fortunate enough to be staying at the hotel, are recommended to pay it a visit: no other large resort hotel in Sri Lanka is comparable.

BENTOTA BEACH, NORTH

Immediately facing the Exotica, the sandy beach is picturesquely strewn with rocks, from which there are excellent views in both directions. Looking northward, the isthmus ahead is straight, and where it ends appears to face a high island. The hotels along this stretch are concealed most effectively, and it is difficult to believe that together they can accommodate around 1,400 tourists.

Next to the Exotica is the rather smart **Padi International Diving Centre**, equipment may be rented and tuition is available. Along this stretch of beach every hotel has a swimming pool, and all their bedrooms are air-conditioned but, apart from the Taj Exotica, standard rooms do not have a TV or a mini-bar. The **Lihinya Surf Hotel** and **Hotel Serendib**, which follow, are similar middle-price establishments.

Lying some way back from the sea, but with a serene river estuary frontage, the large **Bentota Beach Hotel** was formerly regarded as the resort's finest. In 1999 the hotel was closed while extensive remodelling and upgrading took place. Check the situation with a travel agent or on arrival. Clients of this hotel and those that lie to its north are transported to their accommodation by private ferries from Alutgama.

Two more clubs for sports enthusiasts – **Club Intersport** and **Club Paradise** – flank **Hotel Ceysands**, which is a similar middle-range hotel to the first two hotels passed, and accommodates UK package tourists. The beach ends just past the **Robinson Club**, its 150 rooms giving it the second largest hotel capacity in Bentota. Almost all the clients appear to be German, and only a fully inclusive tariff is offered. For some reason, the establishment bars entry to Sri Lankans.

Bentota's 'island'

It will now have become apparent that the heavily wooded 'island' ahead is not an island at all, but a rock connected by a strip of land to the isthmus. A small Buddhist temple, the **Pancha Kapa Dupa** occupies the hill, which is therefore regarded as holy. Visitors are made welcome, but should be respectably dressed and behave with decorum. There is no entry charge, but most leave a small donation in the box provided. Beside the hill, boatmen conduct visitors to the Beruwala side of the estuary.

BENTOTA BEACH, SOUTH

At the Taj Exotica, the beach swings abruptly eastward, curving slightly until it ends below the high promontory. At first sight, this appears to be a virgin beach, as the few small establishments built on it have been sited well back, along the Galle Road, which here returns to the shore, while the rail track has swung inland. Closest to the Taj, but in complete contrast, is **Club Villas**, a charming 19th century villa, which has a shady garden and, surprisingly, a swimming pool. It has 15 rooms, 4 of them air-conditioned, and its beach front restaurant specialises in Italian food. **Villa Taprobane** and **Grandview Beach Hotel**, both guest houses, follow. At the end of the beach, set on the promontory, is one of Sri Lanka's jewels.

Although small, the exquisite five-star **Saman Villas Hotel** is undoubtedly the most luxurious resort hotel in Sri Lanka. Understandably, it is a member of the Small Luxury Hotels of the World association. Each of the 27 air-conditioned suites (there are no standard rooms) comprises a living room with a veranda and a raised sleeping area – its dividing screen electronically operated from beside the bed! Fittings include not only a mini-bar and satellite TV, but also a CD system. The courtyard bathroom is supplemented by a separate dressing room.

Dramatically located, the swimming pool's overflow at one end disappears, apparently but not in actuality, as a giant waterfall into the ocean below. In spite of its small size, Saman Villas has two bars, two restaurants, a sauna and nightly entertainments. Needless to say this luxury does not come cheap. As at the Taj Exotica, even if not staying at the hotel, a visit is highly recommended. Transport, if required, can be arranged at the hotel.

Guest houses

Behind the Taj Exotica, **Resort Road** runs towards the river, parallel with the railway line. Several guest houses and restaurants have been built overlooking the railway, which, as at Mount Lavinia, must be crossed by foot in order to reach them. As may be expected, accommodation, food and drink are much more economically priced than at the beach front hotels, and this is where younger tourists, including a handful of backpackers, are usually to be found.

Just south of the Exotica, the **Goldi Seafood Restaurant** and guest house has first floor rooms with en-suite bathrooms and good sea views. Northward, **The Pub** and **Wunderschön Seafood Restaurant** offer economical fare but no accommodation.

Just before Bentota Railway Station, and lying back much further than the other establishments, the **Susantha Guesthouse** is probably the best option for those seeking cheap but clean rooms with private bathrooms in the Bentota/Beruwala area. Guests must cross the railway line to reach the beach, but there is direct access to Galle Road from the rear of the complex.

Just south of Susantha, on the Galle Road, the **Hotel/Restaurant Athula** is another economy establishment. Further north along Galle Road a pretty pond to the left is romantically overlooked by the **Golden Grill Restaurant**, which can be reached from the strangely-named **National Holiday Resort**,

an arcade of shops, which includes a branch of **Laksala**, the state-operated crafts emporium; also incorporated in the scheme is the **Refresh Restaurant**. Apparently, the development was built as long ago as 1969 in connection with the establishment of the Bentota Beach Hotel.

Facing the junction of Galle Road and Resort Road, Aida Gems forms part of a terrace of shops; above it, the food served in the **Aida Restaurant** is some of the most highly-rated in Bentota; Sri Lankan curries are always available, a rarity in the area. The restaurant is reached by following the path, right, to the rear of the complex.

INDURUWA

Whilst staying in the area or en route to **Hikkaduwa**, some may like to visit the wide, fast-developing beach of Induruwa village, just 3 miles (5 km) south of Bentota, where accommodation is somewhat cheaper than can be found in its Beruwala and Bentota equivalents. Particularly good value is the new four-star **Induruwa Beach Resort**, with all 90 rooms air-conditioned and fitted with TV and mini-bar; terms are bed and breakfast or half-board.

The one-star **Emerald Bay Hotel**, **Whispering Palms** and **Venus Tourist Beach Resort** are in the economy range, even though the Emerald Bay has a pool and some air-conditioned rooms. At the south end of the beach, visitors are welcome to visit the **turtle hatchery**. Southward from here there are several similar hatcheries, the largest being at **Kosgoda** (see page76).

Kosgoda & Hikkaduwa

Hand-carved masks, a feature of Ambalangoda, are popular tourist souvenirs

The beach of Kosgoda fishing village, 3 miles (5 km) south of Induruwa, is best known for its turtles, and it is here that Sri Lanka's oldest turtle hatchery may be visited. Occupying a prime position on the beach, the three-star Kosgoda Beach Resort has 52 air-conditioned rooms and a pool.

TURTLE HATCHERY

Established in 1981 to protect Sri Lanka's turtles from extinction, the hatcheries pay fishermen for eggs that they collect at night along the 1 mile (2 km) long sandy beach.

Visitors are shown two huge tanks filled with newly-born but lively hatchlings, looking for all the world like battery-driven plastic toys. Having been fed, all will be taken to the sea and released when they are 2-3 days old. Some deplore the fact that this is not done immediately after hatching, thereby eliminating the 'taming' process, and even worse, that they are not always released during the safer hours of darkness.

The main reason for keeping the hatchlings seems to be to attract the necessary finance from tourists. The eggs are buried in sand, and all that can be seen are the identity tags that protrude above each one: all somewhat reminiscent of a Second World War graveyard in the Egyptian desert. Although October to April is the main laying season, some eggs can be found at Kosgoda throughout the year, even during the monsoon, when frenzied waves lash the beach.

Examples of mature Loggerhead turtles, one of them a rare albino, are displayed in an adjacent tank, which is hardly large enough to permit sufficient exercise. Within another structure, four additional square tanks contain even larger turtles. There seems no reason for the unnatural confinement of the creatures apart from providing a spectacle for tourists.

Within the complex, the small cafeteria does not include turtle soup, mock or real, on its menu!

Sri Lanka's turtles

Species may include the Green, Leatherback, Hawksbill, Olive Ridley and Loggerhead. At Kosgoda, up to 20,000 eggs may be laid in a fortnight, each turtle burying as many as 200 at a time in the sand as quickly as possible. The eggs, soft and leathery, are enthusiastically consumed by a variety of predators, including stray dogs and fishermen, who can dig them out of the sand with ease.

Mature turtles are considered a culinary delicacy, and are served as steaks or soup. It is said, surprisingly, that they don't taste fishy – more like beef. The shells are also prized, particularly that of the beautiful Hawskbill.

It takes 48-65 days for an egg to hatch, depending on the species, and immediately the hatchling has broken through its shell – usually at night – it scurries to the sea. Those that make it swim frantically to the relative safety of deep water before beginning to feed on plankton and small fishes.

Green turtles, Sri Lanka's most common variety, rarely swim more than 1-2 miles (2-3 km) out to sea, but other species migrate up to 62 miles (100 km) distant. Loggerhead turtles can live from 200-300 years, the largest measuring up to 6 ft (2 m) in length and weighing 220 lb (100 kg).

AHUNGALLA

Approximately 10 miles (15 km) further south, Aitken Spence's five-star **Triton Hotel** overlooks the enormous bay of Ahungalla. Designed by Sri Lanka's famous hotel architect, Geoffrey Bawa, the hotel, which opened in 1981, has 160 air-conditioned rooms, each with TV and mini-bar. Tennis courts and facilities for table tennis, billiards and badminton, together with a gym, appeal to keep-fit enthusiasts, who are able to cool down in their choice of two swimming pools.

Immediately south of the hotel, the Galle Road passes the **Ambaga-hapitaya Temple** at Welitara village. Beyond here is the **Pushparama Temple**, where monks not only train boys in Buddhist beliefs but also provide a general education. The 19th Cen. building in which they are taught looks like a former church, but it never was. Apparently the Dutch architect who designed the building had not mastered Buddhist styles; extensive renovation should be completed by 2000. The vihara was built in 1945, but the white dagoba dates from around 1850.

BALAPITIYA

Located at Balapitiya, 3 miles (5 km) further south, **Lotus Villa Resort** specialises in ayurvedic treatment, special diets are catered for. The **Maha Ganga** river, adjacent to the town, is popular for river trips, and many hotels in the area will arrange picnic excursions. Wildfowl in abundance is attracted to the uninhabited islets that dot the water with their greenery. Ambalangoda is located a further 3 miles (5 km) south on the Galle Road.

AMBALANGODA

Known as '**Mask Village**', **Ambalangoda** is famed for traditional Sri Lankan dance masks which are made and sold here in profusion. The masks follow centuries-old designs; all are garishly painted, but sizes and the quality of craftsmanship vary greatly. Attracted by their exotic appearance, it is possible that almost as many masks are bought by tourists for display in their European homes as they are by Sri Lankans to enliven their festivals.

There are many mask shops, particularly on the main road at the north end of the town. Two sons of the late Ariyapala, a renowned mask-carver, each own a shop on the roundabout, one of which incorporates a **Mask Museum**. Other notable establishments include **Southland Masks**, 353 Nairn Street and **M.H. Mettananda's Masks Centre**, 142 Patabendimulla.

Masks purchased by tourists in Ambalangoda are not necessarily cheaper (and are often dearer) than elsewhere in Sri Lanka, particularly Colombo. Prices range from 100 to 50,000 rupees, depending on complexity. Almost any shop can arrange a visit to see carvers at work, however, it is rumoured that some 'carvers' only start to work when tourists arrive, and stop immediately they leave.

It is easy to pass through Ambalangoda without appreciating that the town has an excellent beach. This is because it is hidden from the road by a 'village' of fishermen's shacks, the narrow paths of which must be negotiated in order to reach the sand; the locals don't seem to mind tourists passing through their backyards.

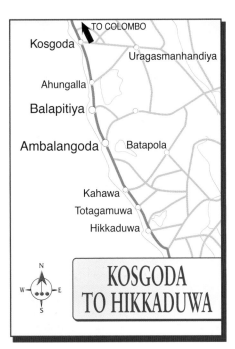

Kosgoda
TO COLOMBO
Uragasmanhandiya
Ahungalla
Balapitiya
Ambalangoda   Batapola
Kahawa
Totagamuwa
Hikkaduwa

N
W · E
S

KOSGODA TO HIKKADUWA

Above: Hikkaduwa's flotilla of glass-bottomed boats

Below: Hikkaduwa combines a tranquil resort to the north with lively surfing to the south

Sun Oriental Resorts specialise in ayurvedic treatments, has a swimming pool and 30 non air-conditioned rooms. It is the only hotel-class accommodation in Ambalangoda, a town that has never aspired to beach resort status. There are, however, small guest houses for those who choose to stay here; recommended are the **Blue Horizon Tour Inn** and the **Shangrela Guest House** which are both close to the beach.

Hikkaduwa lies 7.5 miles (12 km) further south on the Galle Road.

HIKKADUWA

The town of Hikkaduwa is the most southerly in Sri Lanka that can be classed as a major beach resort. It would be hard to find a more varied beach, which stretches southward from the Harbour. In sequence, well-defined sectors accommodate: fishermen, excursion boats, bathers, sun worshippers and surfers. In spite of its size, Hikkaduwa has only one four-star hotel, and only three with more than 50 rooms; it is therefore, less package-tour orientated than the other resorts. Rates are also lower, thereby attracting a much higher proportion of youngsters.

NORTHERN BEACH

Hikkaduwa's largest hotel, the **Coral Gardens**, marks the south end of the half mile (1 km) north-

Hikkaduwa's coral

Until a few years ago, Hikkaduwa's great attraction was its living coral, but gradually most of this was chipped away, either for burning to provide building lime, or for sale to tourists as souvenirs. To conserve what remained, a coral sanctuary between the shore and the reef, which protects the north part of the beach, was established. A flotilla of glass-bottomed boats enabled non-diving tourists to view the exotic coral 'garden' and the equally brightly marked tropical fish that swam around it.

In 1998, disaster struck: the temperature of the shallow water soared to previously unknown heights (El Nino was blamed), and the coral died. Now, all that remains is a coral cemetery; darkened husks a sad reminder of the tiny creatures' fragility.

A few tropical fish may still be seen within the sanctuary; these are fed by boatmen, who are desperate to keep them there so that they have something for the tourists to see. Nevertheless, one wonders how long Hikkaduwa's glass-bottomed boat industry can last; live coral could not reappear for several hundred years, and the tropical fish will probably tire of eating bread in a somewhat briefer period of time.

It is claimed that divers with the necessary equipment, which can be rented locally, can still see live coral further out to sea where the water is much deeper, and therefore remained cooler. Check the situation locally.

ern sector of the beach. It has four stars, and all the 156 air-conditioned rooms overlook the sea. Strangely, none are provided with balconies, an unforgivable oversight in a hotel constructed as recently as 1986. General upgrading of the rooms seems to be due, and perhaps something will be done to overcome this unusual drawback.

From the beautiful gardens, the bulky 5-floored building, with its series of shallow, curved roofs, resembles a squashed Chinese pagoda. No other hotel in Hikkaduwa has comparable grounds or such an extensive pool (separate pool for children). However, those who want a sunlounger and parasol must be up early, insufficient are provided by the hotel, but a generous token of gratitude to an attendant can work wonders.

From the Coral Gardens hotel, the coral reef which gives this part of the beach its swimming-pool calm curves northward in a wide arc to a distance of up to 656 ft (200 m); the water never exceeds 13 ft (4 m) in depth within its compass.

Galle Road runs very close to the beach at Hikkaduwa, but much of its traffic is hidden from view by beach front hotels and restaurants. A stream enters the sea just before the **Coral Seas Beach** restaurant/ guest house (with 8 letting rooms). Its small, open restaurant overlooks the beach, and the helpful proprietor will provide dishes to order; he also operates glass-bottomed boats at reasonable rates.

Four more hotels follow, of varying standard; each confusingly includes the seemingly obligatory 'coral' in its name at present, but perhaps with the sad demise of Hikkaduwa's coral some will eventually be re-christened. **Coral Rock Hotel** provides some of the best value accommodation on the coast, all its balconied rooms overlook the sea and are air-conditioned. The **Coral Reef Beach Hotel**, which follows, is also competitively priced; it has 32 rooms overlooking the sea but none are air-conditioned. Next comes the attractive **Blue Corals Hotel**, somewhat higher in standard; the 52 rooms overlook the sea, six of them air-conditioned, but not all have balconies. An attractive garden incorporates a swimming pool and a children's pool.

Just behind this group of hotels, Waulagoda Road, which runs inland from Galle Road, has several cheap guest houses just a short walk from the sea.

Returning to the beach, **Coral Sands Hotel**, three-star rated, has 20 air-conditioned and 30 non air-conditioned rooms, all with sea views and balconies; there is also a swimming pool. The beach virtually ends at the fairly new two-star **Hikkaduwa Beach Hotel**; its 16 air-conditioned and 36 non air-conditioned rooms all have sea views and balconies. The small garden incorporates a secluded swimming pool from which there are views across the waterfront.

Hikkaduwa Town

Behind Hikkaduwa Beach Hotel, Galle Road crosses a stream and leads northward to the town. Here there is very little of tourist interest unless the railway station is sought. The harbour, although large, cannot be described as picturesque. Just south of the station, Baddegama Road leads to **Telwatta**. Until recently this was a bird sanctuary of some renown, but apparently something has upset the birds, which have ungratefully turned up their beaks at the sanctuary and flown elsewhere. Many three-wheelers can be rented around the station, thus avoiding a walk back to the beach hotels.

SOUTHERN BEACH

To continue southward along the beach from the Coral Gardens Hotel it is usually necessary to follow Galle Road immediately behind the building before making for the sand. The reason for this is that an evil-smelling outpouring of fluid at one side of the hotel rushes out to meet rocks which, except when the tide is out, are buffeted by waves. As this is the only interruption to one's progress along the entire beach it seems strange that nothing has been done to create a rock bridge over the obstacle – either by the hotel or by local government.

Initially, the beach is extremely narrow but further south it widens considerably to provide Hikkaduwa's best sunbathing beach. **JHL Beach Restaurant** looks directly on to the sea and is a particularly attractive (and economical) spot for good English-style breakfasts. Next to it, **Refresh Restaurant** also serves alfresco meals, but in its dining room, more easily approached from Galle Road, the best food in Hikkaduwa is served: the fish, prawns and crabs are good, but the menu is extensive and varied. The two-star **Hotel Reefcomber** is the last of Hikkaduwa's starred establishments. It has 59 air-conditioned

rooms, each with sea view and balcony. Ground floor rooms, however, are sub-standard, and should be declined unless renovation has taken place. There is a swimming pool.

The character of the beach soon changes abruptly; beach-shack bars/restaurants and guest houses run in an unbroken line along the sand, punctuated by batches of sunbeds. Most accommodation from now on tends to be basic and cheap, and this is where the largest congregation of young visitors can be found on the island. Towards the south end, at Navigama, **Sunil's Beach Hotel** has a swimming pool, some of the 62 rooms have air-conditioning.

Even more dramatic is the change in the character of the sea; gone is the swimming pool calm of the north beach, to be replaced by great rollers, which increase in frequency and height as the beach extends further south almost halfway to Galle. Although the roughness of the sea makes swimming impossible for most, it is, of course, a magnet for surfers, and while the east coast remains out of bounds, this is Sri Lanka's only true **surfing beach** accesible to tourists. Surf boards can be rented at several establishments, one of which is **Ranjith's Guest House**.

Although Hikkaduwa's loss of its 'Coral Garden' is tragic, the calm, reef-protected water to the north, the wide beaches and excellent surf to the south, and the good value for money offered by its hotels and restaurants would appear to ensure the resort's continued popularity.

Galle to Dondra Head

7

GALLE

The ancient fortified city of Galle (pronounced 'Gaul') occupies a man-made promontory, polygonal in shape, surrounded by grassy ramparts and lapped on three sides by the sea. Many of Galle's colonial Dutch buildings have survived, and the combination of maritime location and venerable architecture gives the town a picturesque quality unmatched in Sri Lanka.

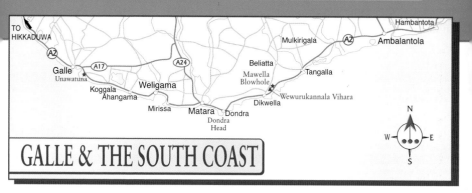

Hambantota
TO HIKKADUWA
Mulkirigala
Ambalantola
Galle
Unawatuna
Beliatta
Mawella Blowhole
Tangalla
Koggala
Ahangama
Weligama
Wewurkannala Vihara
Dikwella
Mirissa
Matara
Dondra
Dondra Head

N
W · E
S

GALLE & THE SOUTH COAST

HISTORY

By tradition, Galle is the biblical Tarshish, from where the jewels were shipped with which King Solomon wooed the Queen of Sheba; however, the town is not recorded with certainty until 1267. A hundred years later, the great Arab explorer Ibn Batout dismissed Galle as a small town. Its present name is believed to have derived from the Sinhalese *Gala*, meaning rock, which was later corrupted by the Dutch East India Company to *gallus* (Latin) meaning cock.

The Portuguese gained the Galle trading rights from the Kandy King in 1503, but the relationship between them was perpetually troubled, and in 1589 the Portuguese fortified the town, which they named Santa Cruz. Within the walls, the 89 acre (36 hectare) area was created by filling in the land between several distinct islands. The Dutch ousted the Portuguese around 1640 and gradually replaced almost all their buildings, including the ramparts of the fort, which was almost entirely rebuilt in 1663. In spite of the difficulties caused by rocks and strong currents, Galle was the only port in Sri Lanka during the Dutch period that could accommodate large vessels, and in consequence it briefly became the island's capital.

As elsewhere in south Asia, the British took over reasonably amicably from the Dutch, who departed from Sri Lanka in 1796. A jetty was soon built at the harbour, which was to play an important part in attracting merchant and passenger shipping to the island. Coach services transported passengers from Galle to Colombo until the late 19th century, when breakwaters were constructed at Colombo, and virtually all the island's maritime trade was diverted to it. The almost perfect preservation of Galle's fort, the finest colonial example to survive in Asia, led to its inclusion, in 1992, as a World Heritage site.

RAMPARTS

Most of the one and a half mile (2 km) circumference of the ramparts remain accessible, and a walk around them can be completed in around two hours; it is best undertaken towards evening or early in the morning. Most visitors, however, will make short detours from the ramparts en route to museums, churches, etc, and an additional two hours should be set aside for them. Vehicular entry to the enclosed area of Galle from the new town to the north is via **New Gate**, which makes a logical point from which to begin a walk around Galle – in an anti-clockwise direction.

North Wall

New Gate, the main entrance to the fort, was inserted in the north wall by the British in 1873. Previously there had been no gate in this stretch of the wall as it faced landward and was therefore the most vulnerable to attack. The Portuguese had excavated a moat outside it, but the three great bastions were added by the Dutch. The most easterly, the **Sun Bastion**, which overlooks the harbour, was a popular duelling point as it faced the sunrise – 'pistols at dawn'; the last duel here was fought in 1810 by two British captains, one of whom perished.

It is best not to ascend the ramparts at this point as they are rather narrow and steep in places, additionally, there is more of interest to be seen from Church Street, the road that swings eastward from the roundabout facing the gate.

CHURCH STREET

As Church Street straightens, a small stone building on the right houses the **National Museum**. It was built in 1656 and served as a warehouse and then the billiard room of the adjacent hotel, eventually opening as a museum in 1986. Items from the Portuguese and Dutch periods are displayed, together with the usual Kandy masks. Of greatest interest to most, however, will be the scale model of Galle.

The **New Oriental Hotel**, next to the museum, was built in 1684 as a residence for the Dutch commander and his officials. It is the country's oldest building to accommodate a hotel, which opened in 1863. Although the bedrooms are in dire need of refurbishing, and more effort might be made to deter mosquitoes, this is an engaging place in which to spend a couple of nights. The atmosphere is decidedly colonial, with an English pub-type bar (check the opening times), airy verandas and a tranquil dining-room in which the most delicious curries in Sri Lanka are served. The choice of the hotel is chicken; a succulent texture and positive taste, which even asserts itself in a fiery curry, proclaim the birds to be free-range.

Mature trees and tropical shrubs encroach on the hotel's pretty swimming pool as if it were set in a private garden; all very non-commercial and delightful.

Dutch Church

The white-painted **Dutch Groote Kerk (Great Church)**, founded in 1640, occupies the site of a Portuguese convent. Dating from 1755, the present building is believed to be the oldest Protestant church in Sri Lanka. It is said to have been commissioned in gratitude to God by the Dutch governor's wife who, after many barren years, gave birth to a son.

Left of the entrance is the best of several Dutch armorial hatchments displayed in the church; another example, facing the pulpit, is dated 1800. Above the entrance, the organ loft and original organ (no longer in working order) survive. Against the north wall are the high-backed pews, originally reserved for important Dutch members of the congregation. The Dutch-style pulpit, made in Galle, retains its enormous sounding board. Dutch tombstones reused from a defunct cemetery form the pavement.

Dutch Reformed Church services are still held, but in Sinhala only.

Immediately south of the church, the single-floored library was built by the British in 1832. Now, it is partly sponsored by the town of Velsen, in Holland, with which Galle is twinned.

Next to it is Galle's most important Catholic church, **All Saints**, designed by James P. Smither in 1871. Smither was also the architect of Colombo's National Museum, which he designed in coolly Classical style. Here he abandons this for Gothic Romanesque, considered at the time to be 'church' architecture. For some reason, the combination of curved, Romanesque and pointed Gothic arches usually results in horror film buildings.

QUEEN STREET

Returning northward, Queen Street bends right from Church Street. On its corner, the former **Dutch Government House** is currently being restyled to provide a hotel, restaurant and shop complex. Above the north-east (Queen Street) doorway, 'Anno 1683' and the cock emblem of the Dutch East India Company are the only reminders of the building's original use.

On the opposite corner facing Church Street, the **belfry and clock tower** was built by the British. It replaced a Dutch structure of 1701 from which a bell had tolled to announce the death of important citizens.

OLD GATE

An impressively long but narrow Dutch-built structure incorporated in the ramparts occupies the north side of Queen Street. This is reached via the archway to **Old Gate**, formerly the only entrance to the fortified town. Carved above the arch, and dated 1669 in Roman numerals, the Dutch East India Company's VOC insignia is flanked by lions and surmounted by the company's cock emblem.

The **National Maritime Museum** is entered immediately left within the archway. Photographs, full-size models of fishing boats, descriptions of the manufacture and use of fishing nets, and tanks containing specimens of maritime life in Sri Lankan waters are the main exhibits.

Above the external face of the gate's north arch, the undated arms of the United Kingdom have been sumptuously carved, an addition probably made before the British created the main entrance to the fort. From the gate, the road swings northward, skirting the waterfront, to the new town of Galle. A short path from the road leads to the jetty, from which local youths like to impress with their diving skills.

Protruding seaward from the rampart, the **Zwart (Black) Bastion** is believed to be a survivor of the Portuguese fort; if so it would be the oldest of Galle's bastions to have survived.

Return to Queen Street, and follow its curve southward, where the thoroughfare's name changes to Hospital Street. On the seaward side, grassy ramparts lead to **Akersloot Bastion**, which is named to commemorate the birthplace of the

Continued on page 88...

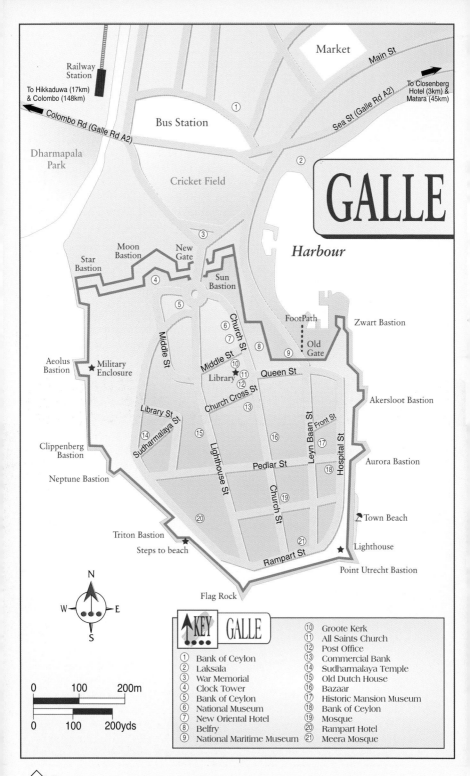

Market

Main St

To Closenberg
Hotel (3km) &
Matara (45km)

**Railway
Station**

To Hikkaduwa (17km)
& Colombo (148km)

Colombo Rd (Galle Rd A2)

Bus Station

Sea St (Galle Rd A2)

①

②

**Dharmapala
Park**

Cricket Field

GALLE

③

Harbour

**Moon
Bastion**

**New
Gate**

**Star
Bastion**

④

**Sun
Bastion**

⑤

FootPath

Zwart Bastion

⑥

Church St

⑦

**Old
Gate**

⑧

⑨

**Aeolus
Bastion**

Middle St

★ **Military
Enclosure**

Middle St

⑩

Library

⑪

Queen St

Akersloot Bastion

⑫

Church Cross St

⑬

Library St

Sudharmalaya St

⑭

⑮

⑯

Leyn Baan St

Front St

⑰

Hospital St

Aurora Bastion

**Clippenberg
Bastion**

Lighthouse St

Pedlar St

⑱

Neptune Bastion

Church St

⑲

Town Beach

Triton Bastion

⑳

Steps to beach

㉑

Lighthouse

Rampart St

★

Point Utrecht Bastion

Flag Rock

N
W ●●● E
S

0   100   200m

0   100   200yds

◇ 86 ◇

Above: *Tiny beaches are reached by steps from Galle's ramparts*
Below: *Girls on a catholic school outing stress Galle's Christian heritage*

Dutch commander who took Galle from the Portuguese.

Facing **Aurora Bastion**, which follows, Pedlar Street leads to Leyn Baan Street, first right, where, on the east side, is the **Historic Mansion Museum**, Galle's museum of greatest interest and a popular attraction (see box below).

RAMPARTS WALK

On returning to Hospital Street, most visitors will opt to walk along the top of the ramparts towards the **lighthouse** ahead. Views eastward are stunning, taking in the waterfront and a green stretch of coastline that is unusually high for Sri Lanka. This is known as the **Rhumsala Kanda Ridge**, and there are great views of Galle from its summit. A fresh water pond at its base is called **Watering Point**, as it was from here that ships obtained their water supplies for a long voyage.

Along Galle's ramparts outside school hours, cheerful groups of boys wielding cricket bats emulate their national sporting heroes on the grassy slopes. Immediately below lies the **town's main beach**, a narrow strip of sand which is reached by a flight of steps next to the lighthouse. The young batsmen continually swipe balls down to the beach below, and surprisingly cheerful fielders expend a great deal of their time and energy in retrieving them. Others appreciating the green swards are herds of goats, most but not all of them tethered, which seem intent on munching the succulent grass to extinction.

• HISTORIC MANSION MUSEUM •

This museum is accommodated in a house built by the Dutch in 1763; its owner, the personable Mr Gaffar, bought the property, then a ruin, in 1985, and spent seven years on its reconstruction. His object was to create a home for the collection of antiques that he had acquired over a 40-year period, and is still augmenting. Designed as a family house built around a courtyard, the original thick walls of coral rock bonded with clay have been retained, but the only other original feature is the courtyard's well, which had been dilapidated before restoration.

The interior generally has been designed to reflect Dutch taste in the 18th century. Most of the doors are from the Dutch period and were obtained from ancient Sri Lankan properties; unfortunately, none had survived in this building.

Exhibits displayed within include gems, colonial furniture, weapons, porcelain and a unique collection of antique coins. Only Mr Gaffar can identify all the items, at present from memory, but an inventory is planned. He warns that virtually all the 'antique' coins for sale in Galle are fakes. A strategically located area beside the exit is devoted to Sri Lankan gems, which are for sale. The processes of polishing and creating them is demonstrated.

Immediately opposite the museum, Mr Gaffar has constructed a private mansion, with decor inspired by Islamic themes – he is a devout Muslim. Although this is not a museum, the owner delights in conducting those who express interest around his idiosyncratic new residence.

The present **lighthouse** was erected beside the **Point Utrecht Bastion** by the British during the Second World War. It replaced an earlier lighthouse that stood beside Flag Rock, Galle's most southerly point, before burning down.

The stretch of rampart between the lighthouse and Flag Rock, the bastion that follows, contributes to the most scenic area in Galle. This incorporates the **Meera Mosque** on Rampart Street, which was constructed around 1900, allegedly on the former site of the Portuguese cathedral. At first glance, as with so many of Sri Lanka's mosques, the building looks more like a church; there is neither a dome nor minarets, the only give-away being the facade's half-moon relief.

At the south end of the adjacent Church Street, a **Muslim area** has developed. Muslim houses, often incorporating purdah screens, add a picturesque touch to the thoroughfare, which begins at its north end with Christian buildings. More goats and some cows enjoy the grass along this section of the ramparts. Here also, more young boys demonstrate their cricketing prowess, even though, when the ball is hit over the ramparts, they may have to demonstrate their climbing and swimming skills as well.

Flag Rock, the point at which this section of the ramparts ends, was actually a Portuguese bastion. Later, the Dutch would flag their ships from here to warn them of the dangerous rocks in the vicinity – hence the rock's name.

TRITON AND NEPTUNE BASTIONS

Steps descend to a tiny beach beside the **Triton Bastion**. At this point, the Dutch installed a windmill to draw up sea water for cleaning Galle's streets, which at that time were unsurfaced. Behind the bastion, in Rampart Road, the **Rampart Hotel** with its colonial-style verandas is actually a modern building; its interior is somewhat gloomy.

At the **Neptune Bastion**, the British constructed a military headquarters, which remained until the outbreak of the Second World War when it was demolished to permit uninterrupted views seaward of any possible Japanese aggressor.

SUDHARMALAYA TEMPLE

Galle's only Buddhist temple of note occupies the Rampart Street/Sudharmalaya Street corner, facing the Clippenberg Bastion. The complex also incorporates a teaching school for novice monks. In its vihara, modern wall-paintings, garishly painted as usual, flank an equally bright reclining Buddha. However, the latter is faced by original, and much more tasteful, late-18th century wall paintings. The temple's Bo-Tree grows within an enclosed green on the opposite side of the road.

Ahead, the **Aeolus Bastion** is fenced off, as the military currently occupy the area. It is worth ascending the ramparts once more at the north range primarily for the views inland. The **Star, Moon and Sun Bastions** of this range, the most important part of the fort's defences, were not replacements of Portuguese work but Dutch additions. It is said that at the opening ceremony they were named by the Dutch commander's wife before igniting the gunpowder to fire a celebratory shot from a cannon. At the foot of

the Moon Bastion, the **Clock Tower** was, as usual, a British addition.

Outside New Gate, the **First World War Memorial** stands in a triangular green. To its rear, Galle's **cricket ground** stages an occasional Test Match. Behind this is the **Bus Station** and, across the river to the west, **Galle Railway Station.**

As may be expected in Sri Lanka's fourth largest city, Galle's new town has a large commercial building and a market place, but little will be of interest to tourists. Some, however, may wish to visit Galle's branch of the state-run emporium **Laksala**, where examples of handmade Galle lace may be purchased.

ACCOMMODATION

Within Galle itself, although there are a handful of guest houses, the only tourist class accommodation is to be found at the New Oriental Hotel, already described. However, just 1 mile (2 km) westward, in the village of Dadella on the Colombo Road (as the Galle Road is called hereabouts), the **Lighthouse Hotel** provides five-star luxury. The

renowned Sri Lankan hotel architect Geoffrey Bawa has designed an ultra-modern building, its minimalist interiors apparently more influenced by Japanese than Sri Lankan traditions. An exception is the main staircase, which is embellished with life-size figures representing the Portuguese settlers of Sri Lanka.

A superb pool and easy access to the sandy beach below encourage the guests to spend a sinful amount of time relaxing. Luxurious bedrooms have all the facilities expected in a hotel of this rating. Most of the 60 rooms (3 of them suites) are allocated to package tour operators, and accommodation is difficult for independent visitors to obtain during the high season.

The **Closenberg Hotel**, located 2 miles (3 km) east of Galle, is renowned for its Sri Lankan curries. Perched on a promontory, the house was built in 1858 for Captain Bailey, a P&O agent, on the site of a Dutch fortress that had protected the entrance to Galle Harbour. Much period charm remains in the public rooms, and some of the antique furniture is of museum standard. Most of the 21 rooms, some with balconies, are located in the modern annexe.

UNAWATUNA

Around 3 miles (5 km) east of Galle the picturesque bay of Unawatuna should not be missed by connoisseurs of fine beaches.

With its gently curving crescent of sand, sense of enclosure and gleaming white dagoba, Unawatuna is most people's idea of the perfect Sri Lankan beach. The scientist and writer Sir Arthur C Clarke rented a house here for many years, only giving it up when he became confined to a wheelchair. In spite of being "rather spoiled by shanties and hippies", the country's most famous overseas resident still regards Unawatuna as the finest beach in Sri Lanka.

ACCOMMODATION

As almost all Unawatuna's accommodation is in economically-priced guest houses, a higher percentage of impecunious youngsters and backpackers (Sir Arthur's 'hippies') stay here than at any other resort in Sri Lanka. An exception is the splendid **Unawatuna Beach Resort** (known as UBR), where in 1998, a block of luxury rooms was opened over-looking the hotel's new swimming pool. The tariff, which includes half board, is rather high, a reflection of the hotel's unique standing at this resort.

Buses stop some distance from the beach, but three-wheelers will deposit and collect visitors more conveniently at the **Happy Banana Restaurant.**

A coral reef protects Unawatuna bay, creating safe bathing, especially at the west end where the water is very shallow. On Sundays, this sector becomes extremely crowded, resembling a municipal swimming pool when a school party has arrived. As cars are able to park nearby, families loaded with food find it convenient to have their extensive picnics here, thereby adding to the crowds. However, the atmosphere is always pleasant, and the friendly locals are delighted to practise their English with foreign tourists.

Headland views

Few visitors will be able to resist ascending to the **dagoba** on the west headland, from where the views over the bay are a delight. The temple below the dagoba is Hindu. From the dagoba, a 20-minute walk along the coast leads to the rocky 'Jungle Beach', secluded and backed by trees, but without a sandy beach. Boat trips to Jungle Beach are also available at 'very special', i.e. rip-off, prices, to tourists. The coastal scenery is spectacular.

At the eastern sector of the beach the sands shelve steeply, and this sector is not suitable for poor swimmers, even though the sea remains calm. However, Unawatuna is popular with wind surfers, who confine their activities to this part of the bay. Scuba divers may rent equipment from the UBR.

Restaurants and guest houses proliferate on the beach itself and along the Devala and Yaddehimulla roads immediately behind it. As may be expected, the further from the beach, the lower the tariff. It should be remembered that many of Unawatuna's guest houses do not have bedrooms with private shower/ WC and most lack hot water. Apart from UBR, accommodation of a reasonable standard is available at: **Rumassala Hotel** and **The Strand**. Of similar standard are: **Unawatuna Beach Bungalow, Sunny Beach Hotel, Full Moon Inn, Amma's Guest House, Weliwatta** and **Golden Ente**.

Recommended restaurants include **UBR, Happy Banana** and **Hot Rock**.

As might be imagined in such a young orientated resort, a highly amplified, computerised rhythm is likely to provide the accompaniment to evening meals, particularly on Friday and Saturday nights, and older visitors (i.e. those over 30) may not find this a particularly attractive feature of the resort. However, earplugs, combined with the careful selection of accommodation and restaurant (moving if necessary), usually enables most to overcome this problem.

UNAWATUNA TO KOGGALA

Eastward from Unawatuna to Koggala, 6 miles (10 km) distant, the main road keeps very close to the beaches, and the coastal views are some of the best that a motorist can enjoy on the island. Lying northwest of the resort village of Koggala are its lake and airport; the latter, laid out by Britain's Royal Air Force during the Second World War, once again military. It is said that 1,000 homes were demolished to make space for the airport, an act that still rankles locally.

KOGGALA

Koggala's beach stretches for half a mile (1 km). Although the sea can

be rough, rocks form a natural, shallow pool for bathers. The **Club Horizon**, a Confifi Group hotel, accommodates guests in 51 rooms and 22 separate bungalows, all air-conditioned. Terms quoted are fully inclusive. There are two swimming pools (one for children). Also with a swimming pool, the tariff at the much larger **Koggala Beach Hotel** is half that of the Club Horizon; there are 79 air-conditioned and 110 non air-conditioned rooms.

WICKRAMASINGHE MU-SEUM

Immediately after passing the Club Horizon hotel's entrance, a left turn is signposted to the **Martin Wickramasinghe Museum of Folk Art and Culture**. In a long career Wickramasinghe wrote more than 80 works, and is regarded as Sri Lanka's finest writer. Within the complex, in addition to the Folk Museum containing Wickramasinghe's collection of artefacts, stands the pretty bungalow in which he was born. The grounds themselves are planted with a variety of tropical trees.

Exhibits in the museum are eclectic but captioned, which is just as well because none of the staff speak English. Many will be amused by the education section, with its economical examples of perforated slates for learning arithmetic, and a sandboard on which children practised writing.

Wickramasinghe's bungalow lies to the rear of the boat in the garden. In the first room are family photographs – all ten of the author's children were born and lived here. The small room in which Wickramasinghe himself was born lies right off the dining-room and is apparently unaltered. An extension to the rear houses exhibits relating to events in the author's life; included is the MBE awarded to him by Queen Elizabeth II in 1953. Martin Wickramasinghe died in 1979.

KOGGALA TO WELIGAMA

TEMPLES

On the east side of Koggala, a side road leads from **Kataluwa** inland 2 miles (3 km) to the **Purvaramaya Temple**. Note that there are several temples in the area and ensure that the driver understands exactly which one is being sought: he must not turn off the main road before Kataluwa.

The temple's vihara was built in the 18th century, but it is its ambulatory, added in 1881, that is of particular interest. Murals painted on the internal wall depict scenes that relate the gruesome story of a cannibal king. The tale is extremely lengthy and complicated, but an enthusiastic attendant is usually on hand to explain as many of the paintings as each visitor's time permits. It is interesting to observe that Europeans depicted in the murals wear late-19th century dress.

AHANGAMA

Ahangama's beach is really a continuation of Koggala's. Its **Hotel Club Lanka**, with a huge pool, has 33 rooms; none are air-conditioned, but the value for money is exceptional.

En route to Weligama, the name of **Count de Maunay's Island**, a small islet just off shore, commemorates the French aristocrat who purchased it in 1932.

Stilt fishermen

It is entirely due to the stilt fishermen that Ahangama, a small village, has come to prominence. Uniquely, these fishermen wait for a fish to bite whilst perched in line on the crossbars of their respective poles, which have been fixed securely in the sand. Sometimes they will sit for hours, resembling a row of predatory storks.

The best times to observe this strange sight are usually 7.30am to 9am and 3.30pm to 6.30pm, but as soon as a tourist arrives on the scene, no matter when, a stilt fisherman can be expected to appear from nowhere to pose on his pole for a photograph. It is said that more money is earned from tourist tips than from selling fish. Stilt fishermen can be seen anywhere along the coast between Ahangama and Weligama (but not in Weligama itself).

Along Galle Road, teams of young girls can be observed making lace by hand in the traditional way. A range of delightful objects that they have produced, from place-mats to tablecloths, are offered for sale.

WELIGAMA

Taprobane Island, which can be reached on foot at low tide, contributes to the picturesque quality of Weligama's wide bay. Novelist Peter Bowles wrote 'The Spider's House' during a sojourn in the house on the island, in 1952. Accommodation is available at the **Weligama Bay Inn**, where young Sri Lankans learn catering skills, but it should be noted that the Galle Road rather noisily skirts the beach.

From the bay, a road leads half a mile (1 km) inland to the upright, 8th century figure of **Bodhisattva** (a Buddha to come) carved in a deep niche out of the rock.

MIRISSA

Past the next headland, Mirissa has an excellent beach, where the sea, outside the south-west monsoon period, is nearly always calm. Eastward from here there are no more protective reefs, and the sea becomes very much rougher – usually too rough for most swimmers. At the west end of the beach, the main road lies reasonably well back, but returns to skirt its east end.

The **Mirissa Beach Inn**, comprises five bungalows, and the larger **Paradise Beach Club**, with twelve bungalows, has a good restaurant and an attractive pool. Both provide adequate if not luxurious accommodation, and it is preferable to stay at either than spend a night in the large town of **Matara**, 6 miles (10 km) distant, where the limited accommodation is extremely basic and aimed at local visitors.

MATARA

Sri Lanka's eighth largest town has little of tourist interest and does not merit an overnight stay, however, its 18th century Dutch-built **Star Fort** has been well restored. This lies on the north side of the Nilwala Ganga, and was built to protect the much larger but now ruined fort originally built by the Portuguese on the peninsula to the south.

The bridge immediately south of the fort crosses the river to the peninsula, in the middle of which stands Matara's main fort.

Founded by the Portuguese in the

Star Fort

The coral rock walls of the Star Fort form the shape of a six-pointed star, hence of course its name. A pretty, 'toy town' portal bears the arms of the Dutch governor, Baron Redoute van Eik, who commissioned the fort in 1763. Set in its pediment above is the Dutch East India Company's VOC monogram. A wooden bridge across the moat gives access to the interior. Living quarters built around the courtyard are once more occupied. Take care not to fall in the central, unprotected well! The fort's small Dutch period museum was renovated in 1999. A walk along the rampart overlooks the moat, which recently has been filled with water.

mid-17th century, the Dutch rebuilt the fort in 1780, a date commemorated on the north entrance. The ramparts can be explored, but views are somewhat marred by the chaotic appearance of the bus station. The fort's clock tower, of course, was a British addition. During the Second World War, the complex served as an ammunitions store.

Some visitors will find Matara's **bus station** particularly useful, as it is from here that all buses on this part of the coast commence their journeys, thus giving passengers a rare chance of getting a seat – few will find strap-hanging all the way to the Hill Country a pleasant experience! Find out departure times in advance, arrange for a porter to guard any large bags or cases, and join in the 'rugby scrum' to board the vehicle as soon as it approaches – then reserve a seat and reclaim the luggage. Even better, pay the porter to do all this for you.

Matara marks the end of the railway line, and its terminal lies nearly half a mile (1 km) north-west of the Star Fort – most, therefore, will need transport from the railway station. There are, of course, three-wheelers and taxis, but some may prefer to experience the *hackerie*, a small cart now drawn by oxen but previously by men (as were rickshaws) until the arrival of the Dutch.

Matara beach

Matara's beach is surprisingly appealing for such a busy town, but in spite of some protection from its high, off-shore island, the sea is usually too rough for bathing. Skirting it, Beach Road retains some colonial buildings and provides an attractive promenade.

Right: Although an 18th century foundation, the figure of Buddha is a more recent feature of the Wewurukamala Vihara

Below: Dondra Head is the most southerly point in Sri Lanka

Beside the beach but facing the bus station, the Matara Rest House, reputedly the best accommodation in town, has basic rooms; there is no hot water and the mosquitoes seem to know exactly where every hole in the nets around the beds are to be found. Only for the desperate.

THE SOUTHERN COAST

Between Matara and Tangalla there are an exceptional number of

locations of tourist interest, but all are difficult to reach without a car. Shortly after leaving Matara a road leads inland for 2 miles (3 km) to the enormous **Weherahena Temple** (this can be reached by 349 bus from Matara).

Weherahena Temple

Sheer size is the attraction of this relatively modern temple, built in 1906. A russet and yellow painted Buddha, 128 ft (39 m) high, faces the courtyard and is backed by an enormous, very tall vihara, its two wings extending protectively to flank the figure.

After depositing shoes, a clockwise tour is recommended, ending in the courtyard. Of greatest interest internally is the subterranean section of the vihara where, from its steps, a skylight gives a clear view of the Buddha's chin high above. Ahead, a mirror reflects the temple's relics and treasures. The walls of the shrine are brightly painted with scenes from the Buddha's life.

Passed en route to Dhondra Head, the modern, beautifully sited complex of the **University of Rohuna** overlooks a lake and the sea.

Devinurawa Temple

This modern temple is of no particular interest apart from its 38 ft (11.6 m) high Buddha cast in concrete, it is a copy of the famous granite Aukana figure sculpted from rock, which many will visit between Dambulla and Polonnaruwa.

DONDRA HEAD

Dondra Head is Sri Lanka's most southerly point and, for this reason alone, much visited. On the headland stands one of the most splendid of the series of **lighthouses** constructed by the British from Colombo southward along the coast. It became operational on Queen Victoria's birthday in 1889. A scramble over the rocks provides the best view of the structure, which is now partly hidden by trees on the landward side.

Maha Vishnu Temple

A major Hindu temple devoted to Vishnu, built on the headland in the 7th century, was almost entirely demolished by the iconoclastic Portuguese soon after their arrival. Fortunately surviving is an exquisitely **carved stone gateway**, the finest of its type on the island. Excavated columns have been re-erected to run in two parallel lines from the entrance to the modern sector of the temple.

Dikwella (or Dickwella)

Cashew nuts and copra items such as rope and mats are made locally. Almost all the guests at the **Club Dikwella Village Resort** are Italian, as reservations are promoted in Milan. Just east of the town, overlooking the bay, the **Dikwella Beach Hotel**, with 10 rooms, has an economical tariff.

From Dikwella take the Beliatta road to see the country's largest figure of Buddha.

WEWURUKANNALA VIHARA

As the complex is approached, trees and houses give scale to the enormous head of Buddha that towers impressively above them. Founded in the 18th century, the temple's 160 ft (50 m) high Buddha is a comparatively recent addition.

As might be expected, the religious paintings within the vihara are bright and somewhat naive in style. The Buddha's head-dress apparently represents bands of a curled-up cobra, not an inverted ice-cream cornet as has been irreverently suggested. It is possible to ascend to the Buddha's head for views of the surrounding countryside.

MULKIRIGALA ROCK TEMPLE

From Beliatta clock tower, a road indicated leads to the **Mulkirigala Rock Temple**, which can alternatively be reached directly from Tangalla 10 miles (16 km) if more convenient. Those who intend to visit Dambulla's cave temples, which are similar but of much greater interest and extent, may prefer to give this excursion a miss.

The summit of the rock is 290 ft (210 m) high, and 510 steps must be climbed to reach it. Caves passed on the way up are decorated with murals depicting the usual Buddhist subjects, and contain reclining Buddha images. Most of the work was carried out in the 18th and 19th centuries. Ancient writings in the Pali language discovered in one of the caves in the 19th century, enabled experts to translate the *Maharamsa*, which chronicles the country's early history. Pali, after falling into disuse became reserved for Buddhist canonical tracts. A white dagoba has been erected on the summit, from which there are good coastal views eastward; in

clear weather, Adam's Peak can be seen rising spectacularly to the north.

Returning to the coast, 3.7 miles (6 km) east of Dikwella a path leads from the road to a famous Sri Lankan natural phenomenon.

MAWELLA BLOWHOLE

Outside the period of the southwest monsoon the sea is rarely sufficiently rough for this natural marvel to function; even so, tourists are often brought here, only to be disappointed. The blowhole is a fissure leading down from the cliff top to an open cave and, when waves crash in, the water is forced through to form a high spout. Hawkers sell cashew nuts and mangoes to visitors from their stalls throughout the year.

Additional Information

Places to Visit Galle

Historical Mansion Museum
31-39 Leyn Baan Street
Open daily 9am-6pm (closed Friday 12.30pm-2pm)

Maritime Museum
Queen Street
Open daily 9am-4.30pm

National Museum
Church Street
Open Tuesday-Sunday 9am-5pm

Places to Visit Koggala

Martin Wickramasinghe Museum of Folk Art & Culture
Open daily 9am-1pm and 2pm-5pm

The South-East Coast & Yala National Park

From Dondra Head, Sri Lanka's coastline at last changes direction, and the beaches face south-east rather than south-west. In addition, as far as Tangalla (or Tangalle), they are backed by low cliffs and rocks, which form a series of bays. Many people judge this part of the coastline to be the most picturesque in Sri Lanka, but as the road keeps slightly inland for most of the route the scenery can only be appreciated fully by exploring it on foot.

TANGALLA

COASTAL WALK TO TANGALLA

Nearly 2 miles (3 km) north of Tangalla a short track leads from the main road to **Palm Paradise Cabanas**, a bungalow development on a pretty beach that is extremely popular with German tourists.

Room facilities are basic and there is a Robinson Crusoe atmosphere that appeals to some.

A stunning coastal walk northward from the Palm Paradise comprising a series of headlands and coves terminates after around 1 mile (2 km) at Tangalla Bay. The **Tangalla Bay Hotel** provides an immediate visual impact, its white, Art Deco-inspired bulk giving the

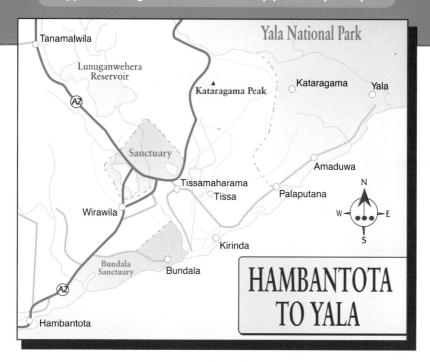

Tanamalwila

Lunuganwehera Reservoir

Yala National Park

▲ Kataragama Peak

Kataragama

Yala

A2

Sanctuary

Amaduwa

Tissamaharama

Tissa

Palaputana

N

Wirawila

W   E

S

Kirinda

Bundala Sanctuary

Bundala

HAMBANTOTA TO YALA

A2

Hambantota

appearance of a beached transatlantic liner of the 1930s. Its architect was profligate with his treatment of surfaces within and without, as all are painted – and twice yearly monsoons are not kind to paintwork. Once the nautical kitsch has been accepted, most guests enjoy their stay – the rooms are comfortable, the food good and the huge areas of glass create a bright, cheerful ambience. The small but adequate swimming pool is very important, as only the bravest will wish to enter Tangalla's rough seas.

Although not quite so idyllic as the coastal walk to the south, the walk from the hotel northward towards Tangalla town is most attractive, the bright green grass of the headlands combined with black

rocks and golden sandy beaches. Sri Lanka's south-east beaches are occasionally red, as if the wine had been spilled by guests at a jolly picnic that had got out of hand – there are good examples on both sides of the hotel. Turtles lay their eggs on some of the beaches at night, as emphasised by the name of Turtle Landing Restaurant just north of the hotel.

TANGALLA TOWN
The coast turns left towards the harbour, passing Tangalla's **Rest House**, once the residence of the local Dutch administrator, which provides a good halt for refreshments on its veranda. Facing the building, a narrow strip of sand leads to a promontory that is sheltered on one side by a semi-circle of

rocks, creating a natural bathing pool. Although the water is too shallow for swimming, this is the only section of Tangalla's beaches where a dip can be taken in safety at all times.

Tree-fringed **Medaketiya Beach** can be seen sweeping northward from the quay, but security restrictions now entail a long detour in order to get to it. Three-wheelers are usually available, but although there are guest houses along the beach, the sand shelves very steeply and the sea is usually too rough for swimming. The town itself is of little interest.

Between Tangalla and Hambantota the cliffs and trees are replaced by scrub. The dry zone of the island, which avoids much of both the south-west and the north-east monsoons' rainfall, has been entered.

HAMBANTOTA

Although this is the largest town on Sri Lanka's south-east coast, little of its energy is devoted to tourism, a high proportion of the 9,000 population being involved in fishing and agriculture. Many of the fishermen are Muslims with Malay ancestry, and 'hamban', as in Hambantota, is a corruption of 'sampan', the name of a Malay fishing boat. The beach, partly of red sand, is rather bleak and treeless and it quickly becomes obvious that Hambantota is no seaside resort. It is the town's proximity to Sri Lanka's two most important wildlife safari locations that attracts tourists. **Bundala Wildlife Sanctuary** is virtually on the doorstep but the somewhat more exotic **Yala National Park** lies further east, and those who plan to visit this may prefer to stay closer to it.

The three-star **Peacock Beach Hotel** is a comfortable, modern establishment, some of its air-conditioned rooms having TV and a mini-bar – try to book one of the hotel's two suites if possible: they are beautifully laid out and good value for money. The large swimming pool is set in extensive gardens to the rear of the building.

All that can be seen of interest on the beach facing the hotel is the hauling in of fishing nets; the sand falls steeply and the sea tends to be rough, making swimming and bathing inadvisable. It is marginally more interesting to walk along the beach in the direction of Hambantota town as far as the jetty, returning by three-wheeler. Few tourists spend more than two nights in Hambantota, and virtually all of them devote half a day to a Bundala safari.

BUNDALA SANCTUARY

Hotels will arrange **jeep safaris**, to Bundala Sanctuary for either 6.30am or 3pm departures, both trips take 3 hours: apart from the likelihood of seeing more birds in the morning there is no particular advantage in getting up early.

Jeeps hold up to 5 people, and it is, of course, cheaper to share a jeep if other passengers can be found, but if a vehicle has already been booked through a tour operator additional passengers will not be permitted, even if they are willing to pay a supplement.

The cost including jeep hire for two people is a not inconsiderable nearly 3,000 rupees, almost 800 of which represents the entry charge levied on foreigners by the government. However, this is less than it will cost for two to visit Yala and some choose Bundala simply because it is cheaper. An obligatory charge for a tracker is included in the fee at both Bundala and Yala, but none ever comes – what happens to the unearned money appears to be a mystery!

The Sanctuary (not a national park) is flat, treeless scrubland, in which, with luck, elephants, crocodiles, monkeys, peacocks and storks will be seen, but there is of course no guarantee. Leopards do not live here, Yala suits them better.

HAMBANTOTA TO YALA

Harvesting salt from the sea is a local industry, and heaps of salt appear shortly after leaving Hambantota. The **Yala Safari Beach Hotel** is the most convenient point from which to explore Yala National Park. From Hambantota eastward to the hotel is only around 31 miles (50 km) but the journey will take almost two hours, as the A2 turns inland towards Wirawila and parts company with the coast for good; the minor coastal road is poor. Some may prefer to turn right at Wirawila cross-roads, continuing directly to Tissamaharama.

Wirawila Tank

Wirawila Tank is a large, man-made lake excavated in the 3rd century BC. A popular hotel, the **Tissa Rest House** nestles on the eastern shore of the tank, which is overlooked by some of its rooms. Although there are 60 bedrooms, the hotel is often fully booked in the season by tour operators due to its proximity to Yala National Park. Jeep safaris may be arranged at the hotel which, unlike the Safari Beach Hotel, does have a swimming pool. Tissamaharama can be reached from here via the Kataragama road without returning to Wirawila.

TISSAMAHARAMA

Tissamaharama (Tissa) was the capital of the ancient kingdom of **Ruhuna**, founded by Yatala Tissa in the 3rd century BC. It is also believed to have been the birthplace of Dutugemunu, the Sinhalese liberator and subsequent King of Anuradhapura. Several ancient buildings around Tissa, most of them dagobas, have been restored in recent years.

Between the town and Wirawila Tank, the white painted dagoba, over 150 ft (46 m) high, is said to have been built by Dutugemunu's father, King Karantissa. A statue represents that king's consort, Queen Viharamahadevi (after whom Colombo's park is named). By tradition, Karantissa built the **Sandagiri Vihara** nearby.

The **Yatala Vihara** between Wirawila and Debarawewa is thought to have been the work of King Tissa: if so it is the oldest structure in the region. Ask for directions to the remains of what is known as the **King's Palace** but are almost certainly those of a multi-storey monastery (Tissamaharama means 'Monastery of Tissa'). All that survives are monolithic columns set in rows, as at the Brazen Palace of Anuradhapura , but Tissa's are even more impressive. Excavations in the area continue slowly.

Kirinda

From Tissa a road goes to the coast at **Kirinda**, a small fishing port with a promontory of huge boulders on which a dagoba stands picturesquely. For security reasons the approach road to the beach is closed, but it is only a short walk to it from the nearest road.

AMADUWA

The narrow coastal road leads eastward from Kirinda, crossing a lagoon and the estuaries of small rivers before at last reaching Amaduwa and the **Yala Safari Beach Hotel**. Ten of the hotel's 63 rooms· are air-conditioned, but again, a high proportion are reserved for group tours in the season. As may be expected, everything, including the buffet meals, is geared to north European tastes.

Most tourists stay overnight and are then taken on the early-morning safari before being whisked off to their next destination. This, presumably, is why the hotel has no swimming pool. In consequence, from mid-morning until the evening arrival of the next coaches, independent travellers have the place almost to themselves. Most will be fascinated by the surrealist, boulder-strewn scenery, which is an attraction in its own right.

To the north, a tiny fishing village lies on the other side of the low headland, its shacks backed by more boulders and fronted by fishermen's boats squeezed together like sardines in a tin. Passed on the way to this village, the derelict Brown's Safari Beach Hotel, a depressing sight, has been closed for some years.

RUHUNU (YALA) NATIONAL PARK

Wilpattu National Park, west of Anuradhapura, is regarded as the country's finest wildlife sanctuary, but the military have placed it out of bounds while the troubles continue. Yala, or Ruhunu as it should be called, is the next in importance, and the most westerly 10 per cent of its 400 sq miles (1,000 sq km) remains open to tourists. Foreigners are charged over 1,600 rupees entry fee and jeep hire costs around 2,500 rupees.

The big attraction here is the leopard, which is able to find at Yala, unlike Bundala, rocky ledges and trees from which to locate and attack its prey. However, numbers are very low, and visitors will need luck to see one. Other animals are far more numerous, and it is unusual not to see monkeys, elephants, crocodiles, buffalo and wild boar, although the nocturnal sloth bear is more difficult to locate.

East of the fishing village of Yala, the coastal strip is occupied by many Tamils, and along the road government security measures against the 'Tigers' prevent tourist encroachment as far north as the approaches to Trincomalee, around 93 miles (150 km) away. This means that Arugam Bay and Batticaloa, former resort areas, can no longer be visited. It must be hoped that the situation will change in the near future, not least because this part of Sri Lanka misses the monsoon that rules out the south-west coast for tourists during the summer months.

FROM YALA TO BANDARAWELA

From this end of the coast, tourists usually make for the Hill Country and Kandy, beginning with a stop at Bandarawela, 75 miles (120 km) to the north.

9

The Hill Country & Nuwara Eliya

Tea pickers working in the dramatic scenery

Those who have made the lengthy journey from Colombo to the southern tip of Sri Lanka will be pleased to discover that from Yala it is only around 62 miles (100 km) to the Hill Country, whereas from the south-west coastal resorts twice that distance is involved.

A road leads directly from Tissamaharama to the hills; however, another road runs parallel with it slightly to the east, passing through the three-religion pilgrimage town of Kataragama. Taking the latter route will add around 12.5 miles (20 km) to the journey, which many who follow neither Buddhism, Hinduism or Islam may find unwarranted.

KATARAGAMA

This town, 9 miles (15 km) north of Tissa, ranks with Adam's Peak in importance as a heart of religious pilgrimage for Sri Lankans. It is believed that King Dutugemunu built a shrine on the sacred hill at Kataragama in the 2nd century BC to Skanda, the god of war who is known locally as the 'Kataragama Deviyo'.

The **Maha Devala**, the most important of Kataragama's Buddhist shrines, allegedly incorporates Skanda's lance. Pujas here at 4.30am, 10.30am and 6.30pm are attended by Buddhists, Hindus and Muslims bearing gifts for the god. It will already have been noticed that Hindu gods are regularly included in Buddhist acts of worship, but this is an unusual example of Muslims becoming involved with a pagan god.

Hindu gods, such as Ganesh, are worshipped at various Kataragama shrines, but the oldest structure is probably the 1st century BC **Kirivehera dagoba**. A two-week festival, held in July and August, is primarily attended by Hindus, during which Skanda's relic is bathed in the local river. Many participants demonstrate the depth of their religious fervour by inflicting punishments on themselves in various ways without appearing to suffer pain. The enormous crowds of worshippers who arrive during the festival can prove intolerable to some; in addition, Kataragama is usually very crowded at weekends and on Poya (full moon) days.

TISSA TO BUDURUWAGALA

At the Buttala junction, follow the main road westward to Wellawaya, then turn left. After 3 miles (5 km) a side road leads right to **Buduruwagala**.

Buduruwagala Buddha

Six figures have been carved out of the rock, probably in the 10th century. Now painted white, the Buddha stands 51 ft (15.5 m) high; traces of stucco and orange pigment indicate that at some period the figure was plastered and painted. He is flanked by Avalokitesvara, a bodhisattva (future Buddha) and his consort Tara.

The three minor figures on the right are said to be the work of the main carver's apprentice son, which would account for their different style. Represented are a dancing girl, Maitreya (another future Buddha) and, holding a *dorje* (a Tibetan thunderbolt), the god of agriculture. Coach parties halt occasionally, but rarely stay long; after their departure, independent visitors can expect to have this peaceful location to themselves.

The more direct road from Tissa passes several reservoirs, the most rewarding of which is fed by the Kirindi Oya at **Handapangala**. A hotel entered from the main road borders the reservoir and provides a good location for viewing bird-life (best, as usual, early in the morning). Elephants, also, are numerous in the region – too numerous according to the local villagers, who have suffered damage to their properties from marauding tuskers in recent years. Approximately 6 miles (10 km) ahead, a narrow lane, left, leads to Sri Lanka's largest rock-carved standing Buddha.

THE HILL COUNTRY

West of Wellawaya, the land rises dramatically, indicating the beginning of Sri Lanka's 'hill country', a roughly circular area, 62 miles (100 km) in diameter, of verdant peaks, valleys and reservoirs that lies roughly in the middle of the southern half of the country. At the hill resorts there is no need for air-conditioning or fans; in mid-winter, nights can even be cold enough for heating to be needed.

The branch road to **Bandarawela** passes the 560 ft (170 m) high **Diyaluma Falls**, popular with locals for bathing and washing clothes. Also with some graffiti 'artists', who seem to idiotically need to demonstrate their importance by defacing far too many rocks at beauty spots in Sri Lanka.

BANDARAWELA

At just over 4,000 ft (1,219 m), the market town of Bandarawela is blessed with some of Sri Lanka's most comfortable mean temperatures. However, as is usual in mountainous areas, rainfall can be high, skies generally being at their clearest in the mornings. Fruits familiar to Europeans, such as strawberries and pears, which grow well in the cooler temperatures, make a change from the usual pineapples, limes and bananas.

Colombo-Badalla railway

While Bandarawela offers little of great tourist interest, apart from its views of the surrounding mountains, it is one of the most convenient places for exploring the region either by road or rail. The **Colombo-Badalla Railway** passes through the town, and visitors are urged to make at least one trip on it, either eastward, perhaps as far as **Ella**, or westward, via **Ohiya** (for Horton Plains), to **Nanu Oya** (for Nuwara Eliya). In both directions the views are exceptionally fine – and the fares incredibly cheap.

Colonial hotel

Fortunately, one of the most fascinating 'colonial' hotels in the country, operated by Aitken Spence, has survived in the town. Called, simply, the **Bandarawela Hotel**, it lies back from the main road, fronted by a small garden, which is popular with tour parties for brief morning coffee or afternoon tea halts. Strangely, few appear to stay the night.

Originally built as a tea planters' club, nothing seems to have changed since the 1930s, particularly in the enormous lounge, which is fitted with supremely comfortable, floral

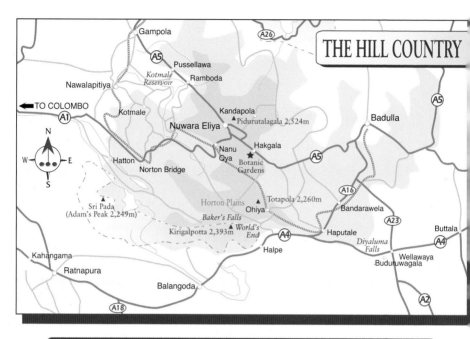

THE HILL COUNTRY

Gampola
A26
A5
Pussellawa
Nawalapitiya
Kotmale
Reservoir
Ramboda
TO COLOMBO
A1
Kotmale
Kandapola
Badulla
A5
Pidurutalagala 2,524m
Nuwara Eliya
N
W — E
S
Hatton
Norton Bridge
Nanu
Oya
Hakgala
Botanic
Gardens
A5
A16
Sri Pada
(Adam's Peak 2,249m)
Horton Plains
Totapola 2,260m
Ohiya
Bandarawela
A23
Baker's Falls
Kirigalpotta 2,393m
World's
End
A4
Haputale
Buttala
A4
Halpe
Diyaluma
Falls
Wellawaya
Buduruwagala
Kahangama
Ratnapura
Balangoda
Halpe
A2
A18

Below; Left: On the route to Bandarawela, the Diyaluma Fall
Right: At World's End, Horton Plains drop vertically 900 feet (274 m) but are worth the scramble for the fit and enthusiastic

Early morning is often the best time for exploring the Hill Country

patterned easy chairs and lovingly preserved antique hardwood furniture. The reasonably-priced bar would not be out of place in an English village. Food is good, and the ambience highly civilised. For some reason, frogs are attracted to the hotel's grounds, and light sleepers may find their nocturnal gurgling somewhat disturbing – take earplugs. A few minutes walk from the hotel, **Woodlands Network** can supply trained local guides for walking tours in the region.

ELLA

At approximately the same height as Bandarawela, Ella is easily reached from the town by road or rail. Passed on the way to the town is the **Rawena Falls**, another popular spot with local bathers. Worth visiting are the gardens of the **Rest House** for their spectacular views of the plain below that stretches to the coast. From Ella southward, a road passes through the **Ella Gap**, and provides a direct route via Wellawaya to the beach resorts.

HORTON PLAINS

The plains, a flat plateau, are located around 25 miles (40 km) from both Nuwara Eliya and Bandarawela, and can be reached by rail (Ohiya station) or road. An early morning start is recommended, as heavy mist often rises to spoil the spectacular view from **World's End** by 10.30am. Low-lying mist may occur during the early stages of the journey from Bandarawella, but this is a sign of fine weather to come, and will be left behind as the road ascends.

Hakgala Botanic Gardens

From Horton Plains car park there is access to the Nuwara Eliya road. A short detour 6.2 miles (10 km) east of Nuwara Eliya enables gardening enthusiasts to visit Hakgala Botanic Gardens, created on a rock in 1861 by Sir Clement Markham as a plantation of cinchona trees, from the bark of which quinine, the malaria palliative, is obtained.

'Hakgala' means 'jaw rock', and, tradition has it that the god, Rama, sent Humayun, the monkey god, to the Himalayas in search of a certain herb with healing properties. Unfortunately, Humayun forgot which herb was required, and so returned with a huge chunk of mountain in his jaw, hoping that its plants would include the herb specified. Whether it did or not is unrecorded, but the chunk of mountain is said to be that on which the botanic gardens have been laid out. Open daily 7.30am to 5pm.

Outside Haputale, **Bambara-kanda Falls**, Sri Lanka's highest at 790 ft (490 m), is unlikely to impress unless heavy rain has fallen recently. It was at **Haputale** that the murderous elephant hunter Major Thomas William Rogers was struck by lightning and killed in 1905 – his grave can be seen at Nuwara Eliya.

Trains from Bandarawela and Nanu Oya will both take around 90 minutes to Ohiya station, from where most rail visitors on their way to World's End will require a taxi. The alternative is a 7.5 mile (12 km) uphill slog, which only hiking enthusiasts will relish.

The name of this saddle of the Haputale mountain range commemorates Governor Sir Robert Horton. Although it is primarily grassland, there are enough trees to attract leopards. Fortunately, there are also sufficient deer, particularly sambar, to keep the big cats well fed. Reassuringly, it is said that leopards have little taste for human beings, even well-fed tourists. Large, purple-faced monkeys with white beards, known as Shaggy Bear monkeys, may look aggressive but are nervous of human beings and keep their distance. Surprisingly, no elephants roam the plains; apparently they did once, but most were shot by hunters, and those that survived migrated elsewhere. Only the southern sector of Horton Plains, which includes World's End, is visited by most tourists.

WORLD'S END

It should be noted that the Farr Inn, at the approach to the World's End pathway, was due to be demolished in 1999 and no replacement is planned. This provided basic but overpriced, accommodation, and its demise is hardly surprising. For access to the Horton Plains National Park, the Sri Lankan government imposes an outrageous $US12 per person on foreigners, all of whom it seems to believe are obscenely wealthy – Sri Lankans pay just 20 rupees! Whether or not the World's End expedition is worth this rip-off charge, the exertion required and the time involved, is a matter of personal taste. When clear, the view from the top of the 900 ft (274 m) plateau is certainly spectacular but not dissimilar to what can be seen looking down many a steep-sided mountain slope.

From the car park, a 2.5 mile (4 km) scramble along an undulating rocky 'path', which after rain becomes a mountain stream, must be made before World's End is reached. After 2 miles (3 km), **Little World's End**, a slightly less dramatic viewpoint, provides a welcome halt, but the view from World's End encompasses far more reservoirs and, in clear conditions, the Hambantota coastline.

A nearby path leads westward to the waterfall known as **Baker's Falls**, from where another path returns directly to the car park, thus completing a circular tour: only an additional third of a mile (0.5 km) is involved in making this diversion.

From the car park area there are good views westward to Adam's Peak. Much nearer, to the south and resembling a volcano, **Kirigalpotta**, at 7,850 ft (2,393 m), is Sri Lanka's second highest mountain. To the north, **Totapola,** at 7,741 ft (2,360 m), is the country's third highest. Hidden from view behind Totapola, **Pidurutalagala** (Mount Pedro) at 8,278 ft (2,524 m), the highest mountain, overlooks **Nuwara Eliya.**

NUWARA ELIYA

Nuwara Eliya, pronounced 'Nureliya', and meaning 'city of light', is located 6,199 ft (1,889 m) above sea level, which makes it the highest town in Sri Lanka. The cool climate, with temperatures averaging only 57°F (14°C) throughout the year, led to its development as a sanatorium for sick British officers as early as 1818.

Many important rivers have their source in the region, and the Kandy Kingdom relied on them for its water supply. With the construction of surfaced roads and the railway, Nuwara Eliya became reachable from Colombo in half a day and from Kandy in less. Under British rule, the town became an exclusive colonial resort, with a golf course, a race track, a park and a gentleman's club – all have survived. European-style residences were built, a few of which have been converted to comfortable, period-style hotels.

Apart from its very Sri Lankan **New Bazaar Street**, which bisects the town, Nuwara Eliya retains an extraordinarily British ambience, but it is the Britain of the 1930s that is evoked. Sleepy, winding roads, with hardly a car to be seen, immaculate lawns, smoke from tall chimneys and black-and-white 'Tudor' houses with climbing roses are not just a time warp but a cultural warp (if there is such a thing). Is this really the second millennium and are we really just 6 degrees north of the equator? As will be seen on a walk through the town, the surrealism of Nuwara Eliya will continually evoke nostalgia as visitors enter its hotels and clubs, particularly British visitors who have reached middle age.

As the town is entered from the direction of Hakgala, **Badulla Road** leads into town, with the racecourse to the right and a cluster of a dozen guest houses on the left. One of these guest houses may prove useful, as the town's hotels are often heavily booked, particularly on

Continued on page 112...

Tea pickers always look happy – even though they are paid only 100 rupees per day!

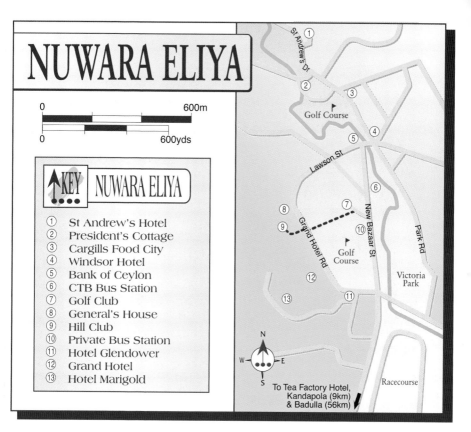

NUWARA ELIYA

```
0                    600m
0                    600yds
```

KEY — NUWARA ELIYA

1. St Andrew's Hotel
2. President's Cottage
3. Cargills Food City
4. Windsor Hotel
5. Bank of Ceylon
6. CTB Bus Station
7. Golf Club
8. General's House
9. Hill Club
10. Private Bus Station
11. Hotel Glendower
12. Grand Hotel
13. Hotel Marigold

St Andrew's Dr

Golf Course

Lawson St

New Bazaar St

Grand Hotel Rd

Golf Course

Park Rd

Victoria Park

Racecourse

N
W — E
S

To Tea Factory Hotel,
Kandapola (9km)
& Badulla (56km)

Nuwara Eliya's mock Tudor Grand Hotel

Fridays and Saturdays, when Colombo executives and their families seek the cooler air of the Hill Country for weekend breaks. During the month of April, in which the Sinhalese New Year is celebrated, it can be almost impossible to secure a room.

A TOUR OF THE TOWN

Nuwara Eliya is a compact town that can be seen on foot easily in half a day. A good place to begin a walk is the roundabout north of the racecourse, from which Grand Hotel Road branches westward.

Seen immediately left is the popular **Hotel Glendower**, with a restaurant that rather surprisingly specialises in Chinese food. The 20-room hotel dates from 1995 but looks as though it must have been running for seventy years at least. Wonderful chintzy furniture in both the public areas and the bedrooms, combined with hardwood fittings and a general spaciousness, reinforces the period look established by the building's black-and-white, timbered exterior.

On Friday nights the Glendower's bar is favoured by western expatriates, most of whom are employed as executives in the local textile factory. Tea is elegantly served on the pretty lawn at the rear of the building. Occupying the bend in the road ahead, and picturesquely framed by enormous trees is the **Grand Hotel**, Nuwara Eliya's pride.

Grand Hotel

The 150-room Grand Hotel is by far Nuwara Eliya's largest and most important building, comprises a unified series of extensions to Barnes Hall, a bungalow constructed for Governor Sir Edward Barnes in 1828 (those who have visited Colombo may recall Sir Edward's statue fronting President's Residence). In 1891, the house was converted to a hotel, but the timbered third floor which gives the Grand its predominantly 'Tudor' appearance, was not added until the 1930s. Corrugated iron roofs painted red or green became popular at Nuwara Eliya towards the end of the 19th century, and remain so, even being incorporated in new buildings so that the appearance of the region is preserved. The Grand Hotel's corrugated-iron roof had to be extended in 1995, when the new 60-bedroom wing was added on the north side.

Now covering 90 acres (36.5 hectares) of grounds, the hotel offers a whole range of accommodation, from standard rooms with fireplaces to enormous presidential suites. A Supper Club offering a high standard of cuisine was added to the facilities in 1998, and its food is now judged the best in town. As may be expected, the hotel is extremely popular with tour operators, and advance reservations in the season are virtually essential. There is, of course, no swimming pool – far too cold. To the rear, Hotel Marigold was under construction in 1999.

Hill Club

A short distance to the north, a private entrance off Grand Hotel Road – there are two but the first is usually locked – leads to the famous **Hill Club**.

Founded in 1876 as a tea planters' club, most of the granite structure is original, but the porch and Tudor-style block were added in 1930. There are 36 letting rooms. Visitors must become temporary members, and men still have to wear a tie in the public areas after 7pm. The set dinner – somewhat highly priced at $US10 – is served by white-gloved waiters in a hushed, formal atmosphere. More casual, but very highly-priced, is the main bar – gentlemen only, until quite recently, but ladies are now welcome. Hunting trophies and old photographs are displayed. Facilities such as the library and billiard room may be used by all members.

On the bend in the road, north of the Hill Club, the neat, white-painted villa still known as the **General's House** was formerly the residence of the Commanding Officer of the British troops. It now provides accommodation for state visitors.

Return southward to the second (locked) entrance to the Hill Club, facing which, the public footpath on the opposite side of Grand Hotel Road crosses the south sector of the Golf Club's links.

Nuwara Eliya Golf Club

The Club's extensive links run through the town to the hillside beyond. Unusually, they are crossed by roads, which divide them into three sectors. Located in the south sector is the **Club House**, to which visitors are made welcome. The Gordon Highlanders founded the golf club whilst on a visit to Nuwara Eliya in 1889, and it is still one of Asia's finest. Members are permitted to join on a daily basis, but male players are required to wear a shirt with collar, socks and trousers – or shorts of reasonable length.

A great attraction to visitors is the bar, with its timber ceiling and wainscoting; the names of trophy winners are recorded in gold leaf on wooden boards. Vintage photos of Nuwara Eliya displayed in the

Lightning strikes thrice

Beneath a tree in the golf club's disused cemetery, one of a cluster of tombstones has been cleft in two. It is difficult to define the name on the stone, but apparently this records **Major Thomas William Rogers**.

Rogers shot elephants for 'sport', claiming to have dispatched 100 every year for 12 years – a figure that has been disputed as being impossibly high. At the age of 41, during a storm at Haputale, Rogers was struck by lightning, dying instantly. His body was buried in Nuwara Eliya's cemetery, but lightning struck again, damaging the major's tombstone, which was quickly repaired.

It is hard to believe, but apparently a bolt of lightning in 1988 hit the tombstone once more, creating the present cleavage, which, this time, it seems, will not be repaired. There are locals who believe that divine retribution from the elephant-headed god, Ganesh, is responsible – if they are right, some may think that this Hindu deity deserves universal applause. Visitors to the golf club might be advised to keep a wary eye on the sky just in case a storm is brewing!

adjacent lounge include a record of the 1947 floods. In addition to the bar, day members may also use the badminton court, library, dining hall and putting greens. There are excellent views over the 18th green from the veranda of the clubhouse. To the rear is a disused cemetery.

The commercial area

A drive leads from the rear of the club house to New Bazaar Street, the town's commercial area. On the left, the pink brick **Post Office** would not look out of place in an English country town. Almost opposite, the **CTB bus station** was originally the railway station; it is rumoured that there are plans to bring the railway back to Nuwara Eliya in the near future.

Modern shops have replaced areas that were badly damaged by anti-Tamil riots in 1983 – in spite of the fact that the Hill Country Tamils, who were bought to the area by the British to work on the tea plantations in the 19th century, have never supported the Tamil Tigers.

The **Windsor Hotel**, a modern three-star establishment with 50 rooms, overlooks the multiple road junction ahead. It is popular with tour operators, for whose clients the restaurant menu caters. To its left, Kandy Road continues northward, passing **Cargill's Food City** supermarket, and soon branching left between the golf links. On the left, **President's Cottage** was formerly the summer residence of the Governor General, when it was known as Queen's Cottage.

St Andrew's Drive, the right branch from Kandy Road, leads to the two-star, 52-room **St Andrew's Hotel**, looking as sternly Scottish

Colonial remnants

Victoria, as a location name, survives much more frequently in Sri Lanka than in India. Similarly, the names of other British dignitaries who were remembered in the same way, often former governors, are still to be found on the island.

This is in contrast to India, where almost all have been changed, partly due to fervent Hindu nationalism and partly to India's struggle for independence, which was far more bitter than Sri Lanka's. Visitors to Sri Lanka, most of whom are usually defeated by the tongue-twisting local names, will be grateful for such moderation.

as its name, which pays homage to the Royal and Ancient (golf) Club at St Andrews in Scotland. Again, this is popular with tour operators. Return to the Post Office, and cross New Bazaar Street to enter **Victoria Park**.

Victoria Park runs parallel with the golf course, the two verdant spaces forming a welcome space in the middle of the town. It is best in spring and late summer, when the flowers bloom, but the park is rather spoilt by the apparent need to cover large areas of plants with protective thatch.

Rising above Nuwara Eliya, to the north, is **Pidurutalagala** mountain, usually referred to as Mount Pedro. At 8,278 ft (2,524 m) this is Sri Lanka's highest peak, which is why the highest television transmitter on the island has been erected on its summit. Because of this, access to the area is no longer permitted.

The exit from the park faces the somewhat neglected **racecourse**, where horse racing now only takes place in April.

Although Nuwara Eliya, due to its height, is always at least 50°F (10°C) cooler than Colombo, from February to May and October to November it is significantly drier and sunnier. These conditions are ideal for growing fruit and vegetables that are usually found only in more temperate zones. Many of the market gardens have replaced the lawns laid out by the British around their colonial residences before independence.

Above: *One of the grand-looking streets in Nuwara Eliya*
Below: *Tea on the lawn at Hotel Glendower, Nuwara Eliya*

THE TEA FACTORY HOTEL

Although Nuwara Eliya has now been explored, a new development of great interest to tourists overlooks the adjacent small town of **Kandapola** – a former tea factory converted to a luxury hotel. Even if not staying at the **Tea Factory Hotel**, an excursion to it is highly recommended; the journey takes half an hour by taxi.

Nuwara Eliya is surrounded by tea estates, and many factories where the plucked green leaves become tea ready for the pot will have been observed at intervals. These buildings are virtually identical in appearance, each one being designed for the processes of withering, rolling, fermenting, firing and grading the leaves. No extraneous embellishments to these tall, rectangular blocks with their low-pitched roofs are employed, and as each floor is almost entirely enclosed by huge windows, the factories evoke the Bauhaus period of architecture, with which many of them are contemporary.

A derelict factory dating from the 1920s was discovered by hotel group Aitken Spence, which saw its potential as a tourist attraction. The building was painstakingly converted to a hotel, with minimum structural changes a stipulation. Views over the tea plantations from the bedrooms, with their huge windows, are stunning, and cleverly reflected on the walls by mirror glass. As may be expected, fifth-floor rooms have the best views, particularly the suites at each end. Another advantage of occupying a top-floor room is that nothing could be done to soundproof the flooring between each level, and some guests on lower floors have been disturbed by movement above. Earplugs are available at reception.

Small quantities of high quality tea are still produced on the estate, and limitless sachets of two varieties are provided in the bedrooms for tea-making whenever required; tea taken black is recommended, as the powdered milk supplied interferes somewhat with its delicate taste.

Preserved in the basement of the hotel is the original engine that powered the factory. Still in working order and switched on every evening, electricity now drives the motor rather than oil as formerly. Visitors are shown around the small factory adjacent to the hotel, where the tea grown on the estate is dried and graded. It will be pointed out that 'high grown' tea, as at Nuwara Eliya, is the finest and most sought after. Packets of tea and other souvenirs may be purchased. Few will forget being surrounded by the intense lime-green of the neat tea bushes, and the cheerful smiles of the Tamil ladies who pluck their leaves – for a hardly munificent 100 rupees per day!

As elsewhere in the mountains, skies are generally clearer in the morning, but the location is so high that hotel guests often look *down* on the clouds. Taxi excursions to Nuwara Eliya can be arranged by the hotel.

ADAM'S PEAK ASCENT FROM DALHOUSIE

Adam's Peak and its ascent from Ratnapura has already been described, but the easiest approach is from Dalhousie village, 20.5 miles (33 km) south-west of

Hatton. The village has bus services in season, direct from Nuwara Eliya, Kandy and Colombo. Allow around 3 hours for the climb.

NORTHWARD TO KANDY

The A5 road from Nuwara Eliya gradually descends to Kandy, Sri Lanka's second largest town, located 50 miles (80 km) to the north. It is possible to make the journey by rail (from Nanu Oya station), but the train takes 4 hours, one hour longer than direct buses. Express buses to Colombo take 4.5 hours, and trains 6 hours. There is also a once daily coastal bus, via Hambantota, to Matara.

After 9 miles (15 km), **Mackwood's Labookellie Estate** tea factory, on the left, welcomes visitors to observe the processes involved (not Sundays). The tea here is still classed as high grown, even though the plantations are lower than those around Nuwara Eliya. Surprisingly, during the 19th century a member of the Rothschild family grew Assam tea experimentally in the region, but it proved undrinkable. If rainfall has been high, visitors may find little happening in the factory, especially on Saturdays. As may be expected there is an adjacent shop from which Mackwood's teas and other souvenirs may be purchased.

Seven waterfalls are passed on route to Kandy, all of which the driver will enthusiastically point out; some are a short distance away from the road but others are adjacent. The **Ramboda Falls** is one of the most spectacular, and refreshments can be obtained at a hotel nearby. Further on, the road twists and turns as it descends steeply through the **Ramboda Pass**. Here, there is an amusing game to play: at the first bend a smiling boy will offer flowers for sale, which most decline, but lo-and-behold the same boy will be waiting at the next bend, having raced down an almost vertical path to get ahead. This may continue up to five times, and at the end few will have the heart to refuse to make a purchase – don't forget, the exhausted lad must now climb up the steep path to its beginning in order to repeat the procedure.

There are good views westward of the **Kotmale Reservoir** from **Hellbode Waterfalls**, where acquisitive monkeys are likely to be seen; keep an eye on valuables.

At **Pusselawa** 5.5 miles (9 km) further, the half-way point in the journey has just been passed, scenery flattens out and the drop in altitude becomes much gentler.

Gampola, the largest town on the route, served briefly as the island's capital in the 15th century. A black elephant frieze decorates the white walls of its Buddhist temple. In this region the British established the first coffee plantation on the island around 1835. Results were excellent, but in 1869 disease struck and the entire crop was lost. Tea proved to be such a successful replacement that attempts were never made to grow coffee again on a large scale. Some coffee trees, however, can still be seen in the region.

Kandy

O n a first visit to Kandy, most people are immediately struck by the uniformly white-painted buildings, the shimmering lake in front of the Temple of the Tooth and what remains of the former royal palace. It is more like arriving at a resort than the second largest city in the country. But of course, unlike Colombo, Kandy is a resort in addition to being a commercial city.

Although Kandy is understandably defined as one of Sri Lanka's three ancient capitals, it should not really be bracketed with the other two, **Polonnaruwa** and **Anuradhapura**, both of which pre-date it by many centuries and have long been deserted (the towns attached to them and bearing their names are certainly occupied, but they are simply appendages of recent date). In addition, the country has had several capitals since Polonnaruwa was abandoned in the mid-13th century.

Although Kandy is still 1,602 ft (488 m) above sea level, the temperatures reached are much higher than those at Nuwara Eliya, and the better hotels have installed swimming pools.

Arriving in Kandy

Travelling from Nuwara Eliya, the road enters Kandy from the southwest, passing the famous **Botanic**

Backed by hills and fronted by its lake, Kandy is Sri Lanka's most attractive city

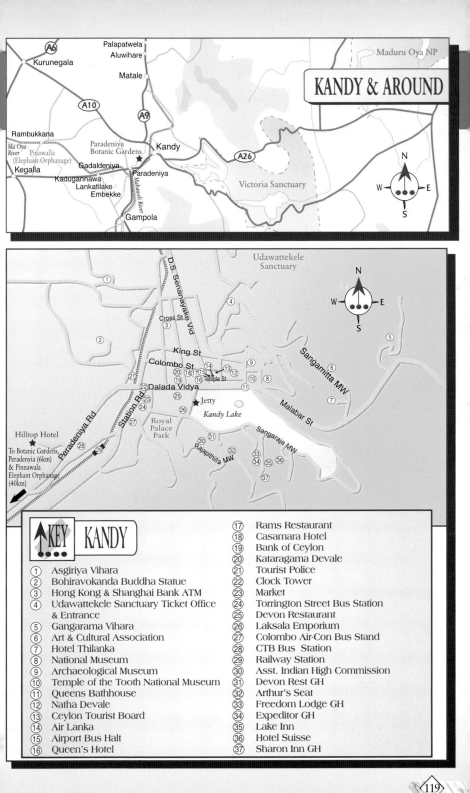

KANDY & AROUND

Maduru Oya NP

A6
Kurunegala
Palapatwela
Aluwihare
Matale
A10
A9
Rambukkana
Paradeniya Botanic Gardens
Kandy
A26
Ma Oya River
Pinnawala (Elephant Orphanage)
Gadaldeniya
Kegalla
Paradeniya
Kadugannawa
Lankatilake
Embekke
Victoria Sanctuary
Gampola

Udawattekele Sanctuary

D.S. Senanayake Vid

Cross St
King St
Colombo St
Temple St
Dalada Vidya
Jetty
Kandy Lake
Station Rd
Peradeniya Rd
Sangamitta MW
Malabar St
Sangaraja MW
Rajapithilla MW
Royal Palace Park
Hilltop Hotel
To Botanic Gardens, Peradeniya (6km) & Pinnawala Elephant Orphanage (40km)

KEY KANDY

1. Asgiriya Vihara
2. Bohiravokanda Buddha Statue
3. Hong Kong & Shanghai Bank ATM
4. Udawattekele Sanctuary Ticket Office & Entrance
5. Gangarama Vihara
6. Art & Cultural Association
7. Hotel Thilanka
8. National Museum
9. Archaeological Museum
10. Temple of the Tooth National Museum
11. Queens Bathhouse
12. Natha Devale
13. Ceylon Tourist Board
14. Air Lanka
15. Airport Bus Halt
16. Queen's Hotel

17. Rams Restaurant
18. Casamara Hotel
19. Bank of Ceylon
20. Kataragama Devale
21. Tourist Police
22. Clock Tower
23. Market
24. Torrington Street Bus Station
25. Devon Restaurant
26. Laksala Emporium
27. Colombo Air-Con Bus Stand
28. CTB Bus Station
29. Railway Station
30. Asst. Indian High Commission
31. Devon Rest GH
32. Arthur's Seat
33. Freedom Lodge GH
34. Expeditor GH
35. Lake Inn
36. Hotel Suisse
37. Sharon Inn GH

Gardens in the suburbs of Peradeniya.

The **CTB bus station, railway station, Colombo Express bus stand** and the local buses stand are all located in the south-western corner of the city, conveniently close to each other. Most independent visitors will require a three-wheeler from any of them to their hotel.

KANDY'S CONCENTRATED ATTRACTIONS

When the British conquered Kandy in 1815 they discovered that the **royal palace** and its adjacent **temples** were the only historic buildings to have survived the battles between the Kandy Kingdom and its many invaders. In consequence, central Kandy's points of major tourist interest are concentrated on the relatively small area around the **Temple of the Tooth**. All tourists will be shown this famous temple, but many guides neglect to describe the remains of the royal palace or the temples to the west of it, some of which are much older structures.

Only a very small part of the entire complex has been put out of bounds since the Tamil Tiger bomb was detonated in January 1998, all the limited damage caused has now been repaired, and the completion of much-needed restoration unconnected with the explosion is all but completed.

EXPLORING KANDY

An intensive one-day exploration of Kandy's 'highlights' might be completed by a walk around the shores of the lake, followed by a stroll up to **Arthur's Seat** for the best views of the city and a short tour of the shopping streets.

Most independent tourists will spend another day west of the city visiting the **Botanic Gardens, Elephant Orphanage** and, if time permits, three 14th century **village temples**, which lie close to each other a mile (2 km) south of the gardens. Those on escorted tours will often be taken to see all or some of these locations as their vehicles approach Kandy from the west.

HISTORY

Archaeological evidence proves that the Kandy area was inhabited at least 2,000 years ago, but a settlement here is first recorded in a 14th century inscription. Following the destruction of Kotte, its status as Sinhalese capital was transferred to Kandy in 1592, almost 400 years after Polonnaruwa, the second ancient capital, had been abandoned.

The Kandyans wanted to rid the country of the religiously intolerant Portuguese, who had gradually taken over the island since their arrival in 1505, and when the Dutch arrived in 1658 with the intention of replacing them, they received all possible assistance from Kandy. However, towards the end of the 18th century the Kandyans had become disenchanted with the Dutch, and assisted the British to replace them in turn. Knowing the Kandyans' successful history of resistance to their colonising predecessors, primarily due to mountainous terrain, after a few skirmishes the British permitted their kingdom to remain self-governing, even when, in 1802, they decreed the country to be a 'Crown Colony'.

• ESALA PERAHERA •

Sri Lanka's most impressive festival, established for many centuries, takes place annually at Kandy over ten days and nights in late July or early August – the actual dates vary and depend on the full moon. Unfortunately, this is well outside the usual tourist period, and visitors will have to make a special effort to witness the event.

The *perahera* (procession) gradually builds in splendour and length, particularly from the seventh night onward, culminating in the final night, when it is led by the Maligawa Tusker, decorated and in exotic caparison. On his back he bears a canopied replica of the outer casket of the Sacred Tooth relic. As the elephant proceeds, a white carpet is laid for him to step on.

The earlier parts of the festival feature Natha (the Buddha to come) and three Hindu gods: Vishnu, Skanda and Pattini, regarded as patrons of Sri Lanka. In addition to being resplendent, the perahera is also extremely noisy, due to the cracking of whips and the beating of drums by literally thousands of followers. Stands are erected along the route, but the best seats are taken many hours before the event starts, particularly on the final night.

As may be expected, Kandy's hotels are booked up months in advance – at stratospheric rates. The route between the Queen's Hotel and the Temple of the Tooth is usually floodlit, which enhances the lovely appearance of the procession.

Through a stroke of luck for the British, however, the situation was about to change. Vikrama Raja Sinha, King of Kandy, although responsible for many improvements to the city, was an autocratic tyrant, whose sadistic cruelty to those who opposed him was legendary. A conspiracy to remove the despot, led by the Prime Minister, Ethelapola, was supported by the peasant class, local chieftains and Buddhist monks. With their encouragement, and sickened by the King's behaviour, the British attacked in 1815, and Vikrama Raja Sinha was captured. After being forced to cede his kingdom to the British the king was deported to Vellore in India, where he was forcibly detained until his death 17 years later.

Meanwhile, the Kandyans, who were given to believe that Prime Minister Ethelapola would be permitted to take over as leader, came face to face with the duplicity of 'perfidious Albion', which had no intention of returning independence to Kandy after the removal of its king. There was a short-lived revolt, led by the disappointed Ethelapola, but the British easily crushed the rebels, and the former Prime Minister was deported to the island of Mauritius. The British policy of divide and rule had succeeded once again. Nevertheless, it was not until three years later that the last Kandyan rebellion was quelled.

Eventually, Kandy was incorporated in the colonial administrative system of the island and, as in India, the 'British way of life' was introduced to the middle and upper classes. Missionaries were brought from England to act as teachers, and churches were built; however, conversion to Christianity was not high

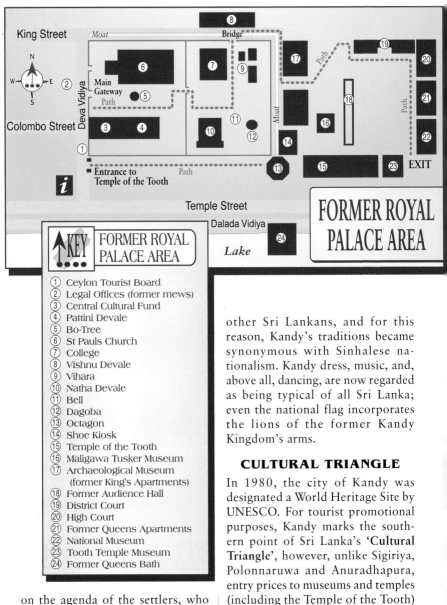

King Street

Moat

Bridge

⑧

N
W—E
S

② ⑥ ⑦ ⑨ ⑰ ⑲ ⑳

Deva Vidiya

Main
Gateway ⑤
Path

Path ㉑

Colombo Street

③ ④ ⑪ ⑱ ㉒

Moat

⑩ ⑫ ⑯

① ⑭

Entrance to ⑬ ⑮ ㉓ EXIT
Temple of the Tooth Path

i

Temple Street

Dalada Vidiya ㉔

Lake

FORMER ROYAL PALACE AREA

KEY — FORMER ROYAL PALACE AREA

① Ceylon Tourist Board
② Legal Offices (former mews)
③ Central Cultural Fund
④ Pattini Devale
⑤ Bo-Tree
⑥ St Pauls Church
⑦ College
⑧ Vishnu Devale
⑨ Vihara
⑩ Natha Devale
⑪ Bell
⑫ Dagoba
⑬ Octagon
⑭ Shoe Kiosk
⑮ Temple of the Tooth
⑯ Maligawa Tusker Museum
⑰ Archaeological Museum
    (former King's Apartments)
⑱ Former Audience Hall
⑲ District Court
⑳ High Court
㉑ Former Queens Apartments
㉒ National Museum
㉓ Tooth Temple Museum
㉔ Former Queens Bath

other Sri Lankans, and for this reason, Kandy's traditions became synonymous with Sinhalese nationalism. Kandy dress, music, and, above all, dancing, are now regarded as being typical of all Sri Lanka; even the national flag incorporates the lions of the former Kandy Kingdom's arms.

CULTURAL TRIANGLE

In 1980, the city of Kandy was designated a World Heritage Site by UNESCO. For tourist promotional purposes, Kandy marks the southern point of Sri Lanka's 'Cultural Triangle', however, unlike Sigiriya, Polonnaruwa and Anuradhapura, entry prices to museums and temples (including the Temple of the Tooth) are very low – even for foreigners – and possession of the Cultural Triangle inclusive entry ticket offers no significant advantages in the city. Nevertheless, those who intend to visit the other cities are advised to purchase their tickets here.

on the agenda of the settlers, who permitted Buddhists, Hindus and Muslims to follow their religions without interference.

Due to their uniquely successful repulsion of the country's invaders, the Kandyans preserved their culture more effectively than any

Above: **A decorative moat encloses Kandy's palace**

Left: **'Kandy-roofed' gateways are a feature of the former royal palace**

Kandy's name – the legends

By popular tradition, the future King of Kandy was told by a Hindu hermit that whilst in the open valley, where Kandy now stands, he had seen a mongoose frightened away by a cobra. This unusual event was regarded as propitious, and the king decided to found a city where it had occurred.

Kandy is an abbreviation of the city's earlier name of 'Senkan-dagala'. As usual, there are alternative suggestions: the name commemorates a king's preferred wife or, a more prosaic, and more likely, explanation, it refers to a rocky (*gala*) mountain (*kanda*). In practice, the local people usually refer to Kandy simply as Nuwara (the city), which should not be confused with Nuwara Eliya.

TEMPLE OF THE TOOTH

Kandy's most popular attraction, the Temple of the Tooth (**Sri Dalada Maligawa**), overlooks the north shore of the lake, a gilded roof effectively distinguishing the relatively small building from others nearby. Sri Lanka's President Premadasa donated this roof, in reality a canopy, to the temple in 1988.

Since the Tamil Tiger driver of a lorry transporting sand – and a bomb – made his stealthy approach to the temple gateway in January 1998, all vehicular access to the building has been blocked. In addition, pedestrians may now only approach the temple from its west entrance, which faces the Tourist Office; as may be expected, there are frequent security checks – but passports are not needed.

The pathway leads straight ahead to the temple through its grounds parallel to the shore of the lake. Most statues passed commemorate Sri Lankan leaders but the second, supported by a pillar, depicts 'that lion-hearted child hero' Madduma Bandara Ethelapola, aged nine, who, together with his elder brother, was beheaded by order of King Vikrama Raja Sinha on 17 May 1814. An inscription records that as he waited for the executioner's sword to fall, the little boy called out "Fear not brother, I will show you how to face death". The youngsters were hostage sons of the former Prime Minister who had defected to the British.

Ahead stands the octagonal dais commissioned by King Raja Sinha early in the 19th century. From this, dignitaries addressed the general public. Only males were permitted to speak, a tradition that has been maintained ever since.

Much rebuilding of the **Patti-rippuwa**, as the dais is called, and the adjacent **shoe kiosk** took place after the bomb had been detonated in the lorry parked in front of them. Little else structurally was damaged, but 26 people died, including the five Tamil Tiger suicide bombers.

Shoes must be deposited before entering the temple, but socks may be worn. Shorts, however, are not permitted. Many like to coincide their visit with the mid-morning puja – check times – although this is not particularly spectacular.

INNER SANCTUARY

The first temple on the site to house the sacred tooth found in the ashes of the Buddha's funeral pyre was built 1687-1707, but this was almost entirely reconstructed 1747-82 in the specific form of a reliquary.

Steps ascend through a painted tunnel vault to the richly carved entrance, at which foreigners must pay (extra for cameras). At the end of another decorated vault is the entrance, framed by four elephant tusks, to the **Drummers' Courtyard**. Here, drums are beaten at dawn and throughout much of each puja, when the drummers are joined by flag wavers and trumpeters.

In the middle of the courtyard the two-tiered shrine houses the tooth relic in a chamber on its upper floor. The relic itself is never seen, nor may it be removed from the temple as it is feared the country would fall – a superstition paralleled at the Tower of London, where it has been said that if the ravens departed, England would be doomed. Staircases ascend from the courtyard to the **Vedahitina Maligawa**, the chamber in which the relic rests. It lies in the smallest of seven bell-shaped gold caskets, which diminish in size so that they fit inside each other in the manner of Russian dolls. All is protected by bullet-proof glass.

Painstaking restoration of the temple took place in 1999 to repair damage caused primarily by monkeys, which are permitted to play in the sacred area with impunity.

New Shrine Room

To the rear of the inner sanctuary, the New Shrine Room, formerly the elephant robing hall, is occupied by a huge seated Buddha. Walls and ceilings are painted with scenes from his life, and the history of Buddhism in Sri Lanka; each bears a caption in English. Particularly apposite is the depiction of the discovery within the ashes of the Buddha's funeral pyre of the tooth that has become Kandy's sacred relic.

TUSKER RAJA MUSEUM

Within the temple enclosure, on the north side, the Tusker Raja Museum pays homage to the country's best-loved elephant. During Kandy's Esala Perahera festival, a caparisoned elephant, called the **Maligawa Tusker**, takes pride of place in the final parade and bears a replica of the tooth relic.

Due to his perfect proportions Tusker Raja, a Thai elephant of 'high caste' captured in the jungle in 1925, was chosen to be Kandy's Maligawa Tusker. In 1984, he was declared a national treasure, and after dying four years later, his stuffed corpse was put on display in this museum, where it remains. There are photographs on one wall taken of Tusker Raja in his prime, and on the other of the elephant immediately after his death.

Temple Treasures Museum

On the east side of the Temple of the Tooth completion of a new museum is expected. Housed in a building designed by an Indian architect, and constructed shortly after independence, this will display many of the temple's treasures. It was due to be opened by the Prince of Wales in January 1998, but the bomb put paid to that.

The portico giving access from the temple to the lake was built as the main entrance to the palace by the last King of Kandy around 1307. Temple elephants can often be seen passing by along this stretch of road,

Kandy's tooth relic is one of two that by tradition were found in the ashes of the Buddha's funeral pyre in 534 BC. The other, now kept in Beijing, was transported to Hong Kong, for a brief sojourn, in May 1999. Some claim a third tooth relic exists, however, most Buddhists do not accept that it is genuine.

But is Kandy's relic genuine? It is said that the tooth was brought to Sri Lanka from India in the 4th century concealed within the tresses of a princess. Buddhism was by then on the wane in India, and it was felt that the relic would be safer in a country where the majority supported the religion. On arrival the tooth was accommodated at Anuradhapura, and later Polonnaruwa.

After the fall of Polonnaruwa an invading army from south India stole the tooth and took it home with them. However, the relic is said to have been returned to Sri Lanka later as part of a dowry paid to a Sinhalese king. It was then kept in various secret locations, one of which was Kotte, but the Portuguese eventually discovered the tooth at Jaffna and shipped it to their Goa colony. At the time, the Portuguese, who were intolerant of all other religions, claimed to have burned the tooth in the presence of their Archbishop and Viceroy in Goa.

This, one might think, was the end of the matter, but the Sinhalese claim that the tooth taken by the Portuguese was a fake, produced specifically to mislead any would-be robber. The genuine relic they said was at Kandy, which neither the Portuguese nor the Dutch were able to capture. The British, as was their policy, respected local religions and Kandy's tooth relic – genuine or not – has remained safe.

which now, conveniently for them, is both traffic and pedestrian free.

Queens (or Royal) Bath House

What may have been the Queen's Bath House protrudes into the lake near the temple exit. Its upper floor was added by the British in the established Kandyan style. Currently used as a police post, water still fills the bath; no doubt this would have once been more enticing.

Although the Temple of the Tooth and its grounds are now completely enclosed, they have always formed an important part of the former palace and temples complex. The remainder may be explored either from the **National Museum**, the pathway adjacent to **St Paul's Church**, or the gateway facing the **Vishnu Devala** on the north side.

Apart from the Temple of the Tooth, which occupies the southern strip, there are four distinct sectors, all of which interconnect. The palace itself, once comprised eighteen buildings, and occupied the two eastern sectors of the enclosure. What survives has been much altered since the arrival of the British, and today hardly suggests palatial splendour.

NATIONAL MUSEUM

To the east, overlooking the lake, the building converted to form the museum in 1978 is said to have formerly accommodated the king's concubines. A plaque outside records the words spoken by the Buddhist missionary Mahinda to King Devanampiya Tissa at Mihintale: "Oh great king, the birds of the air and beasts have an equal right to live and move about in

A Temple of the Tooth elephant takes exercise

any part of this land as you. The land belongs to the people and all other beings, and you are only the guardian". A very 'green' and brave philosophy for the 3rd century BC. Fortunately for Mahinda, the King concurred and was converted to Buddhism.

Kandy-period culture, as may be expected, is the theme of this small museum. There are interesting ayurvedic cures inscribed on palm leaves and a copy of the 1815 Kandy Convention which condemns the cruelty of Vikrama Raja Sinha, and transfers the administration of his kingdom to the British.

To the north, the courtyard building, identified as **Mesa Wasala**, and now an architects' office, was formerly the **Queen's Palace**. Adjacent, further to the north, the imposing **High Court** was built in Baroque style by the British in 1880. Occupying the entire north side of the square, the **District Court** building predates the arrival of the British; its central portico is supported by wooden columns. The Court formerly served as the Kachcheri (Secretariat) and the Royal Armoury.

Audience Hall

Of greater interest, however, is the pillared former **Audience Hall**, which runs north/south enclosing the area. This was built in the late 18th century, although the British extended it in 1875 for a visit by the Prince of Wales, the future Edward VII. At night, the hall was lit by candles, and Kandyan kings, seated on an enormous throne, received their ministers, who had to make their approaches on hands and knees. In this hall also, the king would dispense summary justice, which frequently meant the death penalty. It was here that local chiefs signed the Kandyan Convention, 2nd March 1815, transferring rule from the King of Kandy to the British. Sixty-five beautifully carved pillars of ebony support the building, which, unfortunately, may not be approached closely by visitors.

The path follows the west flank of the District Court, and then slopes down to the next sector of the palace. To the left is the rear of the Tusker Raja Museum and, ahead, the **Archaeological Museum**, located at the north end of the range of buildings that includes the shoe kiosk and the Octagon. It was along this path that the lorry with its bomb was driven in January 1998. After the explosion this section of the path was put out of bounds.

Archaeological Museum

This building originally housed the private apartments of the king and is believed to have been three tiers high before the final British attack on Kandy. All that survives as a reminder of its importance are bas-reliefs of ducks and mythical beasts on the walls of the entrance hall. Exhibits mainly comprise specimens of Kandyan wood carving, which include many examples of lotus blossoms.

By leaving the museum from its west exit, the enclosure's eastern temple sector may be reached.

NATHA DEVALA

Although the **Natha Devala** is a Hindu temple, the buildings immediately ahead, within its precinct, are Buddhist. Two Bo-Trees and various depictions of the Buddha may be seen. This temple is a particularly interesting example of the Sri Lankan merging of Hinduism and Buddhism, which puzzles most visitors, including followers of each faith from abroad. It presumably reflects a desire to have the best of both worlds (or perhaps both *other* worlds).

A vihara, with its dagoba and bell stand close to the domed Natha

Devala in the south-west corner. Much of this south Indian-influenced temple dates from the mid-15th century, and it is, therefore, the oldest building in Kandy. A Buddhist drumming and meditation hall fronts the main structure, its columns carved with identical lions. Original paintings decorate the temple's walls, but there has been much restoration. In the north-west corner, the former **Dharmaraja College**, built by the British in the 19th century, is now a religious and cultural building.

To the east of the building, an ornamental gateway leads to the pathway (part of the bombers' route) and, immediately ahead, a bridge across the moat.

PALACE MOAT

As will have been seen, to the east the moat turns abruptly southward to run parallel with the path between the Archaeological Museum and the Octagon before being conducted underground to the lake. This northern stretch continues westward past **St Paul's Church**, where it terminates. The short length and narrow width of the moat indicate that this was a decorative rather than a defensive feature of the complex. Its wall is not truly castellated but imitates a series of waves, thus repeating the design of the wall around the lake. The bridge leads directly to another Hindu temple, the **Vishnu Devala**, built early in the 19th century by the last King of Kandy for his Hindu wife.

Return through the gateway to the south side of the college, pass the dagoba and continue westward, following the path ahead. On the other side of the wall, the small **Pattini Devala**, immediately left, is the third Hindu temple in the complex: Pattini is the goddess of chastity. North of this, the Bo-Tree, in its enclosure, has been grown from a cutting of Anuradhapura's Sacred Bo-Tree; it was planted by the King of Kandy in 1706.

Exit from the palace complex, right, to the church.

St Paul's Church

Constructed by the British for Anglican worship in 1843, this brick-built church, with its castellated tower, is typical of contemporary Gothic Revival examples erected by Victorians in the United Kingdom. Within, a window and a monument commemorate soldiers of, respectively, the Ceylon Mounted Infantry and the Ceylon Rifle Regiment, who were killed in action.

The lawyers' offices opposite the church have been constructed within stables that formerly accommodated the British administrators' horses.

CENTRAL KANDY

Return southward along **Deva Vidiya** passing, left, a timber-roofed gateway to the palace complex.

The **Central Cultural Fund Office**, which follows, was built by the British in the 19th century, and is distinguished by a Doric portico. Originally a courthouse, the building later became a branch of Laksala, the government sponsored emporium, which has since been relocated to a site overlooking the west shore of the lake.

The portico impressively closes the vista from Colombo Street (officially now Srimath Bennet Soya Vidiya), which it faces in a very European manner. Colombo Street together with King Street (Raja Vidiya) which runs parallel with it to the north, are two of Kandy's liveliest shopping thoroughfares.

South of the Colombo Street junction, the **Ceylon Tourist Board** office is staffed by helpful young ladies who can provide up-to-date information about excursions, opening times, Kandy dance shows and where to purchase Cultural Triangle tickets. On the corner a right turn at Temple Street passes the city's oldest hotel, the **Olde Empire**, with a picturesque veranda that provides superb lake views. However, accommodation is very basic (no private bathrooms), and some of the rooms are rather gloomy.

The **Air Lanka** offices and the stop for direct buses to Bandaranaike International Airport, which follow, will be of use to some independent visitors.

A left turn leads to Dalada Vidya, a street of banks and utilitarian restaurants, the eastern half of which directly skirts the lake, and therefore has no buildings on one side. Since 1999, for security reasons, vehicles have not been permitted to drive along the section of the road that fronts the Temple of the Tooth.

KANDY LAKE

In 1807, King Vikrama Raja Sinha began several improvements to the city, chief of which was the conversion of a large paddy field into an ornamental lake. A great deal of labour was required, and the King coerced local chieftains into providing him with members of their own labour force. It is said that some objected, which seems a rather foolhardy act in view of the ruler's notorious vindictiveness; allegedly they were held prisoner until the excavated site was ready for flooding and then tied to stakes in the lake, slowly drowning as the water level rose.

The wave design of the wall around the lake will be familiar to those who have noted the identical style of the moat's wall in the palace complex. Some believe that after being cremated the King intended that his ashes would be kept on the small island created off the lake's north shore, but this is not certain. However, the island did accommodate the King's harem, to which he was rowed whenever it took his fancy. One wonders if what is known as the Queen's Bath House, rather publicly located but close to the island, may not in fact have served instead as the boathouse.

Overlooking the lake's northwest corner is Kandy's most famous hotel.

QUEEN'S HOTEL

Surprisingly, in spite of its popularity both as a business and a tourist city, Kandy, unlike Colombo, has been unable to attract any of the international hotel groups: in consequence, no four-star or five-star hotels have been built in the middle of the city. The handful of four-star and one five-star hotels that exist to serve Kandy's trade are all located some distance from the city, usually prettily but inconveniently perched on a hilltop.

This is, of course, good news for the centrally-located **Queen's Hotel**, but it has only 55 rooms, in spite of the apparent bulk of the hotel's 19th century building. Some glass was broken when the bomb was detonated nearby and the opportunity was taken to carry out much-needed remodelling of the areas affected.

Although lakeside rooms obviously have excellent views, traffic noise can disturb some, as can the dawn drumming at the Temple of the Tooth if an east-facing room is taken. More tranquil accommodation overlooking the swimming pool at the rear is preferable. All rooms are now provided with airconditioning, TV and a mini-bar.

The large entrance hall and adjacent restaurant are the hotel's most

The Botanic Gardens of Peradeniya, just outside Kandy, are the finest on the island

impressive areas; in the latter, typical package-tour buffets are provided at breakfast and dinner. A separate, rather narrow, Chinese restaurant (with a real Chinese chef) serves well-cooked fish, but with vegetables limited to the usual green beans and carrots.

The reception staff are delightful, speak perfect English and do all they can to help. You will even be advised not to phone long distance from the hotel as it is too expensive, and directed to a much cheaper 24-hour bureau nearby. Independent visitors in particular will discover that relatively few Kandyans speak English, which is presumably why guests at the Queen's who try to communicate with the hotel's room service might just as well be speaking Serbo-Croat. The only words known appear to be "Hallo", or "Excuse me?", both of which will be repeated several times.

The swimming pool is pleasant, but Kandy is renowned for sudden late-afternoon showers, and a swim before 4pm, if convenient, is the best bet.

Kandy's only other truly central hotel of reasonable standard is the two-star **Casamara**. All its 35 rooms are air-conditioned and there is an excellent roof-top bar with fine views over the city. Casamara, just a two-minute walk from the Queen's, is located almost next to the 24-hour telephone bureau referred to above.

WALK TO ARTHUR'S SEAT AND VIEWPOINT

A pleasant, not too strenuous walk from the Queen's Hotel taking in the west shore of the lake and climbing to one of Kandy's best viewpoints, is recommended. Immediately after the hotel is the lake's motor-boat jetty; trips are particularly enjoyable in hot weather as the waters of the lake usually create a breeze after mid-day.

Follow the road ahead which leads uphill to **Royal Palace Park**. Although well kept and attractive, the park, particularly at weekends, has become almost the exclusive preserve of young, very much in love, couples. Few tourists will find a visit worthwhile. The grounds are named Royal Palace Park not for their views of the palace but because they were laid out by the last king of Kandy for his private enjoyment. Follow Rajapihilla MW, which bends eastward, and pass – very quickly – the entrance to the Castle Hill Guest House. Apparently, the three double rooms which are let by this 'private' guest house are clean and beautifully furnished; unfortunately, the female owner keeps – but does not keep under control – a pack of mad dogs, which will intimidate and even bite would-be guests. Give this one a wide berth, however desperate.

ARTHUR'S SEAT

Continue to the bend in the road, from where the finest views in Kandy may be enjoyed. This has long been known as **Arthur's Seat**, a name presumably inspired by that of the famous Edinburgh viewpoint, in spite of there being no obvious connection: no stone slab 'seat' exists and although parts of Sri Lanka's Hill Country can look quite Scottish, Kandy bears no resemblance whatsoever to Edinburgh. From here, the extraordinary greenness of Kandy Lake can be fully appreciated, huge trees around its periphery tower above the temples of the former palace complex, their height is increased by the rising ground.

Return to the lake to complete the walk around its circumference by following Sangaraja MW eastward – allow around two hours. On the first corner, **Devon Rest**, with good lake views, is the closest guest house to the middle of the city, all rooms have shower/toilet and the price is reasonable – extra for lake view rooms.

Occupying the next corner site, the **Malwatte Vihara (Flower Garden) Monastery**, founded by Burmese monks in the 16th century, was restyled around 1750 and its decorative carving and ironwork is their work. Visitors are welcome to witness the ordination of new monks, which takes place annually. This is one of Sri Lanka's two most important monasteries, and its high priests assist in the administration of the Temple of the Tooth.

ACCOMMODATION

Saranankara Road, which branches right, is distinguished by no less than eight guest houses, all of them good value for money. Highly recommended are **Freedom Lodge,** the **Expeditor** and the **Sharon Inn,** which serves good food (ask for a room with private bathroom and balcony).

The **Hotel Suisse** lies back slightly from the lake, over which there are good views from its 100 rooms (60 air-conditioned). A large pool and a floodlit tennis court set in attractive gardens are welcome amenities. As the Suisse is only a fifteen-minute walk from the middle of the city, this is the second most conveniently located large hotel (after Queen's, its sister hotel) in Kandy. The build-ing shows its age, but some up-grading took place in 1999. Hotel Suisse is popular with UK package tour operators and its low-lying position attracts older tourists.

Bohiravakanda Buddha

Although the remainder of the lakeside walk is pleasant, those with limited time may wish to return by three-wheeler. From the west end of Dalada Vidya, where it becomes Peradeniya Road, a street winds upward beside the **Tourist Police Office** to the huge **Bohiravakanda Buddha**, which dominates Kandy. The walk takes twenty minutes and most will prefer to continue in their three-wheeler. The figure, cast in concrete, is modern, and looks its best at night when floodlit. There are all-embracing views over the city.

Grouped around, but high above the east end of the lake are a dozen or so guest houses, plus the two-star, 80-room **Hotel Thilanka**, which has good city and lake views from its pool. As the hotel is popular with tour operators, some guests over-looking its driveway may be disturbed by the arrival and departure of coaches.

WEST OF KANDY

Peradeniya Botanic Gardens, the 'Western Shrines' and **Pinawala Elephant Orphanage** run almost in a straight line west of Kandy, from where they can be visited in one day; however this will involve a reasonably early start and the use of a three-wheeler if the 'western shrines' are to be included.

Travel arrangements

The Pinawala Elephant Orphanage, 25 miles (40 km) distant can be reached from Kandy by bus, with a change at Kegalla. Buses to all destinations on this route depart from the Torrington Street bus station. Trains from Kandy, on the Colombo line, stop at Rambukkana; both this town and Kegalla are roughly equidistant from Pinawala, with which they are linked by local buses. Visitors who have opted to return southward later from Anuradhapura via Kurunegala and Kegalla may find it more convenient to visit Pinawala during that stage of their journey.

It will be seen that the travel options are variable; however, bear in mind that the Botanic Gardens close at 5pm and the Elephant Orphanage at 5.30pm (feeding times at 9.15am, 1.15pm and 5pm); the three temples appear to be open at all times.

Buses from Kandy to Peradeniya complete the 4 mile (6 km) journey in around 40 minutes, depending on traffic.

BOTANIC GARDENS

Peradeniya's gardens, by far the largest and most important in Sri Lanka, open at 7.30am, and the cool freshness of early morning is certainly the best time to make a visit. The area of 147 acres (67 hectares) covered may sound formidable, but is almost precisely half that of Kew Gardens, near London. Vehicles may be driven slowly along the paths, and some tourists may wish to rent a driver who knows the gardens well so that the highlights are not missed (there are no plans available), and all drivers are also certain to know the locations of the three 'western shrines' nearby.

First-rate curry lunches are served in the cafeteria, near the entrance, but make a reservation immediately on arrival, because package tour operators will have booked most of the tables between 12am and 2pm. As most flowers in Sri Lanka bloom in April and May, just after the main tourist season has ended, the majority of tourists will have to be content with early blossoming trees during their visit.

History of the Gardens

In the 14th century, the king of Kandy held court at Peradeniya, which nestles in a sweeping curve of the Mahaweli River. On its banks, the Kandyans defeated the Portuguese in a major battle, and it was probably during this that most of the royal buildings were lost. The gardens were created in the 18th century as pleasure grounds attached to a royal palace, which the king had built at Peradeniya for his occasional use.

Further destruction of buildings took place during a British attack in 1803, and only traces of them have survived. Following their take-over of the country in 1815 the British transferred all their botanical experiments on the island to Peradeniya, which has a significantly cooler climate than the south-west coast, where their first gardens were developed.

More than 4,000 botanical species are said to be represented, but it is the trees, some of them centenarians, which attract most interest. They include spice trees such as nutmeg and cinnamon, specimens from South American rain forests and, a great rarity, Coco de Mer, the double-coconut tree of the Seychelles Islands; the promiscuous form of its double nut, the world's largest seed, has inspired various unofficial names.

Few visitors will want to leave Kandy without seeing a demonstration of traditional dancing. The dances evolved as part of festivals and virtually all have religious themes inspired by south Indian Hindu culture. Whilst male dancers are usually scantily clad to facilitate their athletic performances, the girls wear the sujeewa, a three-piece costume that tourists often mistake for the one-piece sari. Both are worn in Sri Lanka, but the sujeewa has come to be regarded as the national dress and is now de rigeur on important occasions.

A long wail from a conch shell, followed by ceremonial drumming, announces the beginning of the show, which usually includes around a dozen dances and ends with the spectacular fire swallowing and walking on burning coals. The latter is a reference to the legend of Princess Sita who, following abduction by King Ravana, was rescued by her husband Rama and proved her fidelity to him by walking on fire. The male dancers ask Pattini, goddess of chastity, to bless the proceedings.

The dances

Ves Nathuma is a dance in which athletic males perform great leaps and somersaults; the silver decoration of their costumes (*ves*) shimmers to impersonate the rays of the sun.

In the *Raksha Nathuma*, masks of a bird of prey and a cobra are worn by a pair of 'fighting' dancers. It was once believed, and still is by some traditionalists, that those of unsound mind could be cured by witnessing this dance, which had the power to exorcise demons.

Extremely popular is the exotic *Nayura Nathuma* (Peacock Dance), in which female dancers are dressed, rather illogically, as peacocks – the vehicle of the war god Skanda.

Where to see dances

Kandy dance shows, lasting from 60-75 minutes, take place from time to time at major tourist hotels throughout the country – not only in Kandy. Apart from these, regular venues in Kandy, where performances begin at 6pm, include the **Kandyan Arts Association**, in an annexe at the rear with an attached restaurant for dining after the performance, the **Young Man's Buddhist Association**, and the **Red Cross Building**. Highly recommended is the **Kandy Lake Club**, 1 mile (2 km) from the middle of the city, where performances begin in a rear hall at 7pm. Alcoholic drinks are rather expensive.

Near the entrance to the gardens, the Orchid House contains almost 400 local varieties, one of which is called the Kandy Orchid, as the form of its blossom resembles the traditional dress worn by young Kandyan ladies. Enormous bats, known as flying foxes, hang upside down from the branches of the trees lining the main avenue.

Around the Great Circle are trees planted by British monarchs, including Edward VII, George V and Elizabeth II.

A suspension bridge on the west side of the gardens crosses the river to the experimental area, where plants with commercial prospects for the island are developed. Tribes of harmless monkeys cadging food will be passed from time to time, but there are also occasional snakes, some of them venomous, lurking in the patches of long grass, which should therefore be avoided.

TEMPLES OF EMBEKKE, LANKATILAKE AND GADALDENIYA

The 'western shrines', as they are referred to locally, are exceptionally interesting and very different from the temples to be seen either in Kandy or in the other ancient cities. Dating from the 14th century, they display unusually fine craftsmanship, much of it apparently the work of south Indians. The general style is in fact south Indian, and each of the three temples pays homage in varying degrees to both Buddhism and Hinduism.

Embekke Devale

The temple that is usually visited first is the **Embekke Devale**, 4.5 miles (7 km) south of Peradeniya and half a mile (1 km) from Embekke village, to which there is an hourly bus from Kandy.

The name 'Devale' indicates that this is primarily a Hindu temple; it is dedicated to Kataragama, the six-headed god of war and a son of Siva, a deity much venerated in Sri Lanka, where he is generally called Skanda. Although the wooden columns and beams of the entrance porch are finely sculpted it is the exquisite carving of the drumming hall's pillars that is exceptional. Ironwood, a particularly hard timber, was used for the pillars, which accounts for the crispness of the work. Attendants will point out swans, double-headed eagles, musicians, wrestlers, dancing girls and a

Portuguese soldier on horseback. At the time the work was executed, Portuguese soldiers would only have been seen by south Indians, indicating that they must have been responsible for the carving. By tradition, the pillars came from the audience hall of a local king who had become a convert to Hinduism. Note the boldly carved lotus blossom corbels in sets of four bracketing the pillars to the roof.

A semi-circular moonstone fronts the entrance to the hall.

In the adjacent vihara, a seated Buddha provides an alternative image to venerate.

Those without transport will be directed to the path that leads to the **Lankatilake Temple**, 1 mile (2 km) distant but set on a high rock, and many steps must be climbed to reach it. Buses from Kandy to the temple do not pass through Embekke.

Lankatilake Temple

For many, the main interest of this temple, which is again primarily Hindu, is its dramatic position providing comprehensive views over the surrounding paddy fields. Its pagoda-like design is emphasised by wide cornices beneath the eaves, decorated with mythical beasts. Carved elephants protrude from the pale-blue walls.

A seated Buddha is once again the main feature of the vihara; this example is exceptionally well carved, and the wall paintings, which are in good condition, date from the Kandy period. There are several buses from Lankatilake to the **Gadaldeniya Vihara**, located about half a mile (1 km) from the main Kandy road. The alternative is a 2 mile (3 km) walk, which again ends in a climb.

Gadaldeniya Vihara

Also surmounting a high rocky outcrop, this temple, in contrast to the other two, is basically Buddhist with a Hindu annexe. By tradition, 1,000 Indian craftsmen took 30 years to complete the building. The dagoba, seen first, is designed with miniature dagobas at each of its four corners.

Within the porch, a small temple is set aside for worship of the Hindu god Vishnu. It is said that the local ruler at the time was Buddhist but his wife followed Hinduism.

Paintings of elephants and mythical beasts, believed to date from the 14th century, decorate the porch steps.

Within the vihara, the granite Buddha has been gold-plated. The exceptional door retains its original decoration, featuring mythical beasts and suns. An ingenious method of opening and closing it without the use of hinges will be pointed out.

The road from Kandy to Kegalla (for Pinawala Elephant Orphanage) lies half a mile (1 km) north of the Gadaldeniya Vihara. Buses to Kegalla stop at many places along this road; at Kegalla another bus or a three-wheeler must be taken to the orphanage.

HOTELS AROUND KANDY

As has been said, the number of hotels in Kandy is surprisingly limited; however, there are several excellent establishments with a Kandy address that are located some distance away from the middle of the city. Two of the most popular, both 3 miles (5 km) distant, overlook the Mahaweli

This is one of Sri Lanka's most popular attractions, and rightly so. It is open 365 days a year, and only between 12am and 2pm are the elephants not being either bathed or fed. Those who fell in love with Dumbo – and who didn't – will be enchanted by the smaller elephants, although the very youngest are too nervous and well-protected by mother or auntie to permit close proximity.

Of the 60-plus elephants at the orphanage, some were born at Pinawala, but most have been saved from certain death in the wild. Although a few of the male elephants prove to be cantankerous, and their legs have to be chained for safety, the vast majority are docile creatures; nowhere else is it possible to be so close to so many of them in such a natural environment. A staff of 40 care for the elephants, many of them as mahouts (*edhgowwa* in Sinhalese).

The orphanage was opened by the Wildlife Department in 1975 to support six baby elephants who had been trapped in pits and abandoned. It remains state-run, operating as an off-shoot of Colombo Zoo. Income from visitors covers the entire cost of the establishment, and this is one instance where no foreigners are likely to object to paying a higher admission charge than Sri Lankans (who make up half of the visitors).

Feeding time

Feeding the younger elephants is a great attraction which should not be missed. However, elephants abhor hot sun on their nonreflecting backs, and feeding takes place within an open-sided shed that is rather dark – photographers will need flash or fast film. Tourists are permitted to hold a milk bottle while a dreamy-eyed young elephant glugs away. However, the very cutest, the babies, suckle from their mothers and take no part in the feeding. Five packets of powdered milk, which make up around 6 gallons (27 litres) of liquid, are allocated to each young elephant per day for up to 30 months. After six months some greenery is introduced into the diet, and this is increased gradually until an adult consumes 550 pounds (250 kilograms) of leaves and branches every day.

After feeding, the elephants, with the babies, are marched out of the compound to the adjacent Maha Oya, a river that eventually reaches the sea at Negombo. Here they bathe, roll in the mud and squirt water at each other through their trunks. Some astonish the onlookers by actually swimming, an achievement that seems quite miraculous considering their bulk. Most will spend all their lives at the orphanage but some are sold to companies for working; others become respected temple elephants.

Dr Chandana Rajapaksa, the veterinary surgeon in charge of the day-to-day running of the orphanage, unsurprisingly confesses to dreaming of elephants – but they are never pink!

Sri Lankan Elephants

Most people know that the ears of Asian elephants are not as large as those of their African cousins, but the animals themselves are also significantly smaller. Sri Lankan elephants are not quite as large on average as Indian, but otherwise it is hard to distinguish between them. Cared for by humans they can live for up to 100 years, but 30 years less in the jungle. When born in captivity, baby elephants receive more attention from their mother and adoptive 'aunt' than in the wild; surprisingly, as a result of this spoiling they are more difficult to tame. Male elephants can become somewhat aggressive during their annual 2-3 month *musth* period, during which their prime interest is mating.

It may have been noted that there are few genuine tuskers in Sri Lanka. Only four per cent of the country's elephants, all of them male, can grow long tusks, the others, both male and female, have tiny tusks known as 'tushers', which are barely visible. For this reason, many ceremonial elephants, even the Maligawa Tusker, are often obtained from India or Thailand.

In Sri Lanka there are now estimated to be around 2,500 elephants in the wild and 500 in captivity. Through the creation of sanctuaries, it is hoped that their numbers will soon increase, but some herds, although protected, are cut off from their traditional feeding areas by land cultivation and may become extinct.

Captive elephants still play an important part in certain Sri Lankan industries, particularly timber, and fine specimens are eagerly sought after by major temples for ceremonial purposes. Like all pachyderms, elephants are exclusively vegetarian, the branches and leaves of virtually any local tree forming their staple diet, with bamboo particular preferred.

Ganga. To the north, the only five-star hotel in the region, the **Mahaweli Reach Hotel** has 115 rooms, all air-conditioned with TV and mini-bar; set in its grounds, one of the finest swimming pools in the region possesses outstanding vistas across the bend in the Mahaweli Ganga. To the west, the **Citadel** has 120 air-conditioned rooms and a good pool.

Adjacent hotels, both with pools, at Anniewatte, look down on Kandy from the west: **Hotel Topaz**, despite the address 1 mile (2 km) north of the Peradeniya Road, has 75 rooms (36 with air-conditioning) and the **Tourmaline** with 25 air-conditioned rooms.

A four-star establishment located 8 miles (13 km) from the middle of the city, the **Hotel Tree of Life** specialises in ayurvedic treatment. All rooms have air-conditioning, TV and mini-bar, and there is a pool.

Much nearer the middle of the city, the **Hotel Hilltop** is the most convenient of all the hotels for Kandy's railway and bus stations. There are 82 rooms (24 with air-conditioning), and many UK tour operators book their clients here. Situated a five-minute walk up Peradeniya road, the Hilltop's position is not quite as elevated as its name suggests.

As the delightful **Hunas Falls Hotel** is 16 miles (26 km) from the city it can hardly be classed as a Kandy hotel. However, its elevated position beside a tea estate will appeal to those looking for country walks amongst delightful scenery – including, of course, the nearby waterfall.

RESTAURANTS

Kandy is not a restaurant town. Virtually all Kandyans who wish, rarely, to eat out will go to a hotel, and frequently opt for 'Chinese' food. However, at the **Devon Restaurant** (no cream teas!) in Dalada Vidiya, the Sri Lankan curries are good, although only available 11am to 2pm. A great Sri Lankan rarity, an Indian restaurant, **Rams**, can be found at 27 Colombo Street.

Additional Information

Ceylon Tourist Board
3 Deva Vidiy, ☎ 08 222661
Open Monday to Friday 8.30am-
12.30am and 1.30pm-4.45pm,
Saturday 8.30am-1pm

Air Lanka
19 Temple Street, ☎ 08 232494

Places to Visit

Temple of the Tooth
Pujas: 5.30-6.30am, 10-11am,
closed to tourists 4pm

Archaeological Museum
Open Sunday to Thursday
8.30am-5pm

National Museum
Open Saturday to Thursday
9am-5pm

Peradeniya Botanic Gardens
Open daily 7.30am-5pm

Pinawala Elephant Orphanage
Open daily (365 days per year)
8.30am-5.30pm

Opposite page: Many regard this standing Buddha as the finest of the Gal Vihara carvings at Polonnaruwa

F ew will not wish to see, at least on a first visit to Sri Lanka, the famous Ancient Cities of Sigiriya, Polonnaruwa and Anuradhapura, the major components of what is now referred to as the Cultural Triangle.

Anuradhapura, founded in 437 BC, was the country's first capital, and it is here that Sri Lankan art reached its zenith. The site is rich in enormous dagobas, delightfully carved guardstones, moonstones and the sacred Bo-Tree.

Sigiriya involves a strenuous ascent of a flat-topped rock to reach the ruins of the small city that served as the capital from 477 to 495. Welcome halts on the way are made to see the world-famous **Maidens Frescoes** and the **Lion Staircase**.

Polonnaruwa took over from Anuradhapura in 781 as the capital, which it remained for around 500 years. Here, the carvings and ruined buildings are in a much better state of preservation than in the older capital, and for this reason some find it more appealing. Polonnaruwa's highlights are the rock-cut figures of Buddha in the **Gal Vihara**, the **Thuparama Temple** and the **Lotus Bath**.

Before Sigiriya is reached, there is an opportunity to visit the fascinating cave temple of **Dambulla**, packed with literally hundreds of figures of the Buddha. Although its five shrines were created almost 2,000 years ago, most of their present appearance dates from the 18th century.

MATALE

The A9 highway from Kandy northward gradually descends through the lower reaches of the Hill Country, to be followed by flat land interspersed with startlingly high rock formations. Cocoa tree plantations soon dominate the scenery; most of the beans are used to make chocolate locally, the crop being insufficient to export in significant quantity. After 15 miles (24 km), Matale, the most important town on the route, is reached. Encircled by low hills, its chief point of tourist interest, particularly to those who have not visited south India, is its Hindu temple, **Sri Muthumariamman Thevasthanam**. All the carvings are brilliantly painted and the temple's leviathan chariots are exceptional in Sri Lanka.

ALUVIHARA
ROCK TEMPLE

Northward from Matale, many establishments sell batik clothing, wood carvings and spices, focusing their attention on tourists. Insist that any batik purchased is run resistant.

Aluvihara, 5 miles (8 km) north of Matale, is famed for its **cave temple frescoes** and international **Buddhist library**. There are five caves, but two of them are located in the jungle, some distance from the others. As occurs frequently in Sri Lanka, Hindu deities are revered in addition to the Buddha. The three caves that will be shown were created in rocks that appear to have tumbled into the valley from the higher land above. A white wall, inset with carved black elephants, encloses the complex. By tradition, the temples were created in the 1st century BC, and shortly afterwards the Buddha's doctrines are said to have been recorded for the first time in Sri Lanka at this monastery.

Fronted by a building, the first cave accommodates reclining and meditating Buddhas.

The next cave is renowned for its gruesome paintings of sinners in hell being punished by devils. The tormenting of sexual offenders, such as the drawing and quartering of a prostitute, is lasciviously depicted in the spirit of Hieronymus Bosch.

Pali, the canonical language of Buddhism, scripted by the monks, features in the third cave. In the 19th century, the monastery's renowned library was burned down. Works had been inscribed in Pali on palm leaves (*Ola*) and they are being replaced laboriously by monks in the workshop, which visitors are invited to visit. Donations are naturally welcomed.

NALANDA GEDIGE

Around 12.5 miles (20 km) to the north, the main road connects with a bumpy 2 mile (3 km) track, ending at this unusual temple, which, due to its unique charm should not be missed. Unlike a dagoba, a gedige is hollow – just – in spite of incredibly thick walls, and its form appears to be unique to Sri Lanka. Most who visit Nalanda (entry – a high $US5 – is included on the Cultural Triangle ticket) are immediately struck by its similarity to pre-Columbian architecture in Mexico. An even closer resemblance to Kadamba work in south India will be familiar to those who have visited Goa's superb Tamdi Surla temple.

The structure dates from the 8th century and combines both Hindu and Buddhist features, which are rarely found in one building. Although of granite, the temple's carvings have faded badly. Nevertheless, an attendant is sure to draw attention to one of them, which is said to depict, with much guesswork, a man, a woman and a lion engaged in an erotic threesome: the piece of sculpture is now known – surprise, surprise – as the 'Kama Sutra' stone.

There is little of much interest to be seen between Nalanda and **Dambulla**, located roughly 19 miles (30 km) to the north. However, there are a few wayside restaurants where tour parties are occasionally taken for a lunch-time curry: most are rather expensive.

DAMBULLA

In the 1st century BC, invaders from south India captured Anuradhapura; its king, who is referred to as either Walagamba, Valagam or Vatagamini Abhaya – take your pick – fled to Dambulla, where he took refuge in its caves. Some years later, after regaining the throne, in thanks to Buddha he converted the five caves to shrines. Improvements were made by succeeding kings, foremost of whom were Nissanka Malla and Raja Sinha I.

Many people will have seen photographs taken inside Dambulla's caves, showing them gleaming in a bright golden light. The reality, however, is a succession of gloomy interiors in which the splendid contents are hard to make out; additionally, visitors are not permitted to take any photographs within the caves, even without the use of flash. The reason for the first restriction is that bright light has been found to damage the frescoes, and for the second, the tactlessness of a tourist, who posed coquettishly to be photographed with a figure of the Buddha. So incensed were the religious authorities that for some time only Buddhists were permitted to enter the caves.

It should be noted that the entry charge (200 rupees) is no longer included in the Cultural Triangle ticket. Payment must be made at the office, right, within the entrance.

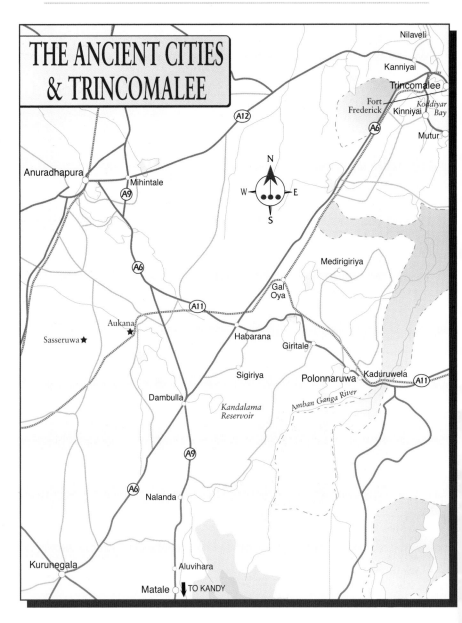

THE ANCIENT CITIES & TRINCOMALEE

Nilaveli

Kanniyai

Trincomalee

Fort Frederick

Kinniyai

Koddiyar Bay

Mutur

A12

A6

Anuradhapura

Mihintale

A9

N

W   E

S

A6

Medirigiriya

Gal Oya

A11

Aukana

Sasseruwa

Habarana

Giritale

Sigiriya

Polonnaruwa

Kaduruwela

A11

Dambulla

Kandalama Reservoir

Amban Ganga River

A9

A6

Nalanda

Kurunegala

Aluvihara

Matale

TO KANDY

Opposite; Top: Entrances to the 500 feet (152 m) rock caves at Dambulla

Bottom: Numerous figures of the Buddha are a feature of the five caves at Dambulla, which date back to the 1st century BC

The caves, basically natural formations, are reached around two-thirds of the way up the 500 ft (152 m) high rock. To reach them, visitors follow a path interspersed with short flights of steps. From outside the caves, extensive views include the enormous rock of Sigiriya, around 12.5 miles (20 km) away to the north-east. As some consolation for photographers, shots may be taken of the views and the exteriors of the caves.

Entrances to the caves run in a straight line, and are numbered from right to left. Within, impressive collections of Buddha images in various positions, together with ceiling and wall frescoes depicting scenes from the life of the Buddha and Sri Lankan history are painted in brilliant hues (which to some degree must now be imagined). Whilst having sympathy with the respect and decorum insisted on by the

religious authorities, it does seem unfortunate that the dominating feature of each cave is a vulgar, brightly-illuminated sign, which reminds visitors that 'photography is strictly prohibited' – something about using a sledgehammer to crack a nut comes to mind.

In spite of the undoubted age of the temple, it is unlikely that any of the figures or frescoes within its shrines predate the 18th century.

Shrines in the Caves

Cave 1

The most impressive feature of this shrine is the 47 ft (14.3 m) long reclining Buddha; frescoes are relatively modern and unimportant. All ceilings in the caves are of plastered rock.

Cave 2

This, the largest and most spectacular of the shrines, was built by King Walagamba. The enormous number of seated Buddhas grouped together may remind some of China's recently discovered 'Terracotta Army'.

Cave 3

King Raja Sinha I greatly extended this cave in the 18th century, adding further images of the Buddha and Hindu gods. The King is represented, right of the entrance, bearded and wearing his crown. A Buddha image reclines on the left wall.

Cave 4

Of less interest, this shrine contains more seated Buddhas and a small dagoba.

Cave 5

Another reclining Buddha dominates this shrine.

ACCOMMODATION

As Dambulla is only 12 miles (19 km) distant from Sigiriya and 41 miles (66 km) from Polonnaruwa, tour operators often use its nearest top quality hotels as a base for visits to all three sites; some even use the same hotel for day trips to Anuradhapura, 40 miles (64 km) to the north. The advantages to their clients, who might otherwise find daily packing and unpacking somewhat tedious, are obvious – but it makes on-the-spot reservations in the most popular hotels difficult for individual visitors.

Five-star rated, the **Kandalama Hotel**, around 6 miles (10 km) east of Dambulla, is romantically sited overlooking the tank. All its 162 rooms are air-conditioned, many of them with a view of the huge rock carving at '**Elephant Rock**'. Sri Lanka's renowned architect, Geoffrey Bawa, was responsible for this Aitken Spence project. Even without the proximity of Sri Lanka's ancient cities, the delightful environment of this hotel, with its two swimming pools, would make a stay worthwhile.

Also overlooking the Kandalama tank, the **Culture Club Resort** is four-star rated, with accommodation in 92 air-conditioned luxury chalets. If both are full, the best option at Dambulla (1 mile/1.5 km from the rock temple) is the **Gimanhala Transit Hotel**. Although there are only ten rooms, all are air-conditioned, there is a swimming pool with views of Kandalama Tank.

SIGIRIYA

Frequent buses from Dambulla to Sigiriya deposit visitors close to the approach to the rock and within reasonable walking distance of the two most popular tourist hotels. The flat-topped rock of Sigiriya, rising 650 ft (200 m) above the jungle, is one of Sri Lanka's most spectacular sights. From its base to its summit, which is actually 1237 ft (377 m) above sea level, are scattered the remnants of a 1,500 year-old royal palace.

Some who have scrambled up Dambulla's rock may be tempted to forgo the much more strenuous effort required at Sigiriya. However, the climb is not as difficult as might appear from the rock's forbidding appearance from a distance. Only the chronically unfit, the very young and the very old are likely to suffer unduly from making the ascent. This is because the path is long and winding rather than steep and various stages are facilitated by cast-iron staircases which have handrails. Come on, think of boasting to your friends – or grandchildren – that you made it all the way to the top! Needless to say, however, very few will wish to climb both Dambulla and Sigiriya on the same day.

Those making their approach from Sigiriya village or Sigiriya hotels on foot must be careful not to take the first, most obvious path to the rock as it leads to an inaccessible side. Be sure to pass the stalls and bus terminal before turning right. An early start is recommended, as the rock can become decidedly hot by 11am.

HISTORY

King Datusena, who ruled from Anuradhapura, 459-73, had two sons, Maggallana and Kassyapa, both of whom claimed the right to succeed to their father's throne. The problem was that the mother of Kassyapa, the eldest, was a palace courtesan, whereas Maggallana's mother was the King's consort. In 473 Kassyapa usurped the throne, by tradition after murdering his father, whom he embedded alive in a wall. Maggallana fled to India, vowing to eventually take his revenge.

Kassyapa soon transferred his capital to Sigiriya, where he built an 'impenetrable' fortress – just in case Maggallana should return. In 491 he did so, backed by a strong force. Kassyapa came out on the back of an elephant to fight his brother, but became trapped in a swamp and was deserted by his army. Unwilling to accept the ignominy of certain capture, Kassyapa slit his own throat. Maggallana now took his rightful place as king, and returned to Anuradhapura, which once more became the capital. Sigiriya's brief, eighteen year period as the Sinhalese capital was at an end.

APPROACHES AND WATER GARDENS

Follow the path clockwise around the ramparts, which are skirted by a moat, which Kassyapa allegedly filled with crocodiles. A bridge between the **Archaeological Museum** and the main car park crosses the moat, and visitors continue directly ahead.

Low brick walls denote the ruins of a miniature water garden on the south side. A similar garden on the north side awaits excavation. Both comprised pools, courtyards and pavilions in a symmetrical pattern. The gardens appear to have been abandoned after Kassyapa's defeat, and were partly built over between the 10th and 13th centuries. A large

Sigiriya's Maidens Frescoes, painted in the 5th century

pond on the right is followed by the ruins of the Dry Season Palaces. A great deal of imagination is needed to appreciate the delightful original appearance of this sector of Sigiriya.

Ahead, great trees and enormous boulders herald the approach to the first steps up the rock proper. By the time that the 40 ft (12 m) high spiral staircase to the **Maidens Frescoes** has been reached, most are surprised, and relieved, to learn that almost half the ascent of the rock has been completed.

The iron staircase is used in both directions and there can be long delays to ascend, particularly when enormous parties of well-behaved schoolchildren arrive (there are so many of them because, unlike tourists, they naturally do not have to pay – but unfortunately their visits do not appear to be regulated in any way). As may be expected, congestion is worse at weekends and during school holidays, which should if possible be avoided.

MAIDENS FRESCOES

Sigiriya's frescoes are Sri Lanka's most famous ancient paintings and most people will already have seen photographs. They are set in a rock gallery protected from sunlight, and comprise 18 portraits of mainly bare-breasted young ladies. All date from the Kassyapa period, and it has been surmised that there may originally have been as many as 500 in the set. It is assumed that the subjects were ladies of the court, but they may have been restricted to the king's wives. Frescoes, of course, must be painted when the original plaster is wet, but restoration took place in 1897 and again following vandalism in 1976: in consequence, although some of the original paint work survives, much of the work is in tempura. Nevertheless, the 1,500 year-old portraits continue to impress, and are rated at least equal in importance with the cave paintings at Ajanta in India, with which they are frequently compared. Photography is permitted.

After descending the staircase the path, excavated from the sheer rock face, is followed northward in the same clockwise direction.

MIRROR WALL

This 10 ft (3 m) high wall of limestone was created as a protective measure for the path. The inner face of the wall was highly polished so that it became smooth as a mirror, hence its name. Sections of the wall still reflect, but it is not clear how much is original work and how much restoration. The graffiti on the wall are as famous as its mirror finish. Probably dating from the 7th to the 11th centuries, much of it relates to the Maidens Frescoes. A book has been published in which 685 of the inscriptions have been deciphered.

Steep steps, perhaps the most tiring part of the expedition, now lead to what is known as the Lion Terrace (or platform).

LION TERRACE

The name of Sigiriya means 'Lion Rock', and the final approach to the summit was originally made up steps which passed through the enormous representation of a lion. Only its paws have survived; apparently the steps originally conducted visitors through the lion's open mouth to the palace buildings. Looking over the edge of the rock closest to the lion's right paw, a lily pond can be seen below. Vendors gather on the Lion Terrace with snacks and cool drinks.

The final stage of the ascent is now made up the iron staircase ahead. It is not particularly tiring, and should only be a problem to sufferers from vertigo.

The Lion Stairs once conducted visitors through the mouth of a huge stone lion to the summit: only the beast's paws have survived

Summit

A surprise to most on reaching the flat summit of Sigiriya is that it covers 3 acres (1.6 hectares) and accommodated not only a royal palace but a small fortified town. Everything, unfortunately, is in ruins, mainly comprising foundation walls of four brick courses. Equally surprising is the existence of trees, which cannot be seen from below. Facing the rising sun on the east side is what is said to be the king's throne – but was probably a military lookout post – visitors are permitted to sit on it. A pool 88.5 ft by 69 ft (27 m by 21 m) excavated from the solid rock was filled in the wet season by rainwater, primarily for bathing, it is believed.

Stupendous views, particularly southward, are perhaps the summit's greatest attraction. Directly below, the **Sigiri Wewa** tank provided the town's main water supply. How water was brought from here to the summit is too exhausting to contemplate.

ACCOMMODATION

Nestling together, close to the Sigiri Wewa tank, both the **Sigiriya Village Hotel** and **Hotel Sigiriya** are within easy walking distance of the rock.

At the three-star Sigiriya Village, the chalet accommodation of 120 rooms was being upgraded in 1999 to provide a high proportion of them with air-conditioning, TV and mini-bar.

Hotel Sigiriya, two-star rated, has 80 rooms, half of them air-conditioned. This hotel's great attraction is its uninterrupted views of Sigiriya rock, particularly from the swimming pool, which the clever architect has laid out so that both rock and pool appear to provide a symmetrically designed unit.

More economical and even more conveniently located is the **Sigiriya Rest House**, just 400 m from the rock each of its 15 rooms has a private shower/WC.

Those who have come to Sigiriya via Dambulla will find that an overnight stay at Sigiriya is particularly convenient if an early assault on the rock is to be made.

Excursions

Apart from Cultural Triangle day trips, Habarana is also conveniently placed for a late afternoon visit to the **Aukana (or Avukana) Buddha**, 18 miles (30 km) to the west, and the **Sasseruwa Buddha**, a further 7 miles (11 km) to the west, two of the country's most celebrated rock-carved statues.

The next destination chosen by most tourists after Sigiriya is Polonnaruwa, 42 miles (67 km) distant. Unfortunately no roads continue either northward or eastward from Sigiriya, and a return must be made to Dambulla, from where there are buses (also from Habarana) to Polonnaruwa.

In spite of its fame, Polonnaruwa has little tourist-class accommodation. Many, therefore, stay overnight at nearby Habarana or Giritale, both of which are passed en route. These hotels can also, of course, be used as a base for visiting Sigiriya.

HABARANA

Habarana is a small village, located at the junction of the A6, A9 and

A11. Its railway station, on the Polonnaruwa and Colombo/Trincomalee lines, is the nearest to Dambulla and Sigiriya. Although there is little of interest around the village, Habarana's central location for visiting the Ancient Cities has made it attractive to package tour operators. Distances by road from the village are: Sigiriya 15 miles (24 km), Dambulla 15.5 miles (25 km), Polonnaruwa 26.7 miles (43 km) and Anuradhapura 36 miles (58 km). Trincomalee, on the east coast, is 80 miles (129 km) away.

ACCOMMODATION

The best hotel is **The Lodge**, 150 air-conditioned rooms with tennis courts and a good pool. **The Village** has 100 non air-conditioned rooms and similar facilities. Both belong to the same group and are fully booked by tour operators in the season.

GIRITALE

Between Habarana and Polonnaruwa, the **Giritale Tank**, a picturesque stretch of water, is overlooked by three hotels. The **Royal Lotus Hotel**, with two stars, has 56 air-conditioned rooms, eight of them designated as 'luxury', and a swimming pool. The **Deer Park Hotel** recently opened, also overlooks the tank and is the most luxurious of the three. Rooms are in cottages, with air-conditioning, TV and mini-bar, and there are four presidential suites. In addition to a swimming pool there is a gymnasium, sauna and three dining rooms, one of which, unusually, specialises in traditional Sri Lankan dishes. All these hotels are 8-9 miles (13-14.5 km) north of Polonnaruwa.

POLONNARUWA

HISTORY

As might be expected, due to a lack of accurate records and the immensity of time involved, not all historians agree on the precise sequence of events at Polonnaruwa (and even less so at Anuradhapura) or the activities of its rulers; some dates, in particular, are controversial.

The **Topawewa Lake** was created around 370, and an early royal residence soon overlooked its shores: the settlement that grew up around it was named Topare, after the lake. There is some evidence that Polonnaruwa, as the city is usually called, had become the effective Sinhalese capital by the middle of the 8th century, although their kings did not completely abandon Anuradhapura until 100 years later.

Towards the end of the 10th century, the Cholas, Tamil invaders from south India, established their capital at Polonnaruwa. It is possible that at that time Anuradhapura was in poor structural shape after its sackings in the 9th and 10th centuries, and an additional incentive to move was that malaria had become a grave scourge, no doubt accentuated by the old capital's numerous water tanks.

The Cholas faced constant threats from the Sinhalese Kingdom, then based at Tissa, in the south-east of the island, and in 1065 they were defeated by its 'poet' king, Vijay I. He decided to settle at Polonnaruwa, which remained the Sinhalese capital until the late 13th century. The city reached its zenith during the reign of King Parakrama, and most

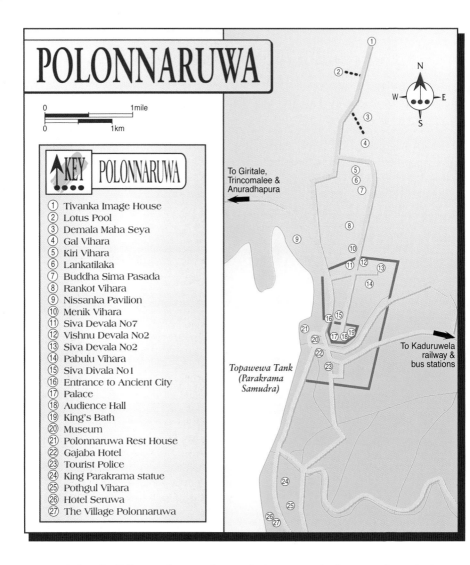

POLONNARUWA

0 _____ 1mile
0 _____ 1km

KEY POLONNARUWA

1. Tivanka Image House
2. Lotus Pool
3. Demala Maha Seya
4. Gal Vihara
5. Kiri Vihara
6. Lankatilaka
7. Buddha Sima Pasada
8. Rankot Vihara
9. Nissanka Pavilion
10. Menik Vihara
11. Siva Devala No7
12. Vishnu Devala No2
13. Siva Devala No2
14. Pabulu Vihara
15. Siva Divala No1
16. Entrance to Ancient City
17. Palace
18. Audience Hall
19. King's Bath
20. Museum
21. Polonnaruwa Rest House
22. Gajaba Hotel
23. Tourist Police
24. King Parakrama statue
25. Pothgul Vihara
26. Hotel Seruwa
27. The Village Polonnaruwa

To Giritale,
Trincomalee &
Anuradhapura

To Kaduruwela
railway &
bus stations

Topawewa Tank
(Parakrama
Samudra)

surviving buildings of note date from this period. Parakrama extended the lake and created parks, palaces, monasteries and temples.

Despite being located closer to the protection of the hills than Anuradhapura, Polonnaruwa could still be reached without great difficulty from the north coast of the island, where the Tamil Indians, based just a short distance away, had been able to make their numerous invasions with ease. In 1288,

Polonnaruwa's dam was breached, and the consequent flooding may have led to the final abandonment of the city. For three hundred years, various locations were designated capitals until the Sinhalese Kingdom became established at Kandy in 1592.

Only a handful of villagers lived at Polonnaruwa for centuries, and jungle quickly took over the ancient buildings as it had already at Anuradhapura. However, during the

1880s, British archaeologists rediscovered Sri Lanka's hidden cities, and much of the jungle was cleared. Restoration, which will take many years to complete, is now co-ordinated between UNESCO and the government's Cultural Triangle Project. Virtually all finance for the work appears to come from abroad – in the form of entrance fees imposed on foreign tourists, together with UNESCO funding.

POLONNARUWA'S LAYOUT

The **Old Town**, where most hotels have been built, lies immediately south of the water channel that bisects the enclosed ancient city; the **New Town**, of little tourist interest, stretches further to the south. Unhelpfully for independent visitors, the **railway and bus stations** are both located a mile or so east of the Old Town, in **Kaduruwela**. Entry to the enclosed area, known as the **Citadel**, is made from the northwest corner of the Old Town, close to the east bank of the Parakrama Samudra tank. Only a few monuments lie outside the south and west walls of the Citadel's enclosure, but many others run 2.5 miles (4 km) northward from its north wall, virtually in a straight line.

Old Town guest houses

The **ticket office**, which is located in the Old Town, just south of the canal, faces a cluster of guest houses, the best of which is probably the **Gajaba Hotel**; all its 10 rooms have attached shower and WC. An **Archaeological Museum** stands in the same road as the Gajaba, slightly to the north and on the opposite side. The museum faces the **Polonnaruwa Rest House**, which is the most con-

veniently sited base from which to visit the Ancient City. In addition, it has wonderful views from a wide terrace across the Parakrama Samudra. Reservations made well in advance are essential as there are only five air-conditioned and five non air-conditioned rooms.

ANCIENT CITY TOUR

PARAKRAMA SAMUDRA (TOPAWEWA)

This tank, covering 5,600 acres (2,400 hectares), was created by Parakrama from three existing tanks, one of which was the Topawewa. Its name, 'Samudra', means sea, and the waters still play an important part in irrigating what is normally one of the country's driest regions.

NISSANKA MALLA'S PALACE

Immediately north-east of the Polonnaruwa Rest House, outside the protection of the ancient city's wall, are the uninspiring ruins of the palace of Nissanka Malla (1187-96), the king who followed Parakrama. Nearest to the Rest House were the **Royal Baths**, to the east stood the **Audience Hall** and, on the north side, the **Council Chamber**.

Council Chamber

Inscribed on the inner face of each of the chamber's columns is the name of the dignitary who sat in front of it.

Apparently, the king conducted proceedings within this hall seated on a great throne, as a 6 ft (1.8 m) high stone lion, believed to be a support for it, was discovered nearby in 1820; this can now be seen in

Colombo's National Museum. Several other buildings have survived at Polonnaruwa from Nissanka's reign, as the king attempted to outdo his predecessor's improvements to the city, almost bankrupting the Sinhalese Kingdom in the attempt.

A low mound near the lake is surmounted by the remains of a royal pavilion.

Those without transport can tour the Ancient City on foot without much difficulty as most of interest lies close to the two parallel roads that now run through it north to south. However, 3 miles (5 km) separate the Royal Palace and the Tivanka Image House, the most northerly monument of importance, and a three-wheeler will obviously speed up a tour; most drivers can identify the monuments without difficulty, but make sure that good English is spoken.

At the entrance to the Ancient City, visitors pass through remains of the stone wall, which encloses the 25 acre (10 hectare) royal and administrative area of Polonnaruwa. At the first intersection, left, stands an important Hindu temple.

Siva Devala No 1 ('Dalada Maligawa')

There are many south Indian-style temples in the city dedicated either to Siva or Vishnu and dating from the Tamil occupations: for identification they are simply given numbers. By tradition, the Tooth Relic, now at Kandy, was briefly accommodated in this early 12th century building. The granite walls, of superb workmanship, have survived, but the brick-built domed roof has collapsed. Within, the Siva lingam is still venerated by Buddhist and Hindu childless

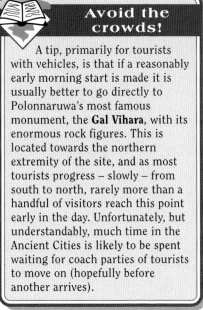

Avoid the crowds!

A tip, primarily for tourists with vehicles, is that if a reasonably early morning start is made it is usually better to go directly to Polonnaruwa's most famous monument, the **Gal Vihara**, with its enormous rock figures. This is located towards the northern extremity of the site, and as most tourists progress – slowly – from south to north, rarely more than a handful of visitors reach this point early in the day. Unfortunately, but understandably, much time in the Ancient Cities is likely to be spent waiting for coach parties of tourists to move on (hopefully before another arrives).

women who offer flowers to the god. Several bronze artefacts discovered here may be seen in Colombo's National Museum.

PARAKRAMA'S PALACE ENCLOSURE

The low wall immediately south of the Siva Devala is part of the enclosure of Parakrama's palace, which comprises three main buildings: the **King's Bath**, the **Audience Hall** and the **Royal Residence**.

King's Bath (Kumara Pokuna)

Water obtained for the bath from the nearby lake was drained into a separate sewage system. Two crocodile-head spouts flank the steps descending to the water. Further south, the steps to the plinth are decorated with lions. The bath had been covered with earth and was only rediscovered in 1935.

Audience Hall

Exuberant carvings of elephants, lions and dwarfs enliven each stage of the hall's platform in ascending order, and a moonstone is set at the base of the north steps. The hall's portals are carved with splendid lions.

Low walls in the building's south-east corner denote a separate dining area.

Royal Residence

Only two floors of 10 ft (3 m) thick walls survive of this once great building, which originally is believed to have been seven floors high. Although the use of lime mortar permitted higher brick edifices to be built at Polonnaruwa than at Anuradhapura, experts believe that above three tiers it still would have been necessary to construct in timber to reduce the load. The surviving levels indicate a building just over 4,300 sq ft (400 sq m) in area, with 50 partitioned rooms on the ground floor. As 30 columns, in addition to the brick walls, were needed to support the floor above, the internal layout would have been somewhat inflexible. Although no roofs have survived, slots in the walls for their beams may be noted.

Proceed northward from the royal enclosure towards a second enclosure – this time religious rather than secular.

QUADRANGLE

Although there are some Hindu references, the Quadrangle's buildings are primarily Buddhist, most of them the work of Nissanka Malla. Nowhere else in any of the Ancient Cities can so many important monuments be found in such close proximity. Just outside the south-west corner is an exquisite gedige.

Thuparama Image House

Probably built by Parakrama, this gedige, although the smallest to survive at Polonnaruwa, where the style was perfected, is possibly the finest; it is the only example to retain an intact roof. Oblong in shape, animal friezes decorate the 7 ft (2 m) thick walls, which are enlivened with bold pilasters and representations of a typical Polonnaruwa building of importance.

Within, particles of the granite of which the large Buddha image is made glimmer like fireflies when illuminated. The faithful still leave flower offerings in front of the figure. Ahead, to the right, near the south wall of the Quadrangle, is one of the finest of Polonnaruwa's buildings.

Vatadage

This circular Buddhist temple, a typical relic house, is known from an inscription to have been built in the 12th century by Nissanka Malla. From an 18 ft (5.5 m) wide stone platform a flight of steps at each of the four compass points leads to the relic house. Its circular walls of brick are fronted by a stone screen, which may have been built later as an afterthought. Nothing survives of the original domed timber roof.

Each flight of steps is flanked by guardstones and preceded by moonstones; the moonstone on the north side is regarded as Polonnaruwa's finest. From within, Buddha figures are also set at the four compass points to look out over each flight of steps; the best preserved is on the north side.

Immediately north of the Vatadage, the **Hatadage** is entered from its south end.

Hatadage

Known as the 'Shrine of Sixty Relics', this reliquary, the work of Nissanka Malla, was allegedly built in 60 days, and is believed to have been commissioned specifically to house the Sacred Tooth relic. Two bands of delicate relief are the only decorative element on the otherwise severe slabs of stone from which the walls have been constructed. At the entrance, however, there are well-preserved examples of guardstones and a moonstone. Originally, the building had an upper floor of timber.

South-west of the Hatadage (but past the Hindu shrines) is one of the city's most unusual enclosures.

Latha (Flower) Mandapaya

What appears to be a post and rail fence of wood but is in reality cut from stone, encloses a tiny dagoba guarded by eight pillars. Each pillar is carved to represent a budding lotus stem, thereby giving the complex its name. To the north, beside the Hatadage, the square building is confusingly known as the Atadage.

Atadage

Allegedly, this was yet another temple in which the Tooth Relic was housed. Like the adjacent Hatadage it also had a timber upper floor. The Atadage is the only structure known to have been built at Polonnaruwa in the reign of Vijay I, the Sinhalese 'poet' king responsible for defeating the Cholas in 1065. On the east side of the Hatadage lies a colossal block of stone.

Gal Potha (Stone Book)

The stone has been carved to represent an inscribed book made from palm leaves (known as *ola*). It measures 27 ft (8.25 m) in length and weighs 25 tonnes. Sri Lanka's largest stone inscription virtually covers its face; most of the Sinhala text glorifies Nissanka Malla, and also informs the reader that the stone was transported here from Mihintale. That town is 71 miles (114 km) distant, and no doubt several elephants would have been needed to drag the stone here.

In the north-east corner of the Quadrangle stands an unusual dagoba, designed as an oriental tower.

Satmahal Prasada

This six tier (originally seven) tower is the most idiosyncratic of Polonnaruwa's monuments. Ascribed to the 12th century, neither its builder nor its precise function are known, although the tower is referred to as a dagoba. The square tiers diminish in size as they progress upwards in the manner of a stepped pyramid. Each face incorporates the figure of a Hindu deity within a niche.

Outer stairs lead only to the first floor, but the internal staircase, which survives, has given rise to the speculation that the prime function of the Satmahal Prasada was to serve as a watchtower

North of the Quadrangle, but still within the Citadel's enclosure, a group of religious buildings comprises a dagoba and three Hindu temples. The dagoba, seen first, lies just off the crossroad, to the right.

CITADEL – NORTH SECTOR

Pabula Vihara

The temple's dagoba, the third largest in the city, was built by Parakrama. Its name, 'Pabula', means coral and may be an allusion to the soft, white appearance of the structure.

The finest Hindu temple at Polonnaruwa lies a short distance to the east.

Siva Devala No 2

This temple was built by the south Indian Chola settlers, probably in the late 10th century, soon after establishing Polonnaruwa as their capital. It resembles the Siva Devala No 1, which followed it a century later, but is in much better condition as the Cholas used no wood in the construction of the granite building. It seems unlikely that any other Polonnaruwa structure predates this temple.

To the west, just right of the main road and nestling close to the Citadel's wall is **Vishnu Devala No 2** and, facing it on the opposite side of the road, **Siva Devala No 7**. Immediately north of the Citadel's wall are passed, left, the **Menik Vihara** and another **Siva Devala**.

ALAHANA PIRIVENA

The grounds immediately north of the Citadel's wall and left of the road were designated by King Parakrama for royal cremations. Known as the Alahana (Crematorium) Pirivena, they lay within the area of a monastic college founded by the same king. Four important college buildings have survived and stand in line ahead for 600 yards (1 km).

Rankot Vihara

Nissanka Malla appears to have built this vihara's enormous dagoba to rival the three larger examples at Anuradhapura, which it clearly resembles in style. The dagoba, which is 180 ft (55 m) high with a circumference of 550 ft (168 m), has recently undergone much restoration by UNESCO. The spire is delicate and the carved figures around the drum can be distinguished without difficulty. To approach closely, however, a large sand courtyard must be crossed after the usual obligatory removal of shoes. Either arrive early in the morning or make sure to wear thick socks, otherwise the sand will be too hot to step on. Ahead rises the tallest building in the Alahana Pirivena group.

Buddha Sima Prasada

This 'House of the Elders' appears to have served as a type of 'chapter house' for monastic assemblies of importance. The building's height and width are both 70 ft (21 m), and its length is 170 ft (52 m). At the far end, the Buddha figure, now headless, was originally around 45 ft (14 m) high.

The remainder of this complex of buildings, known as the **Jetawanarama**, has collapsed into ruins.

Ahead, facing a pillared mandapaya, stands one of the city's most interesting monuments, which, although in ruins, still appears majestic.

Lankatilaka

When built by Parakrama, this gedige was regarded as one of Asia's finest Buddhist shrines. King Vijay IV restored the building, but the roof has since collapsed. The brick walls now reach a height of 53 ft (17 m). Inserted in them, as at the Thuparama, bas-reliefs depict the elevations of domed buildings that are typical of the Parakrama period.

Internally, the long, high 'nave', which is aisleless, evokes an important Christian chapel. At the far end stands an enormous figure of the Buddha, now headless.

The last building in the monastic group is a large brick dagoba.

Kiri Vihara

When 700 years growth of jungle was cleared from around it in the 1880s, this dagoba was found to be in surprisingly good condition. The original lime plaster had not fallen away, and its creamy paint work led to the structure, originally known as the Rapavati Cetiya, being re-named. 'Kiri' means milk-white, but without protection from the monsoons by trees the dagoba has become blackened. Allegedly, it was commissioned by Queen Subhadra, consort of Parakrama.

It is a short walk from here across the road to the **Gal Vihara**, Polonnaruwa's most famous monument.

GAL VIHARA

'Gal', an abbreviation of 'Kalugal', means black rock, presumably a reference to the granite from which the four Buddha figures have been cut. Parakrama commissioned the rock carvings as part of the city's northern monastery, and they are undoubtedly Sri Lanka's finest and best known examples.

All the carvings were executed from one rock face by several craftsmen, probably one for each figure, who skilfully made use of the stone's natural grain so that it followed the contours of the figures. The Buddha is twice represented seated, once standing and once recumbent.

First seated figure

Combining stylistic and natural elements, the Buddha expresses deep wisdom. Note that a slim young man is depicted, not the rotund figure sometimes favoured in Buddhist countries – particularly in the Orient. As with the other figures, the robe is indicated simply by deeply-cut bands. An ugly canopy was added recently to protect the figure from the elements.

Second seated figure (recessed)

Seated within an open-faced cave, this Buddha is the smallest – and some say the poorest – of the set. It is certainly not improved by the wire mesh and glass panel recently added to protect the carving from birds. Hindu gods are depicted watching over the Buddha. A sacred Bo-Tree faces the cave.

Standing Buddha

Possibly the finest of the carvings, the 23 ft (7 m) high figure bearing a sorrowful expression is shown with crossed arms, a rare pose for the Buddha. This led to speculation until recently that Ananda, Buddha's best liked disciple, was represented, grieving at his master's passing, as depicted by the adjacent recumbent figure. However, other carvings, undoubtedly of the Buddha and showing him with crossed arms, have been discovered. It is also apparent from the incisions made in the granite for inserting timber framework that this figure, like the other three, was at one time enclosed separately, and not intended to form part of a tableau.

Reclining Buddha

Many figures of the reclining Buddha will have been seen already throughout the island, but this rock-cut version is by far the longest, measuring 46 ft (14 m), and the best known. The pose represents that adopted by the Buddha immediately prior to losing consciousness the day before he passed to nirvana.

Visitors should note that shoes must be removed before entering the enclosure, and that standing on the wall is prohibited.

Although in general the figure is stylised, subtle realistic touches, such as the pillow's gentle dip beneath the figure's head, have been incorporated. Perhaps, however, it is the sinuous design of the work and its relationship with the adjacent standing Buddha as viewed from various angles that most impresses. Small white 'prayer' flags are left by pilgrims in front of both the standing and the reclining Buddha.

A path leads northward from the Gal Vihara to what appears to be a flat-topped hill but is another dagoba. However, those with transport will be driven closer to it.

DEMALA MAHA SEYA

Parakrama intended this dagoba to be the largest in existence, thus eclipsing those of Anuradhapura. South Indian prisoners provided the labour for its construction. A standing Buddha survives within, but frescoes, which apparently were found in reasonable condition when discovered in 1886, have deteriorated badly. During partial restoration in the late 19th century

it appeared that extensive rubble represented a collapse of upper sections of the structure; however, it is now thought that the dagoba had never been completed. Now around 50 ft (15 m) high, it is set, un-usually, on a tiered base. Recent UNESCO work has cleared the site of the jungle, which once more had taken over.

North of the Demala Maha Seya and a short distance from the road is a pretty pool.

LOTUS POOL

Nissanka Malla commissioned this granite bathing pool for the monks of the **Jetavanarama Monastery.** Measuring almost 25 ft (7.6 m) in diameter, the pool was designed in the shape of a reversed lotus blossom; its concentric steps gently conduct the bather into the water.

The road ends 300 yards (0.5 km) to the north in front of a large image house.

TIVANKA IMAGE HOUSE

Also part of Nissanka Malla's Jetavanarama Monastery, this is the largest of the city's brick-built shrines. Dwarfs and lions decorate the external walls.

Within, frescoes of scenes from the Buddha's former incarnations are now indistinct; the originals were added to by King Parakrama III as part of his attempt to restore Polonnaruwa.

The figure of Buddha is designed so that the head faces one direction and the hips another, known as the thrice-bent position, *tivanka* in Sinhalese, which accounts for the name of the building. Normally, this form is reserved for females.

A direct return southward to the main Habarana road passes, at the first junction, two further Hindu temples: **Vishnu Devala No 4** and **Siva Devala No 5**. At the second (main road) junction, just off the main road are what remains of a pavilion built by Nissanka Malla.

This road must be taken by those proceeding directly either to Anuradhapura and Trincomalee or returning southward. However, there are two additional monuments of interest that lie 2 miles (3.5 km) to the south, on the outskirts of Polonnaruwa's New Town, close to the lake.

King Parakrama I statue

This 13 ft (4 m) high statue is now generally believed to represent Polonnaruwa's builder king – but some disagree. What the bearded figure holds is either the royal yoke symbol or a book, which would indicate a religious teacher – possibly, it is suggested, the Indian philosopher, Agastaga. Formerly, those who held the latter view predominated, and the statue was known simply as 'The Sage'. In appearance, the figure is much more realistic than those that represent the Buddha, which are always stylised to a degree. Unlike the traditional calm serenity of Buddha, the king's expression indicates fatigue.

Just beyond this structure stands Polonnaruwa's most southerly monument.

POTHGUL VIHARA

Surrounded by four small dagobas, the central brick structure, like them, is circular, but unlike them it is hollow. The name Pothgul, meaning 'library', suggests that books were originally stored within. Technically, the shrine is a gedige, even though in appearance it resembles a dagoba.

ACCOMMODATION

Polonnaruwa's two highest-rated hotels face the Pothgul Vihara. Both overlook the lake and are provided with swimming pools. The two-star **Hotel Seruwa** has 40 air-conditioned rooms, all with private facilities; some also have balconies overlooking the lake. The **Village Polonnaruwa** has 36 air-conditioned rooms, either facing the courtyard or in separate cottages.

ROUTES AND PUBLIC TRANSPORT FROM POLONNARUWA

All tourists leaving Polonnaruwa by road for their next destination are likely to take the A11 to **Habarana**. From Habarana, the same road continues north-westward to Anuradhapura and the A6 leads north-eastward to Trincomalee and south-westward to Dambulla.

Buses (from Kaduwela Bus Station)

Bus No 847 links the New Town, Old Town and Kaduwela. There are direct buses to Dambulla, Kandy, Colombo and Anuradhapura from Kaduwela, all via Habarana. Additional services run from Habarana, but it is more difficult to obtain a seat. No direct buses, however, run to Trincomalee, and a change must be made at Habarana (or Anuradhapura).

Trains (from Kaduwela Railway Station)

The service to Colombo is limited to a morning and evening service, and the journey will take significantly longer than by bus. However, those travelling to Trincomalee from Polonnaruwa can board the morning train to Colombo and change at Gal Oya.

ANURADHAPURA OR TRINCOMALEE?

Independent visitors (but few on package tours) now have the option of either taking a short holiday at Trincomalee or exploring Anuradhapura. Some find that a complete rest from cultural activities for a day or so after exploring Dambulla, Sigiriya and Polonnaruwa pays dividends, but others choose to complete the Cultural Triangle first. Distances covered will be the same whichever order is chosen, but those relying on public transport may be swayed by the advantage of Polonnaruwa's direct buses to Anuradhapura (from where there is a limited but direct bus service to Trincomalee).

MIHINTALE

Seven miles (11 km) east of Anuradhapura, at the junction of the A12 and A9 stands the hill of **Mihintale**, a monastic site that remains of great significance to Sri Lankan Buddhists. However, its monuments do not compare in importance with those of Polonnaruwa or Anuradhapura, and 1,840 steep steps must be climbed to reach the summit. In view of this, most tourists give the site a miss.

Many buses ply between Anuradhapura and the town of **Mihintale**, from which the former monastery lies 600 yds (1 km) to the south.

HISTORY

The name of Mihintale, meaning 'rock of Mahinda', commemorates the great Indian Emperor Ashok's missionary son, who converted the Sinhalese King Devanampiya Tissa to Buddhism in 247 BC. By tradition, the king, who ruled from Anuradhapura, was hunting a deer near the great rock when the animal transformed itself into Mahinda and related the doctrine of Buddhism to him. Converted, the king built a monastery at Anuradhapura.

Mahinda, however, lived as a hermit in a cave on the rocky hill until his death at the age of 80. His body was cremated at Anuradhapura, but the ashes and other relics were brought to the hill, which would soon be called Mihintale, and where a monastery would be founded.

EXPLORING MIHINTALE

Many are confused by the complicated layout of the monastery, none of its buildings being identified; in view of this, the services of a local guide are recommended. Most tourists are deposited at the main car park, from where their visit begins, and the following route is described from here. However, some taxi and auto-rickshaw drivers park further south, away from the coaches, and facing the path that leads up to the **Sinha Pokuna**. Those who begin at this point should not have much difficulty in adjusting their route to the one described, as both make directly for the **Refectory**.

Kantaka Chaitiya (or Cetiya)

Now truncated by 59 ft (18 m) from its original height, this dagoba dates from around 55 BC. Until 1932 it was thought that the structure, then covered with earth, was simply a mound, and excavation took three years to completely reveal the dagoba, the base of which has a circumference of 425 ft (130 m). At the four cardinal points stand 'frontispiece' sculpture panels, two of them still in good condition.

Above a cave to the south of this dagoba, the oldest-known inscription in Sri Lanka predates Pali.

Refectory (Eating Hall)

At the top of the steps are the monks' food troughs, which were filled with rice – but probably little else. Two inscribed stone slabs remind the monks of the establishment's strict regulations; these date from the 10th century reign of King Mahinda IV. This is one of the best of several viewpoints on the rock from which to admire the great dagobas of Anuradhapura, 5 miles (8 km) to the east.

A steep flight of steps ascends eastward to a small plateau. At this point, foreigners who thought that there was no entry charge to the complex will now discover their error (the Cultural Triangle ticket does not give free access to Mihintale).

Ambasthale Dagoba

In the middle of the plateau, this dagoba is said to mark the exact point where Mahinda stood when he first met the king. Allegedly, it houses a relic of the missionary.

To the south, a statue of King Devanampiya indicates where he stood at the meeting.

Mahinda's Bed

Steps ascend from the north side of the plateau to an enormous rock, within which is the cave where Mahinda lived, and a stone couch (the 'bed') on which he is said to have slept.

South-west of the plateau, another flight of steps leads to the lst cen. BC **Mahaseya Dagoba**, which is said to contain a hair of the Buddha.

Return to the Ambasthale Dagoba and descend the main steps. Just before the steep flight ends follow the path, left, which passes below the Mahaseya Dagoba and continues to the **Naga Pokuna**. This pool (pokuna) is named after the five-headed snake (naga) carved on its rock face.

Above, on the summit of the hill, are the ruins of a great dagoba, estimated to have been originally 100 ft (30 m) high, and to which, by tradition, the ashes of Mahinda were taken following his cremation. Descend towards the Refectory; just south of its landing is another pool, which should not be missed.

Sinha Pokuna

Delightfully carved, this pool's name derives from the figure of a rampant lion (*sinha*) which surmounts it. Outstanding workmanship makes this one of the finest animal figures in Sri Lanka.

Steps lead back from the Refectory to the main car park; the path from the Sinha Pokuna descends to the smaller car park.

ANURADHAPURA

The enormous, solid brick dagobas of Anuradhapura, now under slow reconstruction, are its most memorable structures. Nowhere else in the world can Buddhist dagobas (or stupas) of comparable dimensions be found. The world's oldest living tree, the sacred Bo-Tree, may still be seen, but a long walk to it is involved.

HISTORY

Anuradhapura is said to have been founded by Anuradha in the 5th century BC, but an alternative belief is that King Pandukabhaya, who made the city Sri Lanka's first capital around 380 BC, named it after the Anuradha constellation. Three kings were responsible for the city's most important monuments, which were constructed during its 1000 year period as capital: Devanampiya Tissa 260-210 BC, Dutugemunu 161-137 BC and Mahasena 276-292 AD.

Frequent battles with Tamil invaders from south India took place throughout much of the city's history; some of them were lost by the Sinhalese and the victors occupied Anuradhapura for varying periods. Elara, one of many Tamil kings, ruled here 205-161 BC, and his ruined cenotaph can still be seen.

Sri Lanka's most important chronicle, the *Mahavamsa*, written in the 5th century AD, records that the city then covered 256 sq miles (660 sq km) and had a radius of 16 miles (26 km). It was well-planned and densely populated – the great monuments now standing in splendid isolation were surrounded by bazaars and dwellings, none of which have survived; similarities with Old Goa in India may come to mind.

Abandonment

When the capital was transferred to Polonnaruwa in 781, Anuradhapura was not completely abandoned, Kings Kasyapa V, Parakrama I and Vijaya I continuing to build or re-build there until the end of the 12th century. Various reasons have been suggested for the Sinhalese kings abandoning Anuradhapura. Not only had the Tamil invaders, who were Hindu, despoiled the city, particularly its Buddhist monuments, but they also occupied it for lengthy periods. Attacks had become easier from the north-west coast beaches due to the clearance of jungle around the city and the construction of roads; little natural protection remained. It is also said that malaria had become rampant, possibly due to three great irrigation tanks excavated around the city: perfect breeding grounds for the anopheles mosquito.

Eventually, all structures of wood disappeared, and many of brick collapsed; what remained were taken over by the jungle, and Anuradhapura became a 'hidden' city. A few settlers have always maintained a small village on part of the site, but not until the arrival of the British was **Anuradhapura New Town**, with its railway station built between the River Aruvi Aru and the Nuwara Wewa tank. In the 1870s, work began on excavating and restoring the great monuments of the ancient city, work that is being continued as part of the UNESCO Cultural Triangle project. As may be expected, an admission fee (of more than 1,000 rupees!) is levied; this is included in the Cultural Triangle ticket. What may not be expected is that additional fees are charged to approach the Bo-Tree and to enter the Isurumuni Vihara.

Before January 1998 it was usual to begin a tour of the Ancient City with the Sacred Bo-Tree and the Brazen Palace; however, following the Tamil Tigers' attack on Kandy's

air-conditioning as it is impossible to sleep through the clattering. Beds are fitted with mosquito nets, which will almost certainly collapse on the sleeper. Mr Upside-Down-Man appears to have been responsible for maintenance: the room key must be inserted the wrong way up and turned right to unlock the door (disconcertingly, the same key is also likely to fit the locks of adjoining rooms), the light switch registers up for on and down for off, the hot water tap runs cold and the cold water tap runs hot. Room service is even more idiosyncratic than usual. However, those with a sense of humour will not be greatly troubled by what are only minor blemishes – the reception staff are friendly and the food

Temple of the Tooth, these can only be approached on foot from the Thipurama Dagoba, a return journey of 1.5 miles (2.5 km).

acceptable. Alcoholic drinks may not be purchased at the Rest House as it is located in a sacred area.

ACCOMMODATION

Located close to the entrance, **Tissawewa Rest House** is still the only accommodation within the area of the monuments and is, therefore, particularly convenient for cyclists or hikers. The building is delightfully colonial, with spacious verandas and high ceilings. Guests may use the swimming pool of the hotel's sister establishment, the **Nuwarawewa Rest House**.

Nevertheless, the dark bedrooms are desperately in need of refurbishing; unless things have changed since 1999 do not pay a supplement for

EXPLORING ANURADHAPURA

Mahasena's Palace lies 3 miles (4.5 km) north of the **Isurumuni Vihara** and between them are numerous ruins, only the most important of which have been restored or are under restoration. The main sites can be seen in half a day, preferably with a rented bicycle or a three-wheeler (cars and coaches are permitted a more limited route), but to explore everything thoroughly can take several days. As at south India's ruined city of Hampi, the longer the time spent,

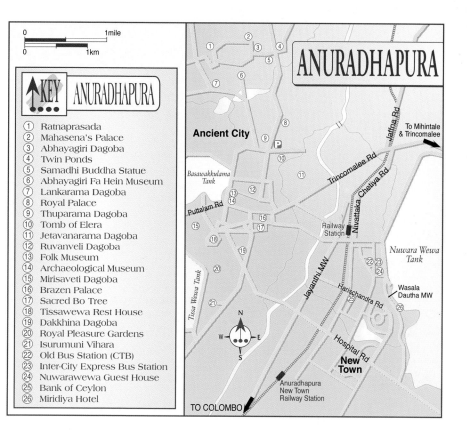

KEY ANURADHAPURA

1. Ratnaprasada
2. Mahasena's Palace
3. Abhayagiri Dagoba
4. Twin Ponds
5. Samadhi Buddha Statue
6. Abhayagiri Fa Hein Museum
7. Lankarama Dagoba
8. Royal Palace
9. Thuparama Dagoba
10. Tomb of Elera
11. Jetavanarama Dagoba
12. Ruvanveli Dagoba
13. Folk Museum
14. Archaeological Museum
15. Mirisaveti Dagoba
16. Brazen Palace
17. Sacred Bo Tree
18. Tissawewa Rest House
19. Dakkhina Dagoba
20. Royal Pleasure Gardens
21. Isurumuni Vihara
22. Old Bus Station (CTB)
23. Inter-City Express Bus Station
24. Nuwarawewa Guest House
25. Bank of Ceylon
26. Miridiya Hotel

ANURADHAPURA

Ancient City

Basawakkulama Tank

Puttalam Rd

Tissa Wewa Tank

Trincomalee Rd

Nivattaka Chetiya Rd

Jaffna Rd

To Mihintale & Trincomalee

Railway Station

Nuwara Wewa Tank

Wasala Dautha MW

Jayanthi MW

Harischandra Rd

Hospital Rd

New Town

Anuradhapura New Town Railway Station

TO COLOMBO

Opposite page & below: Examples of Anuradhapura's exquisite guardstones

the greater the absorption of the atmosphere. Most will wish to see what are known to Sri Lankan Buddhists as the **Eight Sacred Places**: the sacred Bo-Tree, the Brazen Palace, the Abhayagiriya, Jetawanarama, Lankarama, Mirisaveti, Ruanveli and Thuparama dagobas.

Beside the entrance lie the **Archaeological Museum**, also the **ticket office**, and the **Folk Museum**; these and the museum within the **Isurumuni Vihara**, to the south, will be described later, as most will want to explore the great dagobas first.

Jetavanarama (Jetawana) Dagoba

A confusion between the identity of this dagoba and the similar Abhayagiri dagoba to the north arose, probably in the 12th century, and continued until quite recently. Most now believe that the Jetavanarama dagoba is the most southerly of the two. It has been estimated that this dagoba was originally 270 ft (82 m) high; although it now only reaches 249 ft (70 m) it is still the world's second highest (after the Abhayagiri Dagoba). With a diameter of 327 ft (100 m), the solid brick structure is supported by a platform covering 18 acres (7.3 hectares), which itself is raised several feet above the enclosure level.

Writing in a 19th century guidebook, Sir James Tennant estimated that with the bricks a builder could alternatively construct: **1.** 8,000 houses, each with a 20 ft (6 m) frontage; **2.** A 20 mile (32 kms) long railway tunnel; **3.** A 1 ft (0.3 m) deep, 10 ft (3 m) high wall from London to Edinburgh. Take your pick! Restoration, an immense

project, has been continuing for several years – some doubt that it will ever be completed.

King Mahasena began the dagoba in the late 3rd century. Regarded as the last great king of Anuradhapura, Mahasena was responsible for excavating sixteen new tanks and a canal to irrigate paddy fields around the city. This led to prosperity, but the king was never universally popular, as he espoused the less strict Mahayana form of Buddhism, becoming known as 'the heretic king'. The Jetavanarama Dagoba was the most impressive part of a 3,000 strong monastery which had been founded by Devanampiya Tissa in the 3rd century BC but was renamed the Maha Vihara by Mahasena, who transferred great wealth to it from the Abhayagiri monastery. Both monasteries were 'persuaded' to follow the practices of the king's Buddhist sect. Ruins of other monastic buildings can be seen around the dagoba.

North-west of the Jetavanarama Dagoba are the remains of the ruined tomb of the Chola invader King Elera, the best known Tamil ruler of the city, who reigned 205-161 BC. On the opposite (north) side of the road fronting the tomb is a car park, faced by what is certainly the oldest dagoba in Anuradhapura and possibly in Sri Lanka.

Thuparama

It is said that Mahinda, the Buddhist missionary, urged King Devanampiya Tissa to build this dagoba to house the Buddha's right collarbone around 244 BC. Originally designed in the paddy heap (conical) form, the dagoba was converted to its present bell shape by Victorian restorers. Although just 62 ft (19 m) high, this is one of Sri Lanka's most elegant dagobas – it must be hoped that the dreadful yellow sign and corrugated-iron canopy that stood over the entrance in 1999 have by now been removed.

The stone pillars are survivors of the set erected to support the conical roof of a vatadage (circular image house) that was built around the dagoba at some period. By tradition, during its installation ceremony, the Sacred Collarbone, engulfed in flames, ascended from the back of the ecstatic, trumpeting elephant that was transporting it.

No vehicles are permitted to proceed immediately southward from the car park in fear of a terrorist attack on the Sacred Bo-Tree – all must walk the 1,300 yds (1.25 km) involved, and return in the same direction. Fortunately, the **Ruvanveli Seya Dagoba** provides a diversion almost precisely at the half-way point.

Ruvanveli Seya Dagoba

Splendidly restored, this gleaming white dagoba stands in its sanded courtyard surrounded by park-like grounds. King Dutugemunu spent much of his reign in expiation for killing so many in battle, presenting the monks with the Mirisavetiya Dagoba and the Brazen Palace in addition to this dagoba. By tradition, although in 137 BC, when the king lay close to death, the dagoba was still unfinished, his son arranged for the builders to stretch a false top of cloth over a bamboo frame so that his father could appreciate how the structure would finally appear. Another 47 years were to pass, however, before the dagoba was finished. Originally, it was given a water-bubble shape, and

probably stood around 270 ft (82 m) high, but south Indian invaders caused a great deal of damage to it, and now the dagoba, reduced in height to 180 ft (55 m), resembles an inverted bowl.

A passage to the relic chamber was reserved for the king's use. In 1873, fragments of the four chapels, which stood at the cardinal points, were reassembled; the figures of the four Buddhas-to-come are 8th century additions. Carved heads and front legs of elephants protrude from the wall; some of those by the west entrance are believed to be original. A carved figure, south of the dagoba, is said to represent King Dutugemunu. To the south, the Brazen Palace can be reached on foot in just under ten minutes.

Brazen Palace

Like the Ruvanveli Saya Dagoba, the Brazen Palace was built, as part of his atonement, by King Dutugemunu in the 2nd century BC. It was never a royal palace, but formed the nucleus of a Buddhist monastery, which accommodated 1,000 monks and their lay attendants. All that survives are the remains of structural columns from a much later building.

The first palace was roofed with bronze tiles, hence the name given to it. According to the Mahavamsa, it had nine tiers, each provided with 100 rooms, the monks being lodged according to status, the most important occupying the top floor. Apparently, the Brazen Palace was richly decorated internally with gold, silver and precious stones. Due to its height, most of the structure would have been of wood, which almost certainly contributed to the fire that destroyed the building fifteen years after its completion.

the dilapidated **Dalada Maligawa**. Many believe that this was the first temple built in Sri Lanka to accommodate the Sacred Tooth Relic when it was brought from India in 313 AD. This temple lies within the area of the Royal Palace built by King Vijaya I in the 12th century; Anuradhapura had been abandoned by royalty for many years, but it appears that the king wished to regain a royal *pied-a-terre* in what remained of the city.

At the road junction ahead a right turn leads to the finest of the city's ponds.

Kuttam Pokuna (Twin Ponds)

These ponds are believed to have served as bathing pools for the

This pattern of destruction and re-construction recurred several times, and on each occasion a smaller, less sumptuous palace replaced its predecessor.

The last rebuilding took place in the 12th century, after Polonnaruwa had taken over as the capital, King Parakrama I sponsoring the work, possibly after destruction of the palace by south Indian invaders. The 1,600 granite columns, all originally 12 ft (3.7 m) high, are set out in 40 rows of 40 and appear to have supported the lower floors of a square building. Some, however, have suggested that the columns had nothing to do with the palace, and were erected just to record its location.

Immediately south is the **Sacred Bo-Tree** enclosure.

Within easy walking distance, north of the Thuparama Dagoba, is

The Sacred Bo-Tree, now the oldest tree in the world, was brought here as a sapling from the tree in Bodh Gaya, north India, beneath which, around 500 BC, Prince Siddhartha attained enlightenment. Princess Sanghamitta, sister of the Buddhist missionary Mahinda and daughter of the Indian Emperor, Ashoka, accompanied by attendants, is credited with bringing the sapling to Sri Lanka in 240 BC. After the planting ceremony, it is said that this arid region received seven continuous days of rain.

monks from the monastery attached to the Abhayagiri Dagoba nearby. Although both are designed in the same style, the ponds are hardly 'twins', as the northern example is 40 ft (12 m) longer than the southern. In the latter can be seen impressive carvings of a five-headed cobra (*naga*) and a demonic dragon, from the mouth of which water flowed into the pond. There is no such device in the north pond as the water here was obtained from its twin, via a subterranean conduit.

Further west, beneath its canopy, is one of the world's finest statues of the Buddha.

Samadhi Buddha

This 4th century carving depicts the Buddha seated in a meditative position. Apart from damage to the nose, which has been restored, the figure is in excellent condition in spite of being exposed to the elements for centuries – only recently was it given

a canopy. India's first Prime Minister, Jawaharlal Nehru, a Hindu, claimed that a photograph of the Samadhi Buddha comforted him during his imprisonment by the British before Independence. Visitors can approached more closely from a gate to the enclosure on the east side.

On the opposite side of the road, a little further west, an enormous green mound, partly scaffolded, denotes another huge dagoba.

Abhayagiri Dagoba

Standing 246 ft (75 m) high, this is the world's highest dagoba (by 16 ft/5 m), but originally, like the Jetawanarama, it is believed to have been 328 ft (100 m) high. The great structure was built by King Vattagamani Abhaya Valagam, who came to the throne in 103 BC, but was forced to flee the city in the same year by south Indian Chola invaders. They ruled for 15 years

• SACRED BO-TREE (SRI MAHA BODHI) •

For more than 2,000 years expert gardeners have tended the tree, which is therefore the oldest known tree in the world with indisputable credentials. It is a type of fig tree (*ficus religiosa*), and is now showing signs of frailty; in 1950 the Bo-Tree was thought to be dying, but an expert from Washington's Smithsonian Institute nursed it back to health. Smaller Bo-Trees growing nearby all began as saplings taken from their venerable parent and so the life of the sacred tree will continue through its descendants.

Raja Sinha, the last King of Kandy, erected a wall protecting the tree in the early 19th century; the golden rails were added in 1966. Facing a figure of the Buddha is an altar on which offerings are laid by worshippers, particularly at weekends and on Poya days.

Before the Kandy bomb it was usual, and more convenient, for visitors to begin their exploration of Anuradhapura at the Sacred Bo-Tree; it must be hoped that a reversion to this procedure will soon be possible. The long walk back to the car park facing the Tomb of Elera must now be made.

before Valegam returned to drive them out and reclaim the throne. It is almost certain that this dagoba, part of a monastery, was constructed during the main part of the king's reign, 89-77 BC.

By tradition, a Jain hermit named Giri accused Valagam of cowardice; on returning, the king ordered his execution and built a monastery over Giri's hermitage. The dagoba's name is a combination of Abhaya (the king's second name, which means fearless), and Giri (the name of the hermit). The monastery accommodated 5,000 monks, who followed the more liberal Mahayana sect of Buddhism. It is said that the sacred Tooth Relic was housed for a period in one of the temples and ceremonially displayed to the citizens by the king every year – an event reputed to ensure good rainfall for the rice crop.

From 113-125 AD, the structure was enlarged, and its circumference now measures 328 ft (100 m). Flanking the steps are guardstones in the form of shrines, which are believed to date from King Valagam's reign. On the left is Padmanidhi and on the right Santanidhi. To the north-west, **King Mahasena's Palace**, although in ruins, possesses the finest moonstone in Sri Lanka. Unfortunately, the protective railings are so close, viewing and photography is difficult. Nearby, at the entrance to a ruined Image House, an exceptional moonstone has survived. Further west can be seen what is probably the finest guardstone in Sri Lanka.

Ratnaprasada

Protected by railings, which inconsiderately prevent photographs being taken of the complete stone without a wide-angle lens, stands the exquisitely carved 8th century figure of a guardian figure attended by a dwarf. He is crowned with a cobra hood and bears a potted lotus together with the blossoming branch of a tree: symbols of wealth.

The Ratnaprasada (Gem Palace) Temple was the scene of much violence during the 9th century. Members of the Court opposed the king on an issue and took sanctuary within its walls, but his supporters were sent to forcibly evict them for execution. Appalled at this desecration of a holy place, the monks departed. The citizens sided with them and in turn put the king's supporters to death. Eventually, the king apologised for his act and persuaded the monks to return. A small, ruinous dagoba of importance lies to the south.

Lankarama Dagoba

Built in the 1st century BC as part of a *vatadage* (circular relic house) this dagoba, in spite of its poor condition, is classed, surprisingly, as one of Anuradhapura's eight sacred places. If restored, it would no doubt resemble the Thuparama, which predates it by around 200 years. Forming three circles, pillars now of varying height originally supported the roof of the relic house.

A short distance to the north-east, the modern **Abhayigiri Fa Hien Museum**, one of the best in the Ancient Cities, was sponsored by the government of China. Displayed are finds excavated at the Abhayigiri Monastery. Of particular interest is a collection of monks' squatting plates, intended to facilitate their natural functions.

The road southward eventually skirts the **Basawakkulama Tank**, which covers 120 hectares. Excavated probably around the 4th century BC, this is the oldest of the city's tanks. Overlooking it, beside the entrance, are the museums.

Folk Museum

Backing the Ruvanveli Saya Dagoba, the museum demonstrates, with models and artefacts, rural life in this part of the country.

Archaeological Museum

Astonishingly, no entrance charge is made for this two tiered museum, built around a courtyard. However, in 1999 many rooms were closed and few will wish to spend much time here. Of greatest interest, if accessible, are: a model of the Thuparama, showing how this would have appeared with its timber roof; a restored relic chamber and its contents from Mihintale; carved squatting (toilet) plates found when excavating the city's western monasteries, and an outstanding 5th century meditating Buddha. Bronzes and pottery are displayed on the upper floor. Entry tickets to the city are sold here.

South of the museums, near the Tissawewa Rest House, are three monuments of importance, which some may have seen at an earlier stage. They can be visited conveniently in the evening before visiting the main part of the city the following day, particularly by those staying at the adjacent Rest House. North-west of the Rest House is an important, well-restored dagoba.

Mirisaveti Dagoba

This, the first dagoba built by King Dutugemunu, was intended to be the world's largest, but he never completed it. Work began in 161 BC to commemorate Dutugemunu's ousting of the south Indian occupiers of Anuradhapura. The king is said to have stated that the dagoba was named to remind him that once he had eaten a spicy relish (*mirisaveti*) without offering some of it to the monks, as by tradition he should have done.

It is believed that Dutugemunu's sword, which incorporated a relic of the Buddha and served as the royal standard on the battlefield, is buried within the dagoba. Seven days after his victory, Dutugemunu commissioned a water festival, and before taking part he removed his outer clothing and thrust the sword into the ground. On the king's return, the sword, Excalibur-fashion, could not be removed. Dutugemunu ordered that the Mirisaveti Dagoba should be built over it.

King Kassyapa, 921-931AD, rebuilt much of the dagoba and, in 1944 restoration by the state completed earlier work sponsored by a king of Siam. The structure has been painted white, and a finial, as originally, now surmounts the dagoba. Nestling below the embankment of the Tissawewa tank, which covers 395 acres (160 hectares), are two fish ponds.

Royal Pleasure Gardens

King Dutugemunu laid out the gardens over 35 acres (14 hectares). Natural boulders suggested the excavation of two fish ponds between them separated by a relaxation area. The fishes kept were presumably goldfish, as the gardens are sometimes known as Goldfish Park. The second pond retains fine elephant carvings.

Formerly, a platform was erected on the rocks, from which views of the Tissawewa could be gained over its embankment. It is said that in these gardens Prince Saliya, the eldest son of Dutugemunu, first met Asokamala, with whom he fell in love and eventually married. Unfortunately, as she was a commoner, Saliya forfeited his right to inherit the throne. From the gardens, a narrow stream leads a short distance south to Aunuradhapura's last (or first) important monument, a rock temple with a museum.

Isurumuni Vihara

The monastery, founded in the 3rd century BC by Devanampiya Tissa, had been completely lost until British archaeologists cut away the jungle to reveal it in the 1870s. Outside the entrance, to the right, the ceremonial bathing pool is said to have accommodated the monks' pet crocodiles in the early years of the 20th century. Steps ascend to the first rock temple, passing a lotus pond. The carving on the rock face of elephants splashing water is believed to be in its original position; many other important carvings have been transferred to the museum in recent years.

On the right are carved a man with a horse and, below this, an elephant's head.

Within the vihara, to the left, the reclining Buddha figure has been cut from the rock. Within the museum are two famous carvings brought from the rock face. 'The Lovers', a work by the Indian Gupta School (fourth to fifth century), is carved on a slab of stone, and therefore presumed to have come from elsewhere. Allegedly, Saliya and Asokamala are represented, but many

now think that Hindu deities provide the subject matter.

Fixed to the wall, the 'King's family' relief was carved between the 6th and 8th centuries.

ANURADHAPURA NEW TOWN

The New Town lies about one mile (1.5 km) east of the Ancient City and is bounded on its east side by the Nuwara Wewa Tank. Located in the northern sector are the **railway and bus stations**. Several guest houses lie along Harischandra MW and Rowing Club Road, but the best accommodation in the town has views across the tank. The **Nuwarawewa Rest House** belongs to the same group as the Tissawewa Rest House but its building is bleakly modern. There are 70 air-conditioned rooms, some of which have views of the tank, and there is a good swimming pool. The **Miridiya Hotel**, with 38 air-conditioned rooms, has a pool set in a delightful garden fronting the tank. Located just 1.5 miles (2.5 km) west of the Ancient City is the three star **Palm Garden Village Hotel**, by far the best in the area. Its 50 rooms, each with TV and mini-bar include 10 luxurious suites. The swimming pool is enormous.

TRANSPORT

There are two bus stations in the town – the old, for standard CTB buses to Polonnaruwa, Dambulla, Kandy and Colombo; the new, on the opposite side of the road, for air-conditioned buses to Dambulla, Kandy and Colombo, and standard buses to Trincomalee. Trains run from the adjacent railway station to Colombo, Kandy (change trains at Polgahawela) and Galle.

Trincomalee

Pigeon Island, just offshore from Trincomalee, has a rocky shoreline to the east

Trincomalee is the only east coast bathing resort that tourists may realistically visit at present. Although it can be approached directly from either Polonnaruwa or Anuradhapura, many will prefer to fit a visit in between these two Ancient Cities, simply to prevent a touch of cultural 'indigestion', which might otherwise be felt.

However, bear in mind that Trincomalee experiences the north-east monsoon, and rainfall can be high from October to January. If holidaying during this period it is advisable to check the situation at the resort by telephone. The favoured period for a visit to Trincomalee, March to July, is the high season on this coast – but it will be very hot. Attractions here are the white **beaches**, the **British Fort** and **Pigeon Island**, from where live coral 'gardens' can still be seen with ease.

Since 1992, after years of bitter fighting, Trincomalee has been firmly under government control, and there is no reason for tourists to be wary of visiting the area (no matter what they are told by the Tourist Office in Colombo). In 1999, the A6 highway was open at all times, and there were relatively few military blockades until the town was approached; only rarely were tourists asked to show passports.

HISTORY

The name Trincomalee is a corruption of a Sinhalese tongue-twister, even though it sounds as if it commemorates a fishing village somewhere on the Irish coast.

Aryans from north India, probably before Buddhism reached the island, built a large temple on the site of Fort Frederick. Unusually, the Dutch visited Trincomalee before the Portuguese, in 1617, but it was just a reconnaissance and they soon left. Seven years later, the Portuguese, who by then occupied most of the island, arrived at Trincomalee and built a small fort. From 1639, the town was passed in sequence, like a hot potato, between the Dutch, the King of Kandy, the Dutch, the French, the Dutch, the British, the French, the Dutch and finally, in 1795, the British. Trincomalee was, in fact, the first British possession on the island.

During the Second World War, after the fall of Singapore, Trincomalee Harbour, the fifth largest port in the world, became the headquarters of the combined allied fleets in south Asia. It covers an area of 55 sq miles (142 sq km).

When Ceylon gained independence in 1948, the population of Trincomalee was divided almost equally between Sinhalese, Tamils and Muslims. Surprisingly, the British were allowed to control Trincomalee Harbour until 1954, six years after Independence. The future for tourism for the area looked promising, and several hotels were constructed bordering the lovely beaches. However, from the mid-1980s until 1992 bitter fighting took place between the Tamil Tigers and government forces, and tourism came to an almost complete halt. Many Tamil families migrated to south India and their abandoned houses can be seen.

WHAT TO SEE IN TRINCOMALEE

Most tourists who visit Trincomalee will also be visiting the Ancient Cities, but the town is renowned as a resort in its own right by Sri Lankans (mainly from Colombo) and expatriates working in the country. The season here is from April to October, when the rainfall is much lower than in the south-west of the country, and the sea is calm. From a tourist viewpoint, **Fort Frederick** is worth visiting for its Hindu temple and reminders of Trincomalee's colonial past. Views of the **Inner Harbour** and the enormous **Back Bay** are stunning, but the streets and buildings in the town are of little interest. Practically all tourists stay just north of the town at **Nilaveli**, with its white sands and resort hotel from where there are boat trips to **Pigeon Island**, which retains a coral 'garden'.

NILAVELI VILLAGE

Buses run from Trincomalee to Nilaveli Village, but most tourists will opt for a three-wheeler or a taxi. The road passes the shells of many houses that tourists will be assured were fired by Tamil Tigers. The reality is that the properties were owned by Tamils who decided to leave when the fighting began in the mid-1980s. They took everything that could be removed – doors, window frames etc, for re-use elsewhere, which primarily accounts for the derelict appearance of the houses.

Nilaveli Beach

Nilaveli lies 10 miles (15 km) north of Trincomalee town; it is fronted by a beach of soft white – or almost white – sand, which stretches northward for a further 3 miles (4 km) to a lagoon. During the season, the sea is extremely calm and 'gin-clear'. As the sands slope gently the water is safe for bathing, but strong currents can pose difficulties for ambitious swimmers.

Nilaveli Beach Hotel

The **Nilaveli Beach Hotel** opened in 1974 and has bravely refused to close, even when fighting took place nearby. There are 86 air-conditioned rooms and an excellent pool. Whilst this is not the only hotel in the Trincomalee area, it is the only one up to tourist standards, and overlooks the finest beach. On no occasion have visitors been inconvenienced by the civil strife, and here, more than at any other Sri Lanka tourist location it is reassuring to reflect that the Tamil Tiger policy is not to harm foreigners in any way.

Trees growing out of the sand screen most of the building at least partially from the sea, but the hotel's two suites have unobstructed views out to Pigeon Island. For obvious reasons, a limited number of staff are employed for most of the year, and not a great deal has been spent on maintenance. Plans are afoot to bring everything up to standard for the 2000 season. The food, particularly seafood, can be good.

Unlike the south-west coast, the beach is not fringed with palm trees, and there are no rocks or coastal reefs. As may be expected, beach vendors are few – just a handful of Muslims who offer shells and not very exciting boat trips on the lagoon to the north; own transport must be supplied to reach the banks of the lagoon.

PIGEON ISLAND

In calm weather, the hotel arranges motor-boat excursions to this tiny island just a third of a mile (0.5 km) offshore. From Nilaveli Beach it appears that there is just one island, but as the approach is made

it becomes apparent that there are in fact two; passengers are dropped off on the larger, and picked up a few hours later. A morning or afternoon trip will be sufficient for most as no refreshments are available, and bathing from the tiny beaches is not good due to the proximity of rough-on-the-feet coral rock.

It is the coral, however, that is the island's greatest attraction. Non-swimmers with beach shoes can view its coral 'garden', which, unlike Hikkaduwa's, has survived, simply by wading out to it from the landing beach and ducking. Try to rent goggles or, even better, snorkeling equipment, which will obviously extend visibility. The island is very narrow, with pretty sandy coves on both sides; these would be even prettier if Sri Lankan hooligans had not defaced the rocks around them with their idiotic graffiti.

FORT FREDERICK

A small fort was first built at Trincomalee by the Portuguese in 1624, but 15 years later the Dutch strengthened the defences and gave the fort its name. Additions were made by the British after 1795. Fortified walls flank the entrance on either side.

Tourist vehicles must be parked outside the entrance, and no photography is permitted within the complex.

Gateway

Above the portal is inscribed 'Fort Frederick', and the date 1676; the

Opposite page:
A glorious sunset

Right: Trees bring shade to the hot beach at Nilaveli, just north of Trincomalee

British added their coat of arms in 1795. Inscribed on both sides of the wall within the gateway are a pair of fishes, the emblem of the Tamil Pandyan dynasty of south India. Below the fishes on the right an inscription in their language prophesies that the Franks (French) are destined to be the conquerors of Trincomalee. As the Pandyans had left Trincomalee long before any Europeans appeared on the scene it is a mystery who was responsible for this work and when it was executed. The French held the fort briefly in 1672 and maybe a chauvinistic official decided that an 'ancient' prophecy would be appropriate.

A plaque outlines the complex history of Fort Frederick.

The straight road bisecting the fort leads ahead to the Hindu temple one mile (1.5 km) distant at the north tip of the peninsula. Enchanting 'Bambi' spotted deer are permitted to roam freely in the grounds of the fort, apparently in continuation of a long tradition.

At the bend in the road, painted in black lettering on a white wall, is the legend 'When the going gets tough the tough get going. The infantryman has his pride and morale'. It will be noted that many government troops are billeted within the complex in temporary barracks which accounts for the high level of security.

WELLESLEY LODGE

Lying back from the right hand side of the road is an 18th century mansion. In this typically colonial residence, with its wide veranda, Colonel Arthur Wellesley, the future Duke of Wellington stayed in 1799 following his battles with Tipu

Sultan in south India. Wellesley had been taken ill, and did not recover in time to board the ship that would have taken him to Egypt; this proved fortunate for him, as it was sunk in the Gulf of Aden with the loss of all on board. One wonders how history might have been altered had the victor of Waterloo not missed the boat.

SWAMI ROCK

Near this famous rock, which bulges out towards the end of the peninsula, stood the ancient Hindu Temple of a Thousand Columns, dedicated to Siva. The iconoclastic Portuguese destroyed this on their arrival in 1624, using the stonework to build their fort; what was not needed they jettisoned into the sea. A column said to have come from the temple was re-erected on the rock in 1687 by a Dutchman, Van Reede, to commemorate his daughter Francina. According to a Dutch girl, whose father was employed locally as an official, Francina had committed suicide, leaping from the rock after being abandoned by her lover; but evidence later came to light proving that she did no such thing, and in fact married eight years after the column had been erected.

There is no need to remove shoes unless entering the adjacent temple.

Koneswaram Temple

In 1958 this Hindu temple was built as a replacement for the Temple of a Thousand Columns. Within are venerated Siva, Parvathi and their two sons. Unlike the usual gaudy paint work of modern Hindu temples the tones here are a soothing pastel. Scuba divers recently found sections of the ancient temple in water off the rock at a depth of 330 ft (100 m). Amongst their finds was the original Siva lingam, which was hauled out of the water, and is now venerated within the modern building (closed 12am to 5pm). Puja is held daily at 9am, 11.45am, 5pm and 6pm.

From the peninsula there are all-embracing views of the sweeping Back Bay, to the west, and Dutch Bay to the east. Inner Harbour, to the south-west, can be glimpsed from the town, but the area is re-stricted and its once popular sandy beaches can no longer be enjoyed.

St Stephen's Cemetery

Dockyard Road, west of the fort, gives access to the pretty St Stephen's Cemetery. Amongst Brit-ish residents buried here are Charles, the younger brother of Jane Austen, and P. B. Molesworth, an amateur astronomer who is credited with discovering Jupiter's Red Spot at Trincomalee; he be-came the first manager of Sri Lanka's railways and no doubt would still find some of the trains familiar!

KANNIGAI HOT SPRINGS

Natural hot water springs at **Kannigai**, 5 miles (8 km) north-west of Trincomalee (3 miles/5 km south of Naveli), lie on the A12 trunk road to Anuradhapura, and can easily be visited en route to the ancient city.

Bear in mind that it is not possible to bathe in the seven springs, which vary in temperature from 85^{0}F (29^{0}C) to 115^{0}F (46^{0}C). The 'health giving' water can only be appreci-ated by drawing a bucketful, wait-ing for it to cool, and then pouring it over the head and shoulders – a swimming costume is advisable. It must be said that the springs appeal more to Sri Lankans (particularly the military) rather than tourists.

By tradition, the Hindu god Vishnu, in the disguise of an old man, untruthfully told Sri Lanka's Demon King Ravana that his mother had died, and created the springs so that Ravana had a ready supply of water to carry out the traditional mourning ceremony. Apparently, Vishnu's aim was to slow down the progress of Ravana, who was on an evil mission – as is the way with all demon kings.

ROUTES AND PUBLIC TRANSPORT

Once again, in spite of information issued to the contrary by the Tour-ist Board in Colombo, the A12 trunk road between Trincomalee and Anuradhapura, 66 miles (106 km) distant, is open in its entirety throughout daylight hours, but the section between Trincomalee and Mihintale 59 miles (95 km) closes at night to facilitate the movement of military vehicles. Many check-points can be expected on this road.

A limited bus service between Trincomalee and Anuradhapura takes four hours. Buses direct to Colombo take seven hours and to Kandy five hours. An alternative but longer route from Trincomalee to Anuradhapura, in case of unex-pected problems, is via the A6 to Habarana followed by the A11, which branches to Mihintale.

There are also daily trains to and from Colombo but these, as usual, take longer than buses (8.5 hours as against 7 hours) and the morning train from Colombo leaves at a very unsociable hour.

jmc

Dive into the Indian Ocean with JMC

JMC is the only choice for Sri Lanka, offering genuinely different holidays. From its setting in the Indian Ocean, Sri Lanka offers golden beaches, spectacular landscapes, abundant wildlife, unique culture, history and a warm, welcoming service. With JMC you can choose to see as much or as little as you like with holidays to cater for all tastes.

- Sri Lanka & Maldives twin centres
- Tour & Stay holidays
- Exotic Sri Lanka weddings
- All Inclusives, offers for honeymooners & anniversaries & single saver discounts

JMC also offers holidays to Goa, Kerala & the Maldives. For more information call JMC

- 0870 555 044

ACCOMMODATION

Sri Lanka offers a wide range of visitor accommodation, from basic rooms in villagers' homes to luxury hotels with all the expected facilities. A grading system is operated, ranging from one to five stars. All rooms in a star-rated establishment will be provided with en-suite showers and toilets; telephones, mini-bars and televisions are usually only provided in four and five-star hotels. A high percentage of visitors to Sri Lanka will have pre-booked their accommodation via tour operators. If not, it is best to select the resort area and ask advice from a taxi driver or at the beach bars. For those who wish to stay near the more intimate beaches such as Unawatuna, there is little star-rated accommodation available.

During the high season of December and January, prices are slightly higher in all establishments, but considerably higher in the upper-grade hotels. At this time, also, accommodation may be difficult to find in the most popular areas. Individual hotels and guest houses judged suitable for discriminating tourists are described throughout the book.

Hotels

Chapter 1: Negombo

Goldi Sands Hotel,
☎ 031-22021, Fax 031-38227

Royal Oceanic Beach,
☎ 031-24306, Fax 79999

Blue Oceanic Hotel,
☎ 031-24306, Fax 79999

Sea Garden Hotel,
☎ 031-22377

Brown's Beach Hotel,
☎ 031-22032, Fax 24303

Catamaran Beach Hotel,
☎ 031-22206, Fax 075-310046

Interline Beach Hotel,
☎ 031-22350, Fax 3138384

Golden Star Beach Hotel,
☎ 031-33564, Fax 38266

Oceanic Garden Hotel,
☎ 031-77309, Fax 77549

Seashells Hotel,
☎ 031-22062, Fax 074-870768

Club Hotel Dolphin,
☎/Fax 031-77788-9

Ranweli Holiday Village,
☎ 031-22136, Fax 77358

Mario Beach Hotel, Beach Road,
☎ 032-54552/3, Fax 54554

Sanmali Beach Hotel, Wella Road,
☎ 032-54766/7, Fax 54768

Aquarius Beach Hotel, Beach Road, ☎ 032-34888,
Fax 078-60555

De-Phani Beach Guest House,
☎ 031-34359, Fax 38225

Sea Sands Guest House,
☎ 031-23154

Silver Sands Hotel, ☎ 031-22880

Chapter 2: Colombo

Ceylon Intercontinental Hotel,
48 Janadhipathi MW, Colombo 1,
☎ 421221, Fax 447326

Colombo Hilton, Lotus Road,
Colombo 1, ☎ 544644, Fax 54465

Holiday Inn, 30 Sir Mohamed Macan Markar MW, Colombo 2,
☎ 422001, Fax 447977

Hotel Sapphire, 371 Galle Road,
Colombo 6, ☎ 583306, Fax 585455

Taj Samudra,
125 Galle Face Centre Road,
Colombo 3, ☎ 446622, Fax 446348

Galle Face Hotel, Galle Face Green,
Colombo 3, ☎ 541010, Fax 541072

Lanka Oberoi, 77 Steuart Place,
Colombo 3, ☎ 437437, Fax 447933

Chapter 3:
Mount Lavinia

Mount Lavinia Hotel,
100 Hotel Road, Mount Lavinia,
☎ 01-715221/7, Fax 730726/
738228

Berjaya Mount Royal Beach Hotel,
36 College Avenue, Mount Lavinia,
☎ 01-739610-5, Fax 733030

Palm Beach Hotel,
52 De Saram Road, Mount Lavinia,
☎ 01-717484, Fax 712713

Saltaire Beach Resort,
50/5 De Saram Road, Mount
Lavinia, ☎ 01-738713, Fax 508192

Sea Spray Beach Resort,
45 Vihara Road, ☎ 01-730532

Chapter 4:
Wadduwa & Kalutara

The Blue Water,
Thalpitiya, ☎/Fax 34 35067/8

Villa Ocean View,
☎/Fax 34-32463

Royal Palms Hotel, De Abrews
Road, ☎ 034-28113/7, Fax 28112

Golden Sun Resort,
☎ 034-28484, Fax 28485

Rathnaloka Tour Inn, Kahangama,
☎ 045-22455, Fax 045-30017

Tangerine Beach Hotel, De Abrews
Road, Waskaduwa, Kalutara North,
☎ 034-22982/3, Fax 26794

The LTI Sindbad, St Sebastian's
Road, Katukurunda, Kalutara,
☎ 034-26537-9, Fax 26530

Hibiscus Beach Hotel,
Mahawaskaduwa, Kalutara North,
☎ 034-22704/6, Fax 22705

Hotel Mermaid,
Mahawaskaduwa, Kalutara North,
☎ 034-22613, Fax 28572

Chapter 5:
Beruwala & Bentota

Panorama and the **Ypsylon,**
Moragalle, ☎ 034-76132,
Fax 76334

Susantha Guesthouse,
in Resort Road, Pitaramba,
☎ 034-75324, Fax 75590

Confifi Beach Hotel, Moragalle,
☎ 034-76217, Fax 76317

Beach Hotel Bayroo, Moragalle,
☎ 034-76297, Fax 01-439046

Hotel Swanee, Moragalle,
☎ 034-76007, Fax 01-439046

Club Palm Garden, Moragalle,
☎ 034-76039, Fax 01-333324/5

Riverina, Moragalle,
☎ 034-76044/5, Fax 76047

Eden Hotel,
☎ 034-76075/6, Fax 76181

Taj Exotica,
☎ 01-446622, Fax 446348

Lihinya Surf Hotel,
☎ 034-75267, Fax 75486

Hotel Serendib,
☎ 034-75248, Fax 75313

Hotel Ceysands,
☎ 034-750734, Fax 01-447087

Club Villas, 138/15 Galle Road,
☎/Fax 034-75312

Saman Villas Hotel,
(Aturuwella, ☎/Fax 034-75433)

Induruwa Beach Resort,
Kaikawala, ☎ 034-75445,
Fax 75583

Emerald Bay,
☎ 034-75363, Fax 75313

Chapter 6: Kosgoda & Hikkaduwa

Kosgoda Beach Resort,
P.O. Box 01, Nape,
☎ 09-64017/8, Fax 01-345729

Triton Hotel,
☎ 09-64041/4, Fax 64046

Coral Gardens,
☎ 09-77422, Fax 01-439046

Coral Reef Beach Hotel,
☎ 09-77197

Coral Sands Hotel,
☎ 09-77436, Fax 074-383225

Hotel Reefcomber,
☎/Fax 09-77374

Sunil's Beach Hotel, Navigama,
Hikkaduwa, ☎/Fax 09-77187

Chapter 7: Galle to Dondra Head

New Oriental Hotel,
10 Church Street, ☎/Fax 09-35491

Lighthouse Hotel,
☎ 09-23744, Fax 24021

Closenberg Hotel, 11 Closenberg
Road, Galle, ☎/Fax 09-32241

Unawatuna Beach Resort
(known as UBR), ☎/Fax 09-32247

Rumassala Hotel, ☎ 09-34027

The Strand, Yaddehimulla Road
☎ 072-30010, Fax 09-32045

Club Horizon,
☎/Fax 09-83297

Koggala Beach Hotel,
☎ 09-83243, Fax 83260

Hotel Club Lanka,
☎/Fax 09-83361

Mirissa Beach Inn,
☎ 041-50410, Fax 50115

Paradise Beach Club,
☎/Fax 041-50380

Dikwella Beach Hotel,
112 Mahawla Road,
☎ 041-55326, Fax-041 55637

Chapter 8: The South-East Coast & Yala National Park

Palm Paradise Cabanas,
☎ 047-40338, Fax 40401

Peacock Beach Hotel,
Galwala, ☎ 047-20377

Tissa Rest House, ☎ 047-37299

Yala Safari Beach Hotel,
☎ 01-345700, Fax 345729

Chapter 9: The Hill Country & Nuwara Eliya

Bandarawela Hotel, 14 Weliwada
Road ☎ 057-22501, Fax 22834

Hotel Glendower, 5 Grand Hotel
Road, ☎ 052-22501, Fax 22749

Grand Hotel, Grand Hotel Road,
☎ 052-22881, Fax 22265

Windsor Hotel,
PO Box 01, Nuwara Eliya,
☎ 052-22554, Fax 22889

St Andrew's Hotel,
☎ 052-22445, Fax 23153

Tea Factory Hotel,
☎ 052-23600, Fax 22026

Chapter 10: Kandy

Queen's Hotel, Dalada Vidiya,
☎ 08-233290, Fax 232079

Casamara, 12 Kotugodella Vidiya,
☎ 08-234327, Fax 224688

Freedom Lodge, ☎ 08-223506,
Expeditor and the **Sharon Inn**, at
number 59, ☎/Fax 08-225665

Hotel Suisse, 30 Sangaraja MW,
☎ 08-233024-5, Fax 232083

Mahaweli Reach Hotel,
35 PBA Weerakon MW,
☎ 074-472727, Fax 08-232068

Citadel,
124 Srimath Kuda Ratwatte MW,
☎ 08-234365, Fax 01-447087

Hotel Topaz,
☎ 08-224150, Fax 232073

Tourmaline,
☎ 08-232326, Fax 232073

Hotel Tree of Life, Yahalatenna,
Barigama, Werellagama,
☎ 08-499777, Fax 499711

Hotel Hilltop, 200/221
Bahirawakanda, Peradeniya Road,
☎ 08-224162, Fax 232459

Hunas Falls Hotel,
Elkaduwa, ☎/Fax 071-35134

Chapter 11:
The Ancient Cities

Kandalama Hotel, Kandalama,
☎ 066-23475, Fax 23482

Culture Club Resort, PO Box 12
Kandalama, ☎ 066-23500,
Fax 0722-44360

Gimanhala Transit Hotel, 754
Anuradhapura Road, Dambulla,
☎ 066-84864, Fax 84817

Sigiriya Village Hotel, Sigiriya,
☎ 066-30803, Fax 31803

Hotel Sigiriya,
☎/Fax 066-84811

The Lodge,
☎ 072-340201, Fax 01-447087

The Village,
☎ 072-340225, Fax 01-447087

Royal Lotus Hotel,
☎ 027-46316, Fax 01-448849

Deer Park Hotel,
☎ 027-46470, Fax 01-448849

Giritale Hotel,
☎ 027-46311, Fax 46086

Hotel Seruwa,
☎ 027-22411, Fax 01-503504

Village Polonnaruwa,
(formerly the Amalian Nivas),
☎ 027-22405, Fax 01-541199

Tissawewa Rest House, Old Town,
☎ 025-22299, Fax 23265

Nuwarawewa Rest House,
New Town, ☎ 025-22565,
Fax 23265

Miridiya Hotel, Wasala Dantha
MW, ☎/Fax 025-22519

Palm Garden Village Hotel,
Puttalam Road, Pandelagama,
☎ 025-23961, Fax 21596

Chapter 12:
Trincomalee

Nilaveli Beach Hotel,
Nilaveli, ☎ 026-22071, Fax 32297

CURRENCY REGULATIONS

Although funds in excess of $US10,000 should be declared, no enquiries are made when you enter the country. Visitors who wish to extend their stay beyond the visa-free period must have sufficient funds available or possess a major credit card.

ELECTRICITY

Throughout Sri Lanka, voltage is 230-240 AC. All sockets take rounded three-point plugs; bring an adapter.

HEALTH

Currently, it is recommended that visitors to Sri Lanka are injected against typhoid, paratyphoid, tetanus, polio and hepatitis A.

Malaria

During the dry season, few mosquitoes are seen along Sri Lanka's coastal regions, and malaria is rare; nevertheless, many may wish to take precautions. Seek advice on the current situation some weeks before leaving from a pharmacy or a general practitioner. Drugs such as chloroquine and proquanil offer 70 per cent protection, but take insect repellent – and use it.

Some economy hotels provide mosquito nets, which means there are mosquitoes about. Make sure there are no gaps in the net and tuck it in around the mattress. It is also as well to ask for a mosquito coil which should be lit at sundown and all doors and windows closed. Wear clothes that cover the arms and legs during the evening. If particularly worried about health dangers, specialist hospitals will give detailed advice; in the UK contact the Hospital for Tropical Diseases Travel Clinic: ☎ 020 7637 9899.

Rabies exists in Sri Lanka, and visitors are recommended not to pat dogs or hand-feed monkeys. If bitten, seek medical advice immediately.

Usually **stomach upsets** in Sri Lanka are disposed of quickly by proprietary medicines. It is best that these are brought by the visitor so that action can be taken as soon as discomfort is experienced.

Drinking water

Tap water should be rigorously avoided as should any fresh fruit and salad vegetables that may have been rinsed in it. Most luxury hotels supply flasks of purified water, but check with the establishment that it is safe. Ice made from unpurified tap water can also be dangerous, as the freezing process does not kill the microbes that cause the problems. Local people have developed immunity to them and can drink most water without fear. Bottled mineral water is readily available in tourist areas, but should be bought in advance if travelling elsewhere. Ensure that the water is sealed, or it may have been refilled with tap water. It is recommended that teeth are brushed in purified or mineral water whenever possible. Purification tablets should be brought for use in an emergency.

While pharmacies and doctors in the main towns are generally most efficient, it is preferable that any medical supplies that might be required are brought by visitors. Many hotels have an approved doctor on call.

If worrying symptoms develop on returning home, contact a specialist hospital immediately, e.g. in the UK the Hospital for Tropical Diseases, 4 St Pancras Way, London NW1 0PE ☎ 020 7387 4411.

HOLIDAYS AND FESTIVALS

With around thirty annual holidays, both religious and secular, during which banks and government organisations usually close, few tourists are likely to return home without having their holiday coincide with one of them. To avoid any inconvenience, as well as to make the most of the festivals, it is as well to establish their locations and dates, most of them variable, on or before arrival; the Ceylon Tourist Board publishes a helpful Calendar of Events, which makes this a simple matter.

Poya Days

All days of the full moon are celebrated as Poya days by Buddhists, and everything closes. These occur roughly every 28 days, and when they fall on a Friday or a Monday, many Sri Lankans take a long weekend break, visiting friends and relatives, and completely taking over public transport. This is therefore a good time for a tourist to stay put on the beach and relax. On Poya days alcoholic drinks must not be sold, although some hotels turn a blind eye to this where foreign visitors are concerned. Most Buddhist festivals coincide with a Poya Day.

Other religions

Hindus, Muslims and Christians, of course, have their own festivals, many of which are also celebrated nationally. The timing of Muslim festivals varies significantly each year; the most important, *Id-ul-Fitr*, marking the end of the fasting month of Ramadan, will take place in December or November for the next few years. The Christian holidays of Christmas Day and Good Friday are celebrated nationally.

Dates of many Hindu festivals vary slightly each year, but those of secular holidays do not.

Festivals of Importance

January

Poya day: Duruthu Perahera procession from the Kelaniya Paja Temple, 4.5 miles (7 km) east of Colombo. Celebrates the Buddha's alleged visit to Sri Lanka

14th or 15th: Thai Pongal, nation-wide Hindu harvest festival, celebrating the Sun God.

February

Poya Day: Navaham Perahera procession from Colombo's Gangaramayor Temple via Viharamahadevi Park to the Beira Lake district. Fifty caparisoned elephants take part.

4th: National Day marks the country's independence from the United Kingdom, which was gained on this day in 1948. Marked everywhere by parades and dancing.

Late February / early March: Maha Sivarathi. Hindus commemorate Parvathi's successful wooing of Lord Siva.

April

Easter (sometimes late March) is marked throughout the country, but especially in Christian areas along the coast. Just off Negombo, to which it is linked by road, the island of Duwa holds an annual Passion play.

13th and 14th: Sinhalese and Tamil New Year's Eve and New Year's Day are celebrated nationally.

May
Poya Day: (and the day following) Vesak marks the birth, enlightenment and death of the Buddha. Paper lanterns and oil lamps are lit at night throughout Buddhist areas of the country - an enchanting spectacle.

July
Poya Day: (generally late July but occasionally early August) Esala Perahera at Kandy is Sri Lanka's most important festival. Every night, for a 10-day period, a series of processions pays homage to the Buddha's Sacred Tooth relic.

To coincide with Esala Perahera, Hindus hold their Vel festival in Colombo. A procession from the Sea Street temples accompanies the chariot of Skanda, God of War, to Bambalapitiya's temple on the southern outskirts of the city. Expect some rain, it is the rainy season in Kandy. The same god is remembered around the same time at Kataragama in the south, near Yala National Park. Devotees indulge in masochistic activities - skin piercing, fire walking among them, to prove their faith.

October/November
Deepavali: This complicated Hindu Festival of Light commemorates the return of Rama (an incarnation of Vishnu) after his exile, and also honours Laxmi, Vishnu's consort. The lighting of thousands of oil lamps emphasises that good has triumphed over evil.

MONEY

The Sri Lankan currency is the rupee, which has roughly two-thirds the value of the Indian rupee. Notes are in 5, 10, 20, 50, 100 and 1,000 rupee denominations. Coins are in 1, 2 and 5 rupee and in 25 and 50 cent denominations (100 cents = 1 rupee).

American dollars and sterling are the simplest currencies to exchange, whether in notes or travellers cheques/travelers checks. Many hotels in Sri Lanka will change money for their guests, and the rate given is now very little less than that obtainable from banks. Sri Lankan banks have a much simpler and more efficient system for exchanging money than those in India, with very little form filling involved.

Banking hours are: Monday to Friday 9am - 1pm. Ensure that currency exchange forms are given for each transaction, and keep them, for exchanging any remaining rupees when leaving the country. The most welcome travellers cheques/travelers checks are those issued by American Express and Thomas Cook, both in dollars.

PACKING

As no heavy clothes will be needed, apart from a light pullover in the Hill Country, and hotels provide a fast, reliable laundry service, it is unnecessary to pack a large amount of clothing. The standard allowance permitted by most tour operators is 20 kg plus hand baggage. Toiletries, a simple medical kit and camera film (particularly for slides) should be brought, but all clothing is very much cheaper throughout Sri Lanka, much of it of excellent quality, particularly in Colombo.

Be sure to pack an adapter for electrical sockets; also bring spare rechargeable batteries, which can be hard to obtain locally. If staying at an economy class hotel, do not be surprised if there is no plug for the sink in the bathroom; take an adaptable rubber plug.

Thick socks can also come in useful if temples are being visited – shoes must always be removed and the stone can be very hot. For the beach, sandals although generally useful, let in the burning hot sand and canvas shoes are better.

PASSPORTS

All visitors to Sri Lanka must have a passport, valid for six months after their return date. Unless staying longer than four weeks, most western tourists will not need a visa, but those on business will.

TOURIST INFORMATION

Much information can be obtained from hotel reception staff and representatives of tour operators, many of whom make daily visits to the hotels. Tourist Information Centres which can supply information are situated at:

Bandaranaike International Airport, Colombo, 78 Steuart Place
☎ 01-437059
(opposite the Oberoi Hotel)

Kandy, 3 Deva Veediya
☎ 08-22661

Negombo, 12/6 Lewis Place
(no phone).

Ceylon Tourist Offices Overseas

UK
22 Regent Street, London
SW1Y 4OD ☎ 020-7930-2627,
Fax: (171)930 9070

France
19 rue du 4 Septembre, 75002,
Paris ☎ 01-4260-4999,
Fax 428-6494

Germany
Allerheiligentor 2-4, D-6000,
Frankfurt-am-Main 1
☎ 287-734, Fax 288-371

Japan
Dowa Building 7-2-22, Ginza Chuo
Ku, Tokyo ☎ (03) 3289-0771,
Fax (03) 3289-0772

Thailand
5/105-6/105 Soi Rattanaprahm 2,
Sukhumvit Soi 54/2, Bangkok
10250 ☎ 332-9075/ 7761,
Fax (662) 332-9076

India
D19, Defence Colony, New Delhi
110 024 ☎ (011) 460 3124,
Fax (011) 460 3123

Australia
Atutil Pty, Ltd.,39, Wintercorn Row,
Werrington Downs N.S.W.,
Australia 2747 ☎ (2) 47303914,
Fax (2) 6216142

TRAVEL

Air

All aircraft destined for Sri Lanka fly direct to Bandaranaike International Airport; due to the disturbances, there are no internal flights.

Visitors travelling with tour operators will automatically be met at the airport by buses to take them to their resort accommodation. International return flights from Sri Lanka on scheduled (not chartered) aircraft must be confirmed, usually one week in advance of departure.

Taxis are plentiful outside the airport, but there are direct bus services to Colombo or Negombo. In 1999 the fixed price taxi fare from the airport to any address in Colombo was 1,000 rupees. Do not pay extra for luggage, passengers or air-conditioning.

Trains

Trains make frequent and lengthy stops and so always take longer than buses to make the same journey. However, it is usually easier to get a seat, particularly in first class compartments. Fares are slightly higher, but comfort is greater. Between Colombo and Bentota the railway skirts the coast, giving excellent views, whereas the road keeps inland. From Colombo to Kandy observation cars are available (but pre-book). Train journeys in the Hill Country are a delight.

Buses

Just about every town and village of any size in Sri Lanka has a bus service of sorts, and all the coastal areas can be reached with ease. The great problem is getting a seat, which makes it essential to board the bus at the place where the journey starts. Between Colombo and Galle the train is a better bet. Bus travel, apparently, was comfortable in Sri Lanka until the services were nationalised. Privatisation of some services has not yet, however, led to a return to former high standards.

Taxis & three wheelers

Taxis and three-wheelers are unmetered, which puts the tourist completely at the mercy of the driver. It is essential to discover roughly what the fare should be and fix the amount in advance. Tariffs are almost double those in India.

Car & Motorbike Rental

Budget and Hertz have branches in Colombo and there are a multitude of smaller organisations. Those non-resident in Sri Lanka may rent self-drive cars and motorbikes which will save considerably on the cost of hiring a car with a driver. Road signs are quite good and no problems should be experienced on straightforward routes. **Do not, however, attempt to enter Tamil Tiger areas!** Throughout Sri Lanka, driving is on the left. Those intending to rent a motorbike should bring an international driving licence, ensure that full insurance cover is obtained and bring a helmet.

INDEX

A

Abhayagiri Dagoba 167
Adam's Peak 63
Ahangama 93
Ahungalla 77
Alutgama 69
Aluvihara
  Rock Temple 140
Amaduwa 102
Ambalangoda 77
Ancient Cities 139
Anuradhapura 160
Arthur's Seat 131
Atadage 154

B

Balapitiya 77
Bambalapitiya 51
Bandarawela 105
Bentota 66, 72
Bentota Zoo 69
Beruwala 66
Bo-Tree 167
Bohiravakanda
  Buddha 132
Brazen Palace 165
Buduruwagala
  Buddha 104
Bundala Sanctuary 100

C

Cinnamon 28
Clock Tower 42
Colombo 38
Colombo-Badalla
  Railway 105
Cultural triangle 122

D

Dambulla 141
Dambulla's Caves 141
Dehiwala Zoo 58
Demala Maha Seya 157
Diyaluma Falls 105
Dondra Head 96
Duwa Island 34

E

Ella 105, 107
Embekke Devale 135
Esala Perahera 121

F

Fort Frederick 175

G

Gadaldeniya
  Vihara 136
Gal Vihara 156
Galle 82
Galle Face Green 48
Galle Road 41, 49
Galpota 69
Gangaramaya
  Temple 53
Giritale 149
Governor's
  bungalow 55

H

Habarana 148
Hakgala
  Botanic Gardens 108
Hambantota 100
Haputale 61
Hatadage 154
Hendala 34
Henerathgoda
  Botanic Gardens 37
Hikkaduwa 79
Hikkaduwa's coral 79
Horton Plains 107

I

Isurumuni Vihara 170

J

Jami-Ul-Alfar
  Mosque 46

K

Kalutara 59, 61
Kaluwamodara 69
Kandy 118

Kandy Lake 129
Kannigai
  Hot Springs 177
Kataragama 104
Kelaniya 53
Kiri Vihara 156
Kirinda 101
Kirivehera dagoba 104
Koggala 92
Koneswaram
  Temple 176
Kosgoda 75
Kuttam Pokuna 166

L

Lankarama
  Dagoba 168
Lankatilake
  Temple 135
Lion Terrace 147

M

Maha Devala 104
Maha Oya River 37
Maidens Frescoes 146
Maitland, Thomas 56
Mansion Museum 88
Matale 140
Matara 94
Mawella Blowhole 97
Mihintale 159
Mirisaveti Dagoba 169
Mirissa 94
Moragalle 68
Moratuwa 60
Mount Lavinia 54
Mount Lavinia
  Hotel 54
Mulkirigala Rock
  Temple 97

N

Nalanda Gedige 141
Nanu Oya 105
Natha Devala 128
Nathuma 134
National Museum 51
Negombo 26

Nilaveli Beach 173
Nilaveli village 173
Nissanka Malla's
  Palace 151
Nuwara Eliya 109

O

Ohiya 105

P

Pabula Vihara 155
Panadura 60
Pancha Kapa Dupa 73
Parakrama Samudra
  (Topawewa) 151
Peradeniya
  Botanic Gardens 132
Pigeon Island 173
Pinawala Elephant
  Orphanage 137
Polonnaruwa 149
Puttalam 34

Q

Queens
  Bath House 126

R

Raja Maha
  Vihara Temple 53
Ramparts 83
Rankot Vihara 155
Ratnaprasada 168
Ratnapura 61
Ratnapura
  'gem city' 60
Royal Pleasure
  Gardens 169
Ruhunu (Yala)
  National Park 102
Ruvanveli Seya
  Dagoba 165

S

Samadhi Buddha 167
Sigiriya 144
Sinharaja Forest
  Reserve 65

Siva Devala 155
Sri Dalada
  Maligawa 124
Sri Pada 65
St Andrew's Church 50
St Peter's Church 44
St Stephen's
  Cemetery 177
Star Fort 94
Stilt fishermen 93
Sudharmalaya
  Temple 89
Swami Rock 176

T

Tangalla 98
Tea Factory Hotel 116
Temple of the
  Tooth 124
Temple Treasures
  Museum 125
The Hill Country 105
The Pettah 45
Thuparama 164
Thuparama
  Image House 153
Tissamaharama 101
Topawewa Lake 149
Trincomalee 171
Triton and
  Neptune Bastions 89
Turtle Hatchery 76
Tusker Raja
  Museum 125

U

Unawatuna 91

V

Vatadage 153
Vel Festival 47
Viharamahadevi
  Park 52

W

Wadduwa 59, 60
Weherahena
  Temple 96

Weligama 93
Wewurukannala
  Vihara 96
Wickramasinghe
  Museum 92
Wirawila Tank 101
World's End 107, 108

Y

Yala 101
Yatala Vihara 101

LANDMARK VISITORS GUIDES

US & British VI
ISBN: 1 901522 03 2
256pp, £11.95

Antigua & Barbuda
ISBN: 1 901522 02 4
96pp, £5.95

Bermuda
ISBN: 1 901522 07 5
160pp, £7.95

Dominican Republic
ISBN: 1 90152208 3
160pp, £7.95

Pack
2 months
into
2 weeks
with your
Landmark
Visitors
Guides

New Zealand
ISBN:
1 901522 36 9
320pp £12.95

North Cyprus
ISBN:
1 901522 51 2
192pp £8.95

Ticino
ISBN:
1 901522 74 1
192pp £8.95

Orlando
ISBN:
1 901522 22 9
256pp, £9.95

Florida: Gulf Coast
ISBN:
1 901522 01 6
160pp, £7.95

Florida: The Keys
ISBN:
1 901522 21 0
160pp, £7.95

St Lucia
ISBN:
1 901522 28 8
144pp, £6.95

To order send a cheque/Visa/MasterCard details to:

Landmark Publishing,

Waterloo House, 12 Compton, Ashbourne, Derbyshire DE6 IDA England
Tel: 01335 347349 Fax: 01335 347303
e-mail: landmark@clara.net

Provence
ISBN: 1 901522 45 8
240pp, £10.95

Côte d'Azur
ISBN: 1 901522 29 6
144pp, £6.95

Dordogne
ISBN: 1 901522 67 9
224pp, £11.95

Madeira
ISBN: 1 901522 42 3
192pp, £8.95

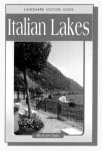

Italian Lakes
ISBN: 1 901522 11 3
240pp, £11.95

Bruges
ISBN: 1 901522 66 0
96pp, £5.95

Riga
ISBN: 1 901522 59 8
160pp, £7.95

Iceland
ISBN: 1 901522 68 7
192pp, £9.95

Cracow
ISBN: 1 901522 54 7
160pp, £7.95

India: Goa
ISBN: 1 901522 23 7
160pp, £7.95

India: Kerala
ISBN: 1 901522 16 4
256pp, £10.99

Vendee
ISBN: 1 901522 76 X
96pp, £4.95

Prices subject to alteration from time to time

Published by
Landmark Publishing Ltd,
Waterloo House, 12 Compton, Ashbourne,
Derbyshire DE6 1DA England
Tel: 01335 347349 Fax: 01335 347303
e-mail: landmark@clara.net

1st Edition
ISBN 1 901 522 37 7

Print: Gutenburg Press Ltd, Malta
Cartography: James Allsopp
Design: James Allsopp

Front cover: Weherahena Temple, built in 1906
Back cover top: Tea pickers, Nuwara Eliya
Back cover bottom: Palm fringed beaches await your arrival

Picture Credits
Taj Exotica Hotel: p66 & p70
All other pictures are supplied by the author

DISCLAIMER
While every care has been taken to ensure that the information in
this book is as accurate as possible at the time of publication, the
publishers and author accept no responsibility for any loss, injury
or inconvenience sustained by anyone using this book.